Global Migration and Social Change series

Series Editor: **Nando Sigona**,
University of Birmingham, UK

The *Global Migration and Social Change* series showcases original research that looks at the nexus between migration, citizenship and social change.

Forthcoming in the series:

Mediated Emotions of Migration
Reclaiming Affect for Agency
Sukhmani Khorana

Migration, Health and Inequalities
Critical Activist Research across Ecuadorean Borders
Roberta Villalón

Out now in the series:

Navigating the European Migration Regime
Male Migrants, Interrupted Journeys and Precarious Lives
Anna Wyss

Visiting Immigration Detention
Care and Cruelty in Australia's Asylum Seeker Prisons
Michelle Peterie

Temporality in Mobile Lives
Contemporary Asia–Australia Migration and Everyday Time
Shanthi Robertson

Find out more at
bristoluniversitypress.co.uk/global-migration-and-social-change

Global Migration and Social Change series

Series Editor: **Nando Sigona**,
University of Birmingham, UK

Find out more at
bristoluniversitypress.co.uk/global-migration-and-social-change

POSTCOLONIALITY AND FORCED MIGRATION

Mobility, Control, Agency

Edited by
Martin Lemberg-Pedersen, Sharla M. Fett,
Lucy Mayblin, Nina Sahraoui and
Eva Magdalena Stambøl

BRISTOL
UNIVERSITY
PRESS

First published in Great Britain in 2022 by

Bristol University Press
University of Bristol
1–9 Old Park Hill
Bristol
BS2 8BB
UK
t: +44 (0)117 374 6645
e: bup-info@bristol.ac.uk

Details of international sales and distribution partners are available at bristoluniversitypress.co.uk

British Library Cataloguing in Publication Data
A catalogue record for this book is available from the British Library

ISBN 978-1-5292-1819-0 hardcover
ISBN 978-1-5292-1820-6 ePub
ISBN 978-1-5292-1821-3 ePdf

Cover design: Andrew Corbett
Front cover image: alamy/Konstantin Kalishko
Bristol University Press uses environmentally responsible print partners.
Printed in Great Britain by CPI Group (UK) Ltd, Croydon, CR0 4YY

FSC
www.fsc.org
MIX
Paper from responsible sources
FSC® C013604

Contents

Notes on Authors

Laura Rosanne Adderley is Associate Professor of History, and also affiliated with Latin American studies and Africana studies, at Tulane University. She is author of *'New Negroes from Africa': Slave Trade Abolition and Free African Settlement in the Nineteenth-Century Caribbean* (Indiana University Press, 2006) and is currently completing a book on life and labour among the very first Africans taken by British authorities from illegally operating slave ships in the Caribbean between 1807 and 1830.

Clayton Boeyink is Research Fellow at the University of Edinburgh (Centre of African Studies). He interrogates the politics, practices and coloniality of refugee self-reliance in Tanzania. His current Displaced Somali and Congolese project focuses on healthcare at the intersection of gender among displaced Somalis and Congolese in Somalia, DRC, Kenya and South Africa. His most recent publication is 'On broker exploitation and violence: from *madalali* to cartel bosses in the food aid resale economy of Tanzanian refugee camps' (*Development and Change*, 2021).

Jerónimo Botero Marino is Dean of the School of Law and Social Sciences at Icesi University in Cali, Colombia. He is Professor of the Department of Humanities and founding member of the Center for Ethics and Democracy, and holds a PhD degree from the University of Barcelona. He is part of Grupo Nexos: Interdisciplinary Group for Sociocultural and Psychological Studies, and specializes in ethics and political philosophy. Publications include for *Signos Filosóficos* and *Topicos*.

Nasreen Chowdhory is Associate Professor in the Department of Political Science, University of Delhi. She is author of *Citizenship and Belonging in South Asia: Contested Terrains* (Springer, 2018) and has edited *Deterritorialised Identity and Transborder Movement in South Asia* with Nasir Uddin (Springer, 2019), *Citizenship, Nationalism and Refugeehood of Rohingyas in Southern Asia* with Biswajit Mohanty (Springer, 2020) and *Gender, Identity and Migration in India* (Palgrave Macmillan, 2022) with Paula Banerjee.

Phillip Cole teaches politics and international relations at the University of the West of England, Bristol. His books include *Philosophies of Exclusion: Liberal Political Theory and Immigration* (Edinburgh University Press, 2000) and, with Christopher Heath Wellman, *Debating the Ethics of Immigration: Is There a Right to Exclude?* (Oxford University Press, 2011).

Lina Ewert is an independent researcher. A sociologist by training, her research interest lies at the cross-section of migration, social inequality and emerging technologies with a particular focus on innovating co-creation processes. Her doctoral thesis combines the themes of intelligence and migration, looking closely at the role of technology firms and security consultancies for data-driven ways of knowing and sorting that appear to colonize humanitarian approaches to displacement. Ewert has published in the *International Journal of Migration and Border Studies* (2020) and for the *SOURCE Network of Excellence*.

Sharla M. Fett is Professor of History at Occidental College in Los Angeles with research interests in slavery, abolition, health and healing in the US South and Atlantic World. Publications include *Working Cures: Healing, Health and Power on Southern Slave Plantations* (University of North Carolina Press, 2002) and *Recaptured Africans: Surviving Slave Ships, Detention, and Dislocation in the Final Years of the Slave Trade* (UNCP, 2017).

Ella Fratantuono is Assistant Professor of History at the University of North Carolina at Charlotte. Her research focuses on migration, settlement, governmentality, social engineering and state-building in the Middle East. She is currently working on her first book project, which explores the development of a centralized immigration regime in the late 19th- and early 20th-century Ottoman Empire. Her articles have appeared in publications such as *Journal of Genocide Research* (2019) and *Middle East Journal of Refugee Studies* (2017).

Leonie Jegen is a PhD candidate at the University of Amsterdam. Her research considers the externalization of European border control in the context of the Senegalese migrant smuggling policy. Previously, she worked at the European Council on Refugees and Exiles (ECRE) and on research projects on West African migration governance at the University of Freiburg and the Vrije Universiteit Brussels (VUB). Jegen has published in the *Journal of Ethnic and Migration Studies* (2020).

Panagiota (Penny) Koutrolikou is Associate Professor at the School of Architecture, NTUA. Her research interests include cities and urban conflicts, urban crises and governance, geopolitics of migration and development, and socio-spatial justice and geographies of rights. She is currently involved in research projects on legal geographies of (un)safety and asylum in Afghanistan, the socio-spatial relations of post-2016 Turkish migration to Athens, redefining spatial justice in Athens as a city in crisis, and govermentalities of urban crises. Koutrolikou has published work in *Citizenship Studies* (2017), *Antipode* (2016) and *Urban Studies* (2012).

Martin Lemberg-Pedersen is Honorary Associate Professor at the University of Warwick, and Head of Policy and Society for Amnesty International, Denmark. His academic research involves interdisciplinary analyses of Western asylum, border and deportation practices, and military-technological-industrial relations. He has focused on EU relations to forced migration in Greek, Turkish and Libyan contexts, Danish externalization policies, and colonial precedents to Western displacement politics. His publications have appeared in *Forced Migration Review* (2021), *Journal of Borderlands Studies* (2021), *Citizenship Studies* (2020), *Global Affairs* (2019), *Questions of International Law* (2019) and *Etikk i Praksis – Nordic Journal of Applied Ethics* (2018).

Lucy Mayblin is Senior Lecturer in Sociology at the University of Sheffield. Her research focuses on asylum, human rights, policy-making and the legacies of colonialism. She is the author of three books: *Asylum After Empire* (Rowman and Littlefield International, 2017), *Impoverishment and Asylum* (Routledge, 2019) and *Migration Studies and Colonialism* (Polity, 2021). She is currently studying crimes of solidarity as part of a Philip Leverhulme Prize fellowship.

Felicity Atieno Okoth is Research Associate at the African Migration and Development Policy Centre and a Tutorial Fellow at Moi University, Kenya, where she teaches International and Intercultural Communication courses. Her research interests include understanding how African migrants' situated practices, specifically intercultural relations, inform their migration aspirations. Okoth has published in *New Media and Mass Communication* (2017).

Nina Sahraoui is Marie Skłodowska-Curie Fellow at CRESPPA, CNRS in Paris where she conducts the project CYBERGEN (2021–22). Her research explores themes at the crossroads of interdisciplinary studies of migration, gender and healthcare. Sahraoui's books and volumes include *Racialised Care Workers and European Older-Age Care* (Palgrave, 2019), *Gender, Work and Migration* (with Megha Amrith, Routledge, 2018) and *Borders across Healthcare* (Berghahn Books, 2020).

Eva Magdalena Stambøl is Postdoctoral Researcher at the Department of Criminology and Sociology of Law, University of Oslo, and at the Otto Suhr Institute for Political Science, Freie Universität Berlin. Her research takes place at the intersection of criminology and international relations and focuses on internal security in EU foreign policy and external relations, borders, transnational criminal justice, and extra-legal governance in West Africa and Latin America. She has published most recently in journals including *Review of International Studies* (2021), *Theoretical Criminology* (2021) and *Punishment & Society* (2021).

Peter Teunissen is Early-Stage Researcher and PhD candidate with the Horizon 2020 Project MOVES, Migration and Modernity at the Freie Universität Berlin, and Universidade do Porto. His research focuses on the intersections between migration industries, b/ordered mobilities, and the infrastructures of exclusion and specifically how this unfolds at the Greek/Turkish borderlands. Peter has published in the *Journal of Borderlands Studies* (2020) and *Social Inclusion* (2020).

Shamna Thacham Poyil is a PhD Candidate in the Department of Political Science at the University of Delhi. Her research focuses on the narrative of statelessness of the Rohingyas and the politics of exclusion. She has authored several book chapters on this topic, the most recent being 'National Identity and Conceptualization of Nationalism among Rohingya' in N. Chowdhory and B. Mohanty (eds) *Citizenship, Nationalism and Refugeehood of Rohingyas in Southern Asia* (Springer, 2020).

Mathias Hatleskog Tjønn holds an MPhil in Modern International and Transnational History (MITRA) from the University of Oslo. He is employed as a research assistant at the Peace Research Institute Oslo (PRIO) and his research interests include Italo-Libyan relations, Mediterranean migration, postcolonialism and transnational history. Recent publications appear in *Babylon – Nordic Journal for Middle East Studies* (2019) and *Global Histories – A Student Journal* (2018).

Elsa Tyszler is Postdoctoral Researcher at the Centre for Sociological and Political Research in Paris. She researches migration control at borders through the lens of gender and race. After the Moroccan-Spanish borders, her current fieldwork focuses on the French borders. Among her publications are 'Humanitarianism and black female bodies: violence and intimacy at the Moroccan–Spanish border' (*The Journal of North African Studies*, 2021); and 'From controlling mobilities to control over women's bodies: gendered effects of EU border externalization in Morocco' (*Comparative Migration Studies*, 2019).

Aurora Vergara-Figueroa is Director of the Afrodiasporic Studies Center at Icesi University, Cali, Colombia, and a W.E.B. Du Bois Research Institute Fellow at Harvard University. She is an Afro-Colombian woman and holds a PhD from the Sociology Department of the University of Massachusetts Amherst. Her main research interests are the sociological study of Afro-Colombians deracinated from the Colombian Pacific coast and the long durée of land dispossession in the world system. She is the author of *Afrodescendant Resistance to Deracination in Colombia: Massacre at Bellavista-Bojayá-Chocó* (Springer, 2018).

Acknowledgements

The editorial team want to express immense gratitude to all contributors to the 'Forced Migration and Postcoloniality' workshop in Copenhagen in December 2019, for the generous and inspiring atmosphere, collective discussions and illuminating debates about the critical potential of engaging with colonialism in forced migration studies. The workshop was made possible with funding from the Independent Research Fund Denmark, but much gratitude is also owed to Martin Lemberg-Pedersen's research assistants Oliver Joel Halpern and Ariadni Zormpa who worked hard and generously to coordinate and liaise with contributors from all over the world in order to make the workshop logistic come together.

For many contributors, this workshop was the last in real and not virtual life before the global COVID-19 pandemic hit, and so still serves as a reminder of the wonderful potential that arises when people are brought together who share a deep desire for exploring the research agenda through interdisciplinary collaboration. While interdisciplinarity is an often-used buzzword at university management levels, the actual support granted to the opening of such spaces between disciplines continues to be the exception rather than the rule, and is far too often left to the individual researcher. This collaboration took place across many different career trajectories, ranging from early career scholars, precarious affiliations and grant pursuits, and to senior scholars embedded in time-consuming administrative work. For this reason too, the editors are thankful to the contributors for carving out time for working on this volume over the span of several years, not least as this required careful balancing acts with the obligations of care work which became so prominent during the global pandemic.

From colleagues, librarians, workshop and seminar organizers, to reviewers, mentors, friends, and persons of knowledge and from social movements, interviewed as part of this research, more people than it is possible to list here have informed, encouraged and helped shape the thoughts and analyses that follow. Some in terms of supporting the idea of an edited volume in itself, others when it comes to inspiration and advice to contributors of the individual chapters. As with any collaborative work, this too stands on top of an underforest of exchanges, sparring, insights, inspiration and generosity. Moreover, the editors also want to thank the series editors from the Global Migration and Social Change book series, as well as the team at Bristol University Press, especially Shannon Kneis and Anna Richardson, who were precise and respectful of the intellectual direction of the volume they facilitated, but also patient when it came to deadlines in the midst of a global pandemic. Also, at key stages in the process, the anonymous reviewers provided insightful feedback on our book proposal, as well as on the entire manuscript.

Series Preface

Nando Sigona
Oxford
29 May 2022

To date, the *Global Migration and Social Change* series has included only single-authored research monographs. With *Postcoloniality and Forced Migration,* we are introducing something new in the series: an edited collection with twenty authors, a mix of early career and more established researchers from a range of disciplinary backgrounds and geographies, and five editors.

What we have not changed is our commitment to offer to our readers cutting-edge research on migration and forced displacement, one that challenges the canon and embedded migration and migration governance in broader societal, political, cultural and economic transformations. This collection contributes to an emerging body of literature in the social sciences that puts at the centre of scholarly research into contemporary forced displacement the legacies of colonialism, revealing and challenging the coloniality and Eurocentrism that shape migration and migration governance today. It is an ambitious project, one that reaches out towards multiple interconnected geographies and colonial histories and draws upon a range of disciplinary traditions and conceptual tools, one that arguably could be achieved only by a group of authors in close dialogue with one another.

Over the years, critical migration scholars have called researchers to challenge the politics of knowledge production in the field and criticized the presentism that underpins mainstream research on refugees, and migration more generally, as well as the limits of a scholarship which too often in its search for policy relevance ends up embracing the categories, frames and research priorities of policy makers in the Global North. This collection, researching the entanglements of forced migration with colonialism in the past and through to the present, contributes to this critical work by bringing forced migration research into conversation with postcolonial and decolonial studies through a fascinating mix of contemporary and historical case studies and theoretical and epistemological contributions. Through historical and empirical research that trace hidden genealogies of migration control and surveillance, through uncovering the colonial legacies that inform the racialized hierarchies that underpin contemporary migration governance, the authors and editors of this volume are inviting all of us to reflect critically on the categories, concepts and questions we ask in our research and to uncover the hidden histories of contemporary forced displacement.

1

Introduction

Martin Lemberg-Pedersen, Sharla M. Fett, Lucy Mayblin, Nina Sahraoui and Eva Magdalena Stambøl

World history is peppered with population displacements, forced migrations and expulsions; and European colonialism was implicated in the forced movement of countless people from the 15th century onwards. From the forced marching of indigenous people across North America (Moses, 2007), to the forced movement of enslaved people around the Atlantic (see Gilroy, 1993), to the division and partition of countries as part of the process of both Empire building and decolonization (Marfleet, 2007), European colonialism was implicated in many involuntary population movements. Equally, the founding of many instruments of international law, including the international refugee regime, which were put in place to support forced migrants, were drafted by colonial powers and informed by colonial logics (Mayblin, 2017). Those logics encompassed ideas of racial hierarchy, including White supremacy, and civilizational difference and gradation. While settler colonialism endures (in, for example, Canada, Australia, New Zealand and the United States of America), and there remain colonized territories around the world, an intensive period of decolonization from the 1940s onwards has shifted global geopolitics. We can no longer talk of the French Empire, the Spanish Empire, or the British Empire as geopolitical entities with world power status. And yet, colonial logics and assumptions about the world and the various peoples who inhabit it have in many ways endured.

From an (underappreciated at the time) start in Third World Approaches to International Law (TWAIL) (Chimni, 1998; Anghie, 2004; Odhiambo-Abuya, 2006), recent years have seen the emergence of a new body of work in the social sciences which seeks to explore the legacies of colonialism for contemporary refugee phenomena (for example, Cazzato, 2016; Danewid, 2017; Mayblin, 2014; 2017; 2019; Gutiérrez-Rodriguez,

2018; Vergara-Figueroa, 2018; Lemberg-Pedersen, 2019; Mayblin and Turner, 2021; Proglio et al, 2021). Collectively, this work draws on the theoretical tools of postcolonialism and decoloniality, in order to challenge the coloniality and Eurocentrism of both the international refugee regime and the field of refugee and forced migration studies itself. This book is a contribution to this emergent research agenda. It explores both histories of colonial era forced migration, and the ways in which colonial legacies continue to shape displacements and our responses to them today. We have set out to conceptualize the linkages between colonialism and forced migration across the world, and across temporal scales, from formal colonial rule to current displacement practices and regimes. In this way, this book is part of the move within refugee and forced migration studies, and migration studies more generally, to begin to take seriously the role that colonialism has played in population movements and responses to them over the past five centuries. Our aim is to contribute to the unsettling of presentist and Eurocentric epistemologies concerning forced migration and in doing so to offer novel insights into the colonial continuities within forced migration governance across the world.

This edited collection emerged out of the 'Postcoloniality and Forced Migration' workshop convened by Dr Martin Lemberg-Pedersen in Copenhagen in December 2019, and funded by the Independent Research Fund Denmark. Unwittingly timed just before the outbreak of the global COVID-19 pandemic, this event provided the kind of inspiring, in-real-life atmosphere, which has since then been challenged by the pandemic and its restrictions. Accordingly, this volume is thoroughly grounded in interdisciplinary inquiry and methodology, and brings together historians, political scientists, sociologists, anthropologists, criminologists and political theorists, both as editors and contributors. Through disciplinary fusions, our aim is to examine the heuristic potential of the notion of postcoloniality, understood as the complex and still ongoing impacts of colonial encounters for both colonized and metropolitan societies, with particular theoretical and empirical attention given to the implications for the governing of mobility.

The aim of this volume is thus to add theoretical and empirical depth to discussions about how the coloniality of power (Quijano, 2000; Mignolo, 2009) affects the politics and study of forced migration. All contributors are attentive to the historicization of their case studies, as we strive to collectively demonstrate the need for a reading of forced migration anchored in history. Some discuss fine-grained archival work, while others offer ethnographic accounts of contemporary policies and migrant trajectories informing our analysis of these power relationships. The theoretical ramifications of this edited volume are ripe with potential for further critical inquiries on race, mobility, imperialism, and methodological and theoretical dimensions across connected histories (Bhambra, 2007). This has informed our selection of chapters which also offer geographic spread, avoiding the common, but narrow, focus on Anglo-American colonialism. The volume thus includes as specific spatial and temporal cases, contexts spanning from India and the Indian Ocean, West, East and North Africa, South America, the Caribbean, North America and Turkey, as well as Europe. In short, by widening the geographic prism of postcoloniality, we seek to ask crucial questions which help unsettle the dominating analytics of Western thinking and geographies about displacement – the nation-state, border control and humanitarianism.

Unfortunately, the rich and nuanced historiographic case material on colonial forced migration policies is often overlooked, over claims about the novelty, singularity or exceptionalism of current migration and asylum policies, a framing that both glosses over and reproduces colonial matrices of power. Overshadowed by literature on current displacement crises, the rich historiography of colonial case material analyses spanning displacements in African, Asian, Southern US, Caribbean or Latin American studies has been left at the wayside of forced migration studies in Western academia. Often, it is placed instead within the geographically delimited traditions of area or specific national and regional studies. A similar fate has befallen important precedents, continuities and contingent parallels between colonial, interwar and present regimes of humanitarianism, profit and control. This tendency also underscores a multi-dimensional absence of cross-disciplinarity that postcolonial forced migration studies is in dire need of addressing. More specifically, these barriers concern the lacking cross-fertilization between different branches of historiography and the extremely fragmented, if not directly severed, links between past and present politics on forced migration. This volume seeks to show that addressing these multi-dimensional barriers through postcolonial interventions holds a breathtaking potential for re-historicizing and re-contextualizing forced migration studies.

Multiple disciplines, multiple omissions

Although heterogenous and wide-ranging, forced migration studies has long suffered from an aversion to history, from a presentist bias, and a concerted ignorance on questions of colonialism in particular (Chimni, 1998; Marfleet, 2007; Walters, 2015; Chatty, 2017; Mayblin, 2017). Far too often, historicity in forced migration studies is taken to mean a starting point somewhere between the interwar years and after the Second World War. Some of the reasons for this self-imposed spatiotemporal reduction of perspectives on displacement include the longstanding overlap between humanitarian practices, labels of displacement policy and the economic and geopolitical interests of states, organizations and corporations. This aversion to history has been reflected across various social science disciplines. Yet a recent 'postcolonial turn' (Koh, 2015; Tudor, 2018) has sought to rectify the situation. Here we sketch out some recent contributions to this agenda from across the social sciences.

IR is one of several disciplines which continues to play a fundamental role in the study of refugee and forced migration dynamics. For a long time, IR exhibited a curious silence on colonialism as an influential factor shaping world power and politics. Despite colonialism and the colonial-imperial slave trade (Tomich, 2004) having such profound and long-spanning impact on world historical events, including the reshaping of forced migration dynamics and international political responses to it, IR scholars for a long time afforded it only cursory mention, if any (for an example of such silence, see Betts and Loescher, 2011). State-centric myths of origin, temporality and difference have shaped analyses of forced migration in past or present contexts often leading to the unstated reaffirmation of an 'insider gaze of the sovereign-capitalist-citizen' that serves to individualize displacement events and obscure their longer patterns of privilege and prejudice (Lemberg-Pedersen, 2022: 129–30). This also spills over into concrete policies, such as a depoliticized understanding of surveillance components in humanitarianism (see Chapter 6), as well as into theory-building in academic disciplines, such as many of the normative guidelines on immigration developed through political theory (see Chapter 11). Comments made in 2000 by Phillip Cole (author of Chapter 11) still to some extent hold true, namely that when we observe works in contemporary liberal political philosophy, and analyses of scholars such as Locke, Hume, Kant, Bentham and Mill, it remains as if 'colonialism and slavery never occurred at all' so that the discipline 'could justifiably be characterised as one vast act of racialised forgetting' (Cole, 2000: 197).

In response to this, a number of recent interventions have questioned such omissions, in what has been called the discipline's 'historiographical turn' (Seth, 2013). Countering abstract conceptual frameworks based on euro- and state centric frameworks, this has allowed for a rich and critical strain of inquiry, including postcolonial analyses of the fundamental, yet often unacknowledged role of imperialisms, colonialisms and notions of race and racism within IR (Long and Schmidt, 2005: 7; see also Anievas et al, 2015). Taking seriously this critique leads to a fundamental paradigm shift that sheds light on previously invisible perspectives.

Across many other disciplines, and cross-disciplinary work, scholars of migration have begun to theorize migratory phenomena and responses to them in light of colonial racism (for example, De Genova, 2018; Vergara-Figueroa, 2018; Davies and Isakjee, 2019). Such critical endeavours have enabled decolonial understandings of borders and of the corresponding modern international order (Cazzato, 2016; Lu, 2019), sustaining a powerful critique of the externalization of migration governance (Afailal and

Fernandez, 2018, Lemberg-Pedersen, 2019; see also Chapter 13). Critical migration scholars have also foregrounded the colonial matrix and racial components underpinning citizenship regimes in the global North (Gil Araújo, 2010; Boatcă and Roth, 2016), and this analytical sensitivity to colonial continuities fostered a critique of the integration framework (Nghi Ha, 2010). Other works have contrasted global practices of border control with the concept of 'sanctuary' and cultures of hospitality (Danewid, 2017; Picozza, 2021; see also Chapter 10).

Another emerging focus of postcolonial forced migration studies is on states' and International Organizations' roll-out of large-scale security and defence technology, as well as dataveillance and humanitarian intelligence operations extracting and monetizing data from populations exposed to protracted displacement. This in effect transforms complex displacement crises in the global South into markets for various corporate and other non-state actors, and border politics to sites of intense activity for lobbyists and interest groups representing such market interests (Lemberg-Pedersen, 2013; Lemberg-Pedersen et al, 2020; see also Chapter 5). Based on analyses of South African politics, Catherine Besteman (2020) has argued that the current militarized technologies which are deployed during displacement operations represent a globalization of apartheid techniques. In her view, this represents a racialized security imperialism because those displaced tend to be construed according to racial hierarchies, and because their subjugation happens in order to secure resources and privilege amassed during previous waves of imperialism by the global North. These technologies also represent privilege in the form of contracts for multinational corporations and conglomerates today. Innovations such as remote sensing, refugee biometrics and machine learning have fast become integral for the management of displaced populations in the global South (Duffield, 2019; Madianou 2019, see also Chapter 6). The postcolonial implications of this are illustrated by the fact that the global North often hosts the biggest donors, organizations and corporate actors partaking in the technological financialization of displaced populations in the global South, people who are often referred to as the 'unbanked populations' of the world (Lemberg-Pedersen and Haioty, 2020).

Across studies of migration stemming from sociology and political science departments, the coloniality lens and historical approaches remain at the margins of these disciplines. Dominant frameworks continue to focus on issues of migrant integration, entrenching Western countries' perspectives on migration and responding to policy-motivated interests. Yet, within the interdisciplinary field of critical migration studies, various engagements with colonial continuities are emerging. Lucy Mayblin's (2017) study into the colonial history of exclusion from refugee rights in the UK and internationally, for example, centres colonialism in understanding the hostility of Western states to asylum seekers today. The sociologist

Encarnacion Gutiérrez-Rodriguez (2018) coined the concept of 'coloniality of migration' drawing on decolonial theory, and in 2018, Aurora Vergara-Figueroa (co-author of Chapter 12) published her monograph *Afrodescendent Resistance to Deracination in Colombia*, a powerful decolonial critique of the discourse of 'forced migration' and 'forced displacement'. She argues that presentist readings of displacement as an immediate crisis erase the histories which make some people, and some territories, spaces in which displacement repeatedly happens, and that in doing so understanding of such phenomena in the sociology of forced migration is impoverished (see also Chapter 12). In a similar vein, Fiorenza Picozza (2021) has also drawn on the decolonial school (notably Quijano, 2000; Maldonado-Torres, 2007) in her powerful ethnography of the consequences of the 2015 'refugee crisis' in Germany. Here, she argues that colonial amnesia facilitated a spectacle of solidarity which is cut through with racialized subjectivities and power relations which can only be understood with reference to the colonial histories of Europe (see also Danewid, 2017).

In criminology, the topics of postcoloniality and forced migration have been treated in two rather disconnected emerging strands of scholarship: on the one hand, post/counter-colonial (for example Agozino, 2003) and Southern (Carrington et al, 2016) criminology have criticized the discipline's Eurocentrism and reproduction of epistemological power asymmetries (see also Black et al, 2021). On the other hand, the emerging field of 'border criminology' (for example Pickering and Weber, 2006; Aas and Bosworth, 2013) has brought attention to the tendency of migration increasingly being governed by Western countries through criminalizing, penalizing and policing the movement of people. Recent contributions have started connecting these two strands in an effort to probe the discipline's engagement with postcoloniality and how it shapes and conditions the current criminalization of mobility (for example Bosworth, 2017; O'Reilly, 2018; Aliverti et al, 2021; Stambøl, 2021).

Continuing the effort to bridging postcolonial and forced migration studies, this book interrogates how the control, securitization, policing and surveillance of mobility follows racialized and geopolitical patterns with colonial and historical roots. Indeed, interdisciplinary inquiries occupy a particularly important role in carving out such critical transcendence. Across disciplines such as anthropology, human geography, sociology and IR and political theory, colonial matrices of power and epistemology have long exercised profound influences, and each discipline has therefore experienced fierce internal debates, as well as positions seeking to justify it. It is therefore not surprising that the interdisciplinary field of forced migration studies faces a formidable challenge of multiplied and mutually reinforcing barriers to critical inquiry.

Postcolonial controversies

Discussions of the relation between colonial and contemporary periods, and the colonial present (Gregory, 2004), and how these should be conceptualized and analysed have been accompanied by controversy in multiple ways. Several debates orbit around the interface between academic research on postcoloniality and current forced migration politics in and beyond governments. First, a common critique identified by Oliver Bakewell (2008) has been the charge that a focus on postcoloniality amounts to 'policy-irrelevant research'. In so far as this charge is successful, it functions as a form of epistemological erasure that privileges those categorizations and policy labels for migration, which reflect present interests of powerful (Western) states and actors (see also Zetter, 1991), while disregarding the relevance of, for instance, colonial precursors and causalities to current and complex policy problems. On the basis of policy irrelevance, postcolonial research is sometimes represented as insignificant. Far too often, refugee and forced migration studies have emulated this topography of political power, but the current edited volume and its critical interventions offer to substantiate and reinstate the relevance of coloniality of power across several case studies. This allows for a decolonial interrogation of the scholarly and political uses of concepts such as 'forced migration' and 'displacement' (Vergara-Figueroa, 2018).

In recent years, the increased cross-disciplinary interest in post- and decolonial approaches to understanding contemporary migratory phenomena is related to broader social and political movements. Internationally, student-led campaigns have coalesced around demands to decolonize the university. Projects such as 'Why is my curriculum white?' and the Black Lives Matter movement have brought questions around the legacies of colonialism, including enduring racisms, to the fore. These agendas have not been without controversy, particularly in settler colonial contexts where anti-colonial struggles over land are still ongoing (see, for example, Tuck and Yang, 2012, as well as Chapter 12). Critics have suggested that projects of decolonizing the university through awareness raising can make people feel that they are doing something radical when nothing is in fact done to change the status quo. This is certainly a debate that both undermines claims of contemporary irrelevance and at the same time challenges academics to consider the role of their work in bringing change. Universities are powerful producers of discourse, and legitimators of certain forms of knowledge (Bhambra et al, 2018, see also Chapter 11). This is without a doubt also the case in forced migration studies, making the active forgetting, erasure, or celebratory narration of colonial histories a pertinent challenge in urgent need of being addressed.

Both of the previous discussions speak to the potential of scholarship to play a role in bringing change in the world, and knowing the histories which brought us to the present is an important part of that. The threat that might be posed by recognizing colonial histories, and understanding that they have shaped the contemporary world in many ways, is illustrated by politicians' keen insistence that we should move past the unpleasantness of history, in order to forge new relations into the future. In this vein, in so far as governmental actors do engage with discussions of postcolonialism, they often interpret the prefix 'post-' as dictating that both previous colonizers and previously colonized populations should let the past be past, and move onwards into a new future. For example, Berlusconi and Gaddafi both framed the 2008 Friendship Treaty between Italy and Libya as 'a page turned on history' (Lemberg-Pedersen, 2019: 2). The Treaty's many provisions relating to migration control at the borders of the EU, and the immensely profitable contracts for oil infrastructure and military exports, illustrate that such understandings of postcoloniality are often also beneficial for states and political actors.

Post- or decolonization discourses can be used for political benefit at the same time as they deny the relevance of colonialism for today's world (see Chapter 8). Thus, European countries have actively used decolonization to frame the birth of the European Union (EU) as a rupture from the crude history of imperial powers, and the Union as a normative, liberal-democratic, decolonial power (Hansen and Jonsson, 2017). This, however, requires forgetting the fact that four out of six founding member states were still colonial powers when the EEC was created via the Treaty of Rome in 1957. It also requires bypassing the fact that the Union's member states currently include many so-called 'overseas territories' in regions such as the North Atlantic, the Indian Ocean and the Caribbean, which also belie claims of a clean onwards movement away from the unpleasantness of colonialism. This example raises important questions about the strategic use of colonial history, and the agendas underpinning such manoeuvres. Certainly, arguments which acknowledge a (brutal) colonial past, but use this acknowledgement strategically to demark the present as an essentially different condition, remain popular among political and bureaucratic actors of former colonizing states. This may in part be because the idea of a substantial rupture between past brutality and present politics minimizes relations of responsibility, and the implications for postcolonial reparations for past harm that this raises (Jones, 2004). Or it may place former colonial powers in advantageous positions *vis-à-vis* their former colonial territories.

Finally, in spite of their marginality and apparent 'irrelevance', scholarly analyses of post- and decoloniality, race, gender and imperialism in forced migration politics are often the targets of fiercely reactionary, nationalistic and right-wing attacks, and delegitimization strategies. This is both at the level of political discourse, but also in mediatized debates, including on social media. For example, during 2020–21, politicians and governments in the United Kingdom, Denmark and France singled out post/decolonial, migration and gender researchers, alongside anti-racist and anti-Islamophobic scholarship. They framed such research as, respectively, unlawful and a threat to society (UK), as biased and unscientific activism (Denmark), or even an "Islamo-gauchist" (Islamo-leftist) form of 'gangrene' to be amputated from French society, in the words of Frédérique Vidal, the Minister of Higher Education, Research and Innovation (Kanji et al, 2021). Similar attacks on this kind of research are also taking place in countries such as Hungary, Poland, Brazil, the United States and India. If nothing else, these efforts to reproduce similar framings about the danger of postcolonial research to society, illustrate that some actors and networks view such scholarship as anything but irrelevant.

Postcoloniality and recontextualizing the present

Across this volume, authors refer to certain literatures and terms which offer theoretical tools for grappling with some of the questions raised by social movements for decolonization within our disciplines (see Mayblin and Turner, 2021 for a more thorough overview). Two such approaches have been postcolonialism and decoloniality, which we name here not to imply that these traditions exhaust the ways in which we can talk about colonialism, power and continuity, nor to imply that they are incompatible. In fact, we find that these represent different focus points, together allowing for a comprehensive critical potential. Indeed, there is a range of other fields of scholarship which centre on colonialism in their analyses, such as Third World approaches to international law, indigenous studies, critical race theory and Black studies. That the contributions to this volume draw primarily on postcolonialism and decoloniality should not therefore be taken to indicate a totality of the theoretical perspectives available for research in this area (see also Conclusion).

As indicated earlier, the 'post' in postcolonialism, somewhat confusingly, does not point to the end of colonialism, but rather to the continuities of colonial ideas, practices and structures, which have continued after colonial encounters and into the present. Leela Gandhi (1998: 4) describes postcolonialism as 'a theoretical resistance to the mystifying amnesia of the colonial aftermath'. It is often associated with the works of Fanon (1965), Spivak (1988), Homi Bhabha (1994) and Said (1995), what we may call the retrospectively assigned canonical figures of postcolonialism. Initially, postcolonialism was associated with the humanities, particularly literature and cultural studies. A major contribution of this body of work has been the theorizing of how colonialism has shaped understandings of cultural hierarchy and difference. For example, Said (1995) identified the production of the imagined space of 'the Orient' by Western scholars, artists and writers, a space which had no meaning for those who lived in so called 'oriental' countries. Postcolonial scholars, then, have contested dominant 'Western' modes of understanding, representing and conceptualizing the world. In doing so, they have challenged the supposed universalism of concepts, categories and theories that have emerged from Europe and the West more broadly. Having emerged from the humanities, postcolonial perspectives were then taken up in the social sciences, initially in cultural studies (Hall, 1992; Gilroy, 1993) but then more widely.

Particularly pertinent to refugee and forced migration studies, postcolonialists contest both the idea that Europeans invented 'human rights', as well as the assumption that European conceptions of individual rights are automatically universal (see Simpson, 2004 on the colonial history of human rights; Cole, 2000 on colonially derived exclusions from universalist ethical theories; and Lowe, 2015 on the emergence of liberalism alongside colonialism). More fundamentally, postcolonialism recognizes the colonial histories which inform ideas of the human today (Wynter, 2003). In making these contestations, we would necessarily need to engage with the ways in which colonialism gave rise to a sense of Western cultural and civilizational superiority. Postcolonialism, then, centres socially constructed ideas of spatial and temporal difference – the idea that some places are ahead in (civilizational) time, while others are behind and need to catch up. This sense of both spatial and temporal difference emerged through and with colonialism, and remains pervasive today (for example, in the discourse of 'development'). The sense of continuity, of a thread linking past and present, is central to postcolonial scholarship. It is about 'the contemporary force of imperial remains' (Stoler, 2008: 196) and central to this is the connection between ideas of racial difference and civilizational hierarchy. This is because the idea of racial difference both legitimated the subordination of colonized people, and provided a system of knowledge through which Europeans invented their own 'superiority' and 'Whiteness' (Hall, 2002). As mentioned previously, academic disciplines were deeply imbricated in the production of these systems of knowledge, and consequently, as postcolonial scholars, it is now our task to trace the connections between these histories, knowledges and contemporary phenomena.

Decoloniality has often been associated with Latin American scholars such as Mignolo (2000), Quijano (2000), Grosfoguel (2007) and Lugones (2007). It focuses on the many ways in which colonial matrices of power continue to dominate, subjugate, dismiss and erase systems of knowledge. In this way, there are many overlaps between the decolonial school and postcolonialism. Decolonial scholars also recognize the enforcement of spatial and temporal distinctions, and they identify the ways in which coloniality (a colonial, hierarchical worldview) emerged at the same time as the idea of modernity.

In particular, this work has uncovered how the idea that Western colonizing countries were modern and superior was seen as a consequence of the enlightenment, the industrial revolution, and the invention of democracy and rights. Decolonial scholars conceptualize this in terms of coloniality and modernity being two sides of the same coin, inseparable from each other, often articulated as coloniality/modernity (Mignolo, 2000).

Decoloniality also holds the explicit ambition to 'de-link' from coloniality/modernity in order to recover alternative knowledge systems, which do not reproduce such power hierarchies (Mignolo, 2007). One way of doing this is 'border thinking' (Anzaldúa, 1987), which, in the words of Mignolo and Tlostanova (2006: 206), is 'the epistemology of the exteriority; that is, of the outside created from the inside'. The border here is understood both in terms of geographical distance from 'modern' places, but also in terms of epistemic difference from the Eurocentric locus of world power. Zapatismo would be one example of border thinking. These emancipatory horizons of decoloniality are not extensively explored in this volume (see, however, Chapter 12) and, indeed, the book is titled 'postcolonial' with the intention of drawing attention to the 'ruins of empire' and their afterlives to borrow from Stoler (2013), see also Davies and Isakjee (2019). Nevertheless, it is necessary in this brief sketch to foreground this important aspect of decolonial scholarship that readers may wish to explore.

Originally, post- and decolonial traditions could also be distinguished by the geographic and temporal scales of their respective inquiries. The former has referred to the Middle East and South Asia from the 18th century onwards, while the latter has had a South American focus and begins from the 15th century. However, subsequent engagements from within these bodies of work have often transcended and combined interventions across these geo-temporal delimitations. Both postcolonialism and decoloniality can be understood as focusing on the complex and ongoing impacts of colonial encounters, the impact of still unfolding matrices of power derived from them, and their influence on societies today (McClintock, 1992; Gandhi, 1998). Of crucial importance to this volume is the implication that this draws our attention to the plurality of colonialisms and different imperial practices across a great many temporal scales and geographic contexts.

The challenge facing post- and decolonial forced migration studies necessarily runs deeper than the unresolved and reiterative imperialist baggage of any one research discipline. As Loren Landau (2012) has argued, North–South academic partnerships on knowledge production often push southern researchers towards policy-oriented research embedded within Northern funding and research priorities. For him, these partnerships risk entrenching the North–South dichotomies and imbalances they purport to address. Productive critiques have challenged the tendency of academic and policy-oriented research to focus on South–North migration and its associated control dynamics (Crush and Chikanda, 2018). The colonial impulses to contain, manipulate and induce the movement of certain populations have therefore also morphed into pluriversal South–South dynamics today. These are entangled across power differentials in ways that can contingently parallel, but also depart from, those of their colonial predecessors (Fiddian-Qasmiyeh and Daley, 2018). The connections between these newer practices and those undertaken in colonial contexts of displacement are evident and in need of further exploration, a current case in point being how migrants under the COVID-19 pandemic have been framed as bearers of disease (Chapter 7). As such, the postcolonial focus of this edited volume complements the emergent literature on centred, recentred or decentred perspectives and categories in the study of forced migration (Achiume, 2019; Fiddian-Qasmiyeh, 2020).

Researching the legacies of colonialism

A range of challenges present themselves to and through postcolonial research: ontological, epistemological, methodological, geographical, financial, institutional and linguistic. In this section we focus on some of the methodological challenges. Over the past few decades, a number of important texts have made challenging anti-colonial provocations to social researchers. Often, these have focused on face-to-face qualitative research. For example, Linda Tuhiwai Smith's (1999) important text *Decolonizing Methodologies* challenges researchers who are working with indigenous communities to consider the coloniality of their practices and the historical harms that research has caused to such communities. It also proposes alternative ways of working and encourages indigenous scholars to use research to further the aims of decolonizing settler colonial contexts. This work is vital in bringing attention to the often-hidden power dynamics between researchers and those that they undertake research with, or even on (see also Chapter 12). While power relations in research practice are a concern for many fields, such as feminist research, decolonial critiques seek to draw out the distinctly colonial dynamics of some social science research. As universities and research institutions increasingly rely on external funds and strategic partnerships, they are also part of and complicit in powerful political-economic constellations (Lemberg-Pedersen et al, 2020). Critical and decolonial awareness of researcher positionality must therefore also be extended to academic institutions as well as their partners. Accordingly, this focus connects to the earlier-mentioned emergent work on power constellations coalescing to extract and monetize data from displaced populations in the global South.

Much less has been written on methods for tracing the past into the present than on researcher positionality. However, the question of empirically identifying continuity – in laws, documents, monuments, and first-hand testimony is pivotal to postcolonial inquiry. So what do we mean by postcolonial continuity? For us, it means to question the 'post' and interrogate colonial continuities in current migration control. This involves the challenge of identifying, establishing and understanding continuity between the epistemologies and practices of colonial pasts and presents. Here, the notion of 'continuity' performs an essential function in crystallizing cross-temporal links, doing important semantic work in post and decolonial analyses, often further conceptualized through terms such as 'nexuses', 'links', 'arcs', or 'trajectories'. Yet, answering questions about what continuity entails, what it *means*, *how* researchers go about establishing it, and *who* instrumentalizes claims about it, is far from straightforward. Tracing historical or colonial continuities of current policies and practices is no simple undertaking. That something occurred before (for example subjugation, racism, exploitation, surveillance) does not automatically mean that current practices are continuations in the form of causal links between the past and present practices. This is a challenge several authors of this volume address when historicizing current migration control and displacement policies and practices, in their particular case studies. In this section we discuss a range of approaches that researchers might use in their work.

First, the German continuity debate may offer some guidance here. It took place within the discipline of historiography when, during the 1990s, German and other scholars increasingly engaged with the controversial and highly politicized topic of connections between colonial rule in German South West Africa (current-day Namibia) and the rise and rationality of the Nazi rule and Holocaust. The postcolonial question posed was therefore the extent to which the totalitarian and racialized Nazi regime was in continuity with the brutal tactics and practices of the earlier German colonial rule. According to the historian Birthe Kundrus (2005), relations of continuity are notoriously difficult to establish, and postcolonial analyses of these can be both over-ambitious and under-determined, assuming certain relations across complex geographic and temporal contexts to be of a decisive, causal and linear character. While certain knowledges, practices and politics travelled between colonial contexts, this was often through intricate dynamics. More specifically, though the Nazi regime did profess inspiration for their KZ camps from earlier German colonial practice, they also, mockingly, referenced the British practice of 'concentration camps' for the displaced Boer population in South Africa as well as US slave plantation complexes. As noted by Kramer (2002: 1316), the 'architects of colonial rule often turned to rival powers as allies, foils, mirrors, models and exceptions'. German and British imperial administrators were adamant that the other was the more brutal colonial power, while American media fiercely lambasted Spanish concentration camps on Cuba, even though the US itself erected similar structures in the Philippines only a few years later.

The sheer multiplicity of these strategic appeals seems to resist any straightforward categorization of linear continuity. Moreover, adds Kundrus, authors who emphasize continuity perhaps fail to take into account the fact 'that people and institutions tend to forget' (Kundrus 2005: 305). However, such forgetting has often also been connected to deliberate epistemological suppression and erasure. Ignorance of the past can also become institutionally sanctioned (Spivak, 1999), and culturally embedded ideas (for example around racial difference) endure even as the facts of their historical application are forgotten. Approaching the question of continuity in the study of forced migration policies therefore requires attention to the formative role of ruptures and non-linearity, and in-depth inquiries into their evolution through particular contexts. Kundrus's own conclusion is ambiguous. She argues against the possibility of establishing narrow and strict notions of continuity, and instead encourages settling for an open-ended understanding of the term, that does not imply causality or finality, but can instead aid in identifying contingent parallels between colonial and later practices. At the same time, she points to colonial-imperial border controls as a case of more stable continuity that may in fact be demonstrable across time. This would then undermine the standard political claim of such practices being exceptions (Kundrus, 2005, see also Chapter 4).

These reflections demonstrate how detailed historiographic research can aid postcolonial researchers in avoiding the risk of claiming continuity by invoking vague or generic notions of colonialism, and then looking for them in the present. Scholars of postcolonialism can instead combine a range of tools, including from historiography, historical sociology, political science and political theory. One approach is to take a number of snapshots, or historical cases, which are used to demonstrate developments over a long time-frame, as Mayblin does in her analysis of colonial ideas in the history of asylum in Britain (Mayblin, 2017; see Hay, 2002 on the diachronic approach). Here, a central theme is also focused upon (such as ideas of differential humanity) and both continuity and change are observed over time. Mayblin (2017) identifies her case studies as 'critical junctures', and historical sociologists and historical institutionalists often use the approach of identifying 'tipping points' – moments of turbulence and change – in order to understand social and political change over long time-horizons. In a similar manner, though referring to his approach as comparative case studies, Lemberg-Pedersen (2019) has operationalized Kundrus's notion of stable, contingent parallels, arguing the existence of colonial precursors to the current European naval patrols and externalization of border control. The series of junctures in his analysis spans rationales and practices in the transatlantic slave trade and its suppression as well as current EU externalization politics. This requires detailed analyses not only of EU politics, but also of 19th-century capture wars, naval and suppressionist border controls. One focus-point of this analysis is the off-shoring of formerly enslaved people to so-called humanitarian colonies in Sierra Leone and Liberia, where they ended up living under extremely harsh conditions, including as forced Black settler militias (Chapter 2). Accordingly, the aim of substantiating such approaches is not to show equivalence between past and present, but to salvage from different temporal scales, important policy lessons and theoretical advances, otherwise ignored (see Hansen, 1996).

Both of these approaches require the in-depth research of historical and current case studies, or critical junctures (for a similar approach, see Chapter 4). When it comes to the historical cases, this can take the form of drawing on secondary studies undertaken by historians, conducting primary research in historical and colonial archives, field and museum visits or the synthesizing of multiple (disciplinary) literatures. Current case studies can rely on archival and repository searches, media and document analyses, different forms of interviews and multi-sited ethnography, including event participation (Marcus, 1995, see also Chapter 13). Both approaches may also involve Andersson's (2014: 284) notion of an extended field site with multiple locales, but where these are, crucially, also understood as *extending back* into (colonial) time. A third approach is the synchronic historical narrative approach which uses process tracing in order to create a 'moving picture' but is necessarily less in-depth (George and Bennett, 2005). These snapshots, in aggregate, have a 'panning' effect over time, used for instance in diaspora and mobilities studies (Kleist, 2019). Diachronic and comparative approaches then differ from the single (and synchronic) historical snapshot, by allowing for the building of a picture of both continuity and change without losing the complexity present in case study research (Amenta, 2009; Hay, 2002).

At the level of theory, Marxist-inspired post and decolonial theories have emphasized the power asymmetries created by global capitalist political structures embedded within and reproduced through colonialism, and enduring from colonial times. Here, Eric Williams's *Capitalism and Slavery* (1944) was seminal in introducing a detailed and productive Marxist political economic lens for the study of British slavery. Other theoretical frameworks, such as neo-colonial theory (Nkrumah, 1965), dependency theory (Amin, 1972) and world systems theory (Wallerstein, 2004) highlight how structural power asymmetries have continued to perpetuate the dependency of the global South on the global North long after formal colonialism ended. As shown in Mike Davis's political ecology analysis of British colonialism in India, *Late Victorian Holocausts: El Nino Famines and the Making of the Third World* (2001), asymmetries made it possible for the former colonial powers (and the global North generally) to continue extracting resources from postcolonies and to dominate their policies. This was done through political conditionality as well as direct interventions such as the toppling or even murder of new socialist state leaders (for example, Patrice Lumumba in Congo). While some of these neo-Marxist perspectives were criticized for a too-strong focus on economic determinism and sweeping generalizations, other post- and neo-colonial scholars complemented the economic-structural focus by giving more weight to psychosocial, cognitive, cultural or even aesthetic endurances of colonial hierarchies after decolonization (Fanon, 1965; Hall, 1996).

The different approaches listed previously illustrate that postcolonial research is not fast or easy. It requires the careful assemblage of social and political theory, historical archival methods, and the methodological and theoretical tools to link those histories to the present. What is distinct about historical sociology, and by extension postcolonial research, as opposed to the discipline of history, is that the aim is not to add to the pool of stories which describe the past. While historians often use their in-depth knowledge of the past in making sense of the present, this is not an explicit aim of the discipline of history (to the extent that one can speak of a whole discipline in such terms). The aim is to understand the past through careful detailed scholarship of particular events, individuals or periods. Accordingly, historical analyses are often not used to problematize current policy constellations (Gabaccia, 2014). Yet, this is of course a central ambition for postcolonial studies. Historical expertise is of vital importance for social scientists because the knowledge produced in most cases far exceeds the knowledge that a social scientist will have of any one historical period or context. Such cross-disciplinary dialogues can therefore function as a powerful remedy to counter processes whereby the repositories of relevant knowledge about forced migration contained in colonial archives, covering centuries-long colonial terrains in Asian, African, Caribbean and American contexts, are being actively forgotten.

Of vital relevance for postcolonial social scientists seeking a historically informed understanding of the present are also the discussions within historiography about the curation of archives, the silences and missing voices within them, in short, the power laden nature of the archive (see Mbembe, 2002; Carter, 2006, Stoler, 2010; Lowe, 2015). That includes how the past is construed, forgotten, remembered and negotiated in the present from available records, documents, literature and memories. As Ahmida (2021) argues, based on his groundbreaking study of the brutal Italian colonization of present-day Libya, colonial archives can also serve as epistemological suppression of oral cultures and traditions of knowledge-sharing among those who were colonized. Links across imperial contexts have often also remained unforged due to linguistic and methodological nationalistic barriers (for this point in migration studies, see Wimmer and Glick Schiller, 2002, for this point in studies of colonialism, see Hansen and Jonsson, 2014: 259–62). But for social scientists, the aim is to then think about the present with the past; and the tool that facilitates thinking across cases and into the present is *theory*. From connected sociologies (Bhambra, 2014), to Orientalism (Said, 1978), from coloniality/modernity (Mignolo,

2000; Quijano, 2000) to necropolitics (Mbembe, 2003), theories are devices for understanding relations between geographically and temporally disparate phenomena, illustrated by the various contributions to this volume.

The contributions in this volume

The chapters of this volume offer wide ranging examples of postcolonial approaches. The next chapter, Chapter 2, takes a selected case study approach to the extraction of military labour from African recaptives – people rescued from illegally operating 19th-century slave ships. Adderley and Fett explore the recruitment of African recaptives into Black British regiments in the Caribbean and into Black settler militias in Liberia. By exploring these two specific case studies, the chapter delineates some common themes of 19th-century slave trade refugee management, with particular attention to coloniality, ideologies of racial hierarchy and the cloaking of policy in humanitarian rhetoric, all themes which serve as illuminating precedents for coercive policies determining the movements and life chances of displaced refugee populations today. In Chapter 3, Fratantuono also explores a historical case, considering themes of expulsion and colonization within the Ottoman immigration story. The Ottoman Empire does not figure prominently in histories of empire and colonization, yet it offers a specific context to pose questions about forced migrants as tools in empire-building. The chapter considers what is relevant in the Ottoman colonization story to Turkey's treatment of Syrian refugees in the 21st century. In keeping with the insights of this volume, the chapter suggests that historicizing the present reveals patterns of exclusion, assimilation and expulsion across regimes and through time. Next, Chapter 4 brings together three case-studies differently situated on the colonial–postcolonial continuum: the Spanish enclaves of Ceuta and Melilla in North Africa, the French overseas department of Mayotte, and Tanzania. Authors Boeyink, Sahraoui and Tyszler explore how racialized hierarchies continue to underpin migration policies in these contexts. They show how French and Spanish colonial powers transmuted practices of mobility control to former and current colonies in Africa. Different historic, political and socio-economic contexts can be seen across the three postcolonial settings, yet it is striking that in spite of local specificities, the colonial legacies of mobility management appear in all cases in contemporary migration policies. Reviewing mobility related practices such as collective refoulement, massive forced removals and strict encampment policies, the authors debunk the narrative of exceptionalism that is often associated with such policies and can be mobilized to legitimate harsh measures and strict regulations.

Also questioning the prevalence of security interests, in Chapter 5, Eva Magdalena Stambøl and Leonie Jegen explore the colonial antecedents of current European mobility control and policing in West Africa. Here, the partly state-owned and partly security industry-owned French company Civipol has come to play a major role in implementing EU development aid redirected for security and mobility control purposes. They undertake a historical exploration of corporate interests, policing and surveillance, as well as the connections between them, from early French colonialism, through the era of post-independence, and through to today. Their key findings are that the distinction between public and private was always blurred and French capital circulated through the former colonies and made it back to France – something which is still the case today, now also encompassing EU aid. Moreover, policing, which tended to be connected to (public as well as private) economic organization and extraction, included surveillance techniques such as carding, fingerprinting, census-taking and registration, including control of colonial migrant labour. This mirrors current European techniques to control migration from West Africa, such as biometric civil registries built by Civipol. Biometric surveillance techniques used to control forced migration are also the topic of Lina Ewert's Chapter 6, which focuses on iris scanning of Syrian refugees in Jordan and their connection to UNHCR control. While outlining the broader trend towards 'surveillance humanitarianism', Ewert also crucially presents us with the perspectives of the Syrian refugees themselves based on fieldwork in Amman. She finds that their knowledge of what happens to their biometric data or awareness of data protection is limited, as data extraction is normalized and bureaucratized. This spread of 'surveillance culture' (Lyon, 2017) into the sphere of refugee encampment, protection and control is approached by Ewert through the concepts of 'technocolonialism' (Madianou, 2019) and decoloniality. This focuses attention on the power asymmetries and relations of dependency within which the extraction of value from data is embedded, to the benefit of (Western) stakeholders. Just like Stambøl and Jegen, Ewert also notes that surveillance techniques visible in forced migration and population control in fact have long colonial and historical roots, and their emergence and operation are deeply entwined with capitalist political economy.

In Chapter 7, Lucy Mayblin focuses on control of forced migration in relation to disease and pandemic control. While migrants have often been presented as bearers of disease, which has justified their exclusion, surveillance and enclosure in camps, it is in fact the much more affluent and mobile populations from the global North who have tended to spread disease across the world. Mayblin demonstrates how this has been the case throughout history, and the deadly implications for refugees that it has given rise to. The aim is to highlight some of the ways in which the almost unfettered mobilities of the world's wealthier inhabitants might in fact be dangerous (rather than benign, if not positive, as it is often portrayed); and to contrast that with the vast and expensive architecture of control erected to prevent or contain Third World mobilities. In recognizing these uneven geographies of fear and control we might then, Mayblin suggests, argue for more just mobility regimes which overcome the embedded racist logics which currently dominate. In Chapter 8, Mathias Hatleskog Tjønn and Martin Lemberg-Pedersen apply a postcolonial gaze on a very specific architecture of trade and control, namely Libyan politics of energy, displacement and forced migration. Recognizing how colonial infrastructures and matrices of power did not end when colonized countries gained independence, and that these can be identified also in current forced migration dynamics, it details the complex entanglements of colonial powers and empires in these Libyan politics, such as Italy, the Ottoman Empire/Turkey and the EU. Spanning from the 1911 Italo-Turkish war that gave rise to the Italian colony of Libya, through to the present, the chapter details linkages between water exploration, settler colonialism and externalized migration control, between Big Oil, EU natural gas pipelines and anti-colonial discourses, and between the Turkish visions of energy corridors through a 'blue homeland'. Tjønn and Lemberg-Pedersen's analysis demonstrates the intricate and strategic uses of postcoloniality, as well as the enduring, but epistemologically erased, effects of brutal colonial suppression in Libya.

In Chapter 9, Peter Teunissen and Penny Koutrolikou explore another geographic area witnessing historic and ongoing struggles between different sovereignties: the Evros/Edirne borderlands between Greece and Turkey. These borderlands experienced numerous wars, conflicts and imperial conquests, resulting in a shifting conception of insiders and outsiders, 'Us' and 'Them'. Being part of the Ottoman Empire from the 13th century, Greek–Turkish borders were drawn up by European imperial powers through the Treaty of Lausanne in 1923. This led to a homogenization and nationalization of the respective polities, and the border became a new marker of animosity. This same border region has now also become one of the first frontiers in the protection of the EU against migrants, giving Greece the role as Europe's 'shield'. The authors analyse how old and new 'Us–Them' imaginaries were mobilized by politicians in the dramatic events of February and March 2020 when Greek police attacked migrants with tear gas, batons, stun grenades, rubber bullets and live ammunition, and violently pushed them back to Turkey. In Chapter 10, Nasreen Chowdhory and Shamna Thacham Poyil take us on a journey through the philosophical and theoretical understandings of sanctuary as well as its performativity throughout history and across the world, but with a particular focus on India. Where this chapter overlaps most closely with the previous two is in their discussion of the Indian 2019 Citizenship Law. This law is based on a nationalist understanding of India as opposed to Muslim 'others', and aims to exclude certain migrants from citizenship as well as from sanctuary. As such, it both focuses (like Chapter 8) on geopolitical-nationalistic struggles between India and its Muslim neighbours, and on how the 'Us–Them' dichotomy plays into migration management and exclusion (as in Chapter 9). In Chapter 11, Philip Cole reflects on how European non-refugee political theorists represent refugee experiences in their work. He discusses some of the vast literature from postcolonial studies which has sought to explore questions of voice and representation and brings this to bear on his own sub-disciplinary field. In Chapter 12, Aurora Vergara-Figueroa and Jerónimo Botero Marino focus on political forgiveness in Colombia, exploring the offering in Colombia of a Black Christ by the FARC authorities to a community who have been the victims of both a massacre and repeated deracinations (forced migrations) over many years. Situating histories of deracination, and how the act of offering forgiveness in this instance can be politicized to repeat histories of colonial exploitation and racial inequality, the authors question what it means to ask for, or give, forgiveness. Chapter 13 is the final empirical chapter of the volume before the conclusion. In it, Felicity Okoth focuses on Kalobeyei Integrated Settlement, a project funded largely by the European Union (EU) to facilitate the local integration of refugees and asylum seekers being hosted in Kenya. Kenya has for a long time been considered a country of transit by forced migrants, given its encampment policy. Consequently, migrants' aspirations are often oriented towards moving to a third country in the global North, as opposed to settling in Kenya. Using a postcolonial lens, Okoth aims to explore the mobility strategies of refugees within Kalobeyei settlement against the backdrop of the delocalization and externalization of Europe's borders. In doing so she draws on the literature of subaltern and postcolonial studies and frames the words, aspirations and actions of refugees in this context in relation to a speaking back to the coloniality of power. This is a powerful closing chapter which balances the tension between efforts to control forced migration with the actual lives, agency and strategies of people on the move.

Finally, in the Conclusion, we draw together insights and discuss seven cross cutting themes that were identified across the chapters: the enduring power of ideas of race and racial hierarchy in responses to forced migration; postcolonial states managing mobile populations in their own interests; states seeking to spatially organize populations along modern/colonial lines; the role of private companies and non-state actors; the role of technologies for surveillance, categorization and control; and finally the fraught politics of sanctuary and hospitality. Drawing on these contributions as well as taking a step back, our final words sketch out a research agenda to further explore what postcolonial perspectives can bring to forced migration and refugee scholarship, an agenda that seeks to consolidate the emerging literature on postcolonial approaches to forced migration so that its insights come to inform critical migration studies more broadly.

References

Aas, K.F. and Bosworth, M. (eds) (2013) *The Borders of Punishment: Migration, Citizenship and the Northern Penal State*, Oxford: Oxford University Press.

Achiume, E.T. (2019) 'Migration as decolonisation', *Stanford Law Review*, 71(6): 1509–74.

Afailal, H. and Fernandez, M. (2018) 'The externalization of European borders: the other face of coloniality Turkey as a case study', *Athens Journal of Mediterranean Studies*, 4(3): 21–3.

Agozino, B. (2003) *Counter-Colonial Criminology: A Critique of Imperialist Reason*, London: Pluto Press.

Ahmida, A.A. (2021) *Genocide in Libya: Shar, a Hidden Colonial History*, New York: Routledge.

Aliverti, A., Carvalho, H., Chamberlen, A. and Sozzo, M. (2021) 'Decolonizing the criminal question', *Punishment & Society*, 23(3): 297–316.

Amenta, E. (2009) 'Making the most of an historical case study: configuration, sequence, casing, and the US old age pension movement', in D. Byrne and C.C. Ragin (eds) *The Sage Handbook of Case-Based Methods*, London: Sage, pp 351–66.

Amin, S. (1972) 'Underdevelopment and dependence in black Africa – origins and contemporary forms', *The Journal of Modern African Studies*, 10(4): 503–24.

Andersson, R. (2014) *Illegality, Inc.: Clandestine Migration and the Business of Bordering Europe*, Berkeley: University of California Press.

Anghie, A. (2004) *Imperialism, Sovereignty, and the Making of International Law*, Cambridge: Cambridge University Press.

Anievas, A., Manchanda, N. and Shilliam, R. (eds) (2015) *Race and Racism in International Relations: Confronting the Global Colour Line*, New York: Routledge.

Anzaldúa, G. (1987) *Borderlands/La Frontera: The New Mestiza*, San Fransisco: Aunt Lute Books.

Bakewell, O. (2008) 'Research beyond the categories: the importance of policy irrelevant research into forced migration', *Journal of Refugee Studies*, 21(4): 432–53.

Besteman, C.L. (2020) *Militarized Global Apartheid*, Durham: Duke University Press.

Betts, A. and Loescher, G. (eds) (2011) *Refugees in International Relations*, Oxford: Oxford University Press.

Bhabha, H.K. (1994) *The Location of Culture*, London: Routledge.

Bhambra, G.K. (2007) *Rethinking Modernity: Postcolonialism and the Sociological Imagination*, London: Palgrave Macmillan.

Bhambra, G.K. (2014) *Connected Sociologies*, London: Bloomsbury.

Bhambra, G.K., Gebrial, D. and Nişancıoğlu, K. (eds) (2018) *Decolonising the University*, London: Pluto Press.

Black, L., Seal, L., Seemungal, F., Malkani, B. and Ball, R. (eds) (2021), Punishment & Society, 23(5) Special Issue.

Boatcă, M. and Roth, J. (2016) 'Unequal and gendered: notes on the coloniality of citizenship', *Current Sociology Monograph*, 64(2): 191–212.

Bosworth, M. (2017) 'Penal humanitarianism? Sovereign power in an era of mass migration', *New Criminal Law Review*, 20(1): 39–65.

Carrington, K., Hogg, R. and Sozzo, M. (2016) 'Southern criminology', *British Journal of Criminology*, 56(1): 1–20.

Carter, R.G.S. (2006) 'Of things said and unsaid: power, archival silences, and power in silence', *Archivaria*, 61: 215–33.

Cazzato, L. (2016) 'Mediterranean: coloniality, migration and decolonial practices', *Rivista di Studi Politics*, 5(1): 1–17.

Chatty, D. (2017) *Syria: The Making and Unmaking of a Refugee State*, London: Hurst & Company.

Chimni, B.S. (1998) 'The geopolitics of refugee studies: a view from the South', *Journal of Refugee Studies*, 11(4): 350–74.

Cole, P. (2000) *Philosophies of Exclusion: Liberal Political Theory and Immigration*, Edinburgh: Edinburgh University Press.

Crush, J. and Chikanda, A. (2018) 'South-South migration and diasporas', in E. Fiddian-Qasmiyeh and P. Daley (eds) *The Routledge Handbook of South-South Relations*, Oxford: Routledge, pp 280–96.

Danewid, I. (2017) 'White innocence in the Black Mediterranean: hospitality and the erasure of history', *Third World Quarterly*, 38: 1674–89.

Davies, T. and Isakjee, A. (2019) 'Ruins of empire: refugees, race and the postcolonial geographies of European migrant camps', *Geoforum*, 102: 214–17.

Davis, M. (2001) *Late Victorian Holocausts: El Niño Famines and the Making of the Third World*, London: Verso Books.

De Genova, N. (2018) 'The "migrant crisis" as racial crisis: do Black Lives Matter in Europe?', *Ethnic and Racial Studies*, 41(10): 1765–82.

Duffield, M. (2019) *Post-Humanitarianism: Governing Precarity in the Digital World*, Cambridge: Polity Press.

Fanon, F. (1965) *The Wretched of the Earth*, London: Penguin Books.

Fiddian-Qasmiyeh, E. (2020) 'Recentering the South in studies of migration', *Migration and Society: Advances in Research*, 3: 1–18.

Fiddian-Qasmiyeh, E. and Daley, P. (2018) 'Conceptualising the global South and South–South encounters', in E. Fiddian-Qasmiyeh and P. Daley (eds) *The Routledge Handbook of South-South Relations*, Oxford: Routledge, pp 1–28.

Gabaccia, D. (2014) 'Time and temporality in migration studies', in C. Brettell and J. Hollifield (eds) *Migration Theory: Talking across Disciplines*, Abingdon: Routledge, pp 37–55.

Gandhi, L. (1998) *Postcolonial Theory: A Critical Introduction.* New York: Columbia University Press.

George, A. and Benett A. (2005) *Case Studies and Theory Development in the Social Sciences*, Cambridge, MA: MIT Press.

Gil Araújo, S. (2010) 'The coloniality of power and ethnic affinity in migration policy: the Spanish case', in E.G. Rodrîguez, M. Boatcă and S. Costa (eds) *Decolonizing European Sociology: Transdisciplinary Approaches*, Surrey: Ashgate.

Gilroy, P. (1993) *The Black Atlantic*, Cambridge: Harvard University Press.

Gregory, D. (2004) *The Colonial Present: Afghanistan, Palestine, Iraq*, Oxford: Blackwell.

Grosfoguel, R. (2007) 'Decolonizing post-colonial studies and paradigms of political-economy: transmodernity, decolonial thinking, and global coloniality', *Transmodernity: Journal of Peripheral Cultural Production of the Luso-Hispanic World*, 1(1): 1–25.

Gutiérrez-Rodriguez, E. (2018) 'Conceptualizing the coloniality of migration', in D. Bachmann-Medick and J. Kugele (eds) *Migration: Changing Concepts, Critical Approaches*, Berlin: De Gruyter.

Hall, C. (2002) *Civilizing Subjects: Metropole and Colony in the English Imagination, 1830–1867*, Cambridge: Cambridge University Press.

Hall, S. (1992) 'New ethnicities', in J. Donald and A. Rattansi (eds) *'Race', Culture and Difference*, London: Sage, pp 252–9.

Hall, S. (1996) 'The West and the rest: discourse and power', in S. Hall, D. Held, D. Hubert and K. Thompson (eds) *Modernity: Introduction to the Modern Societies*, Oxford: Blackwell, pp 184–228.

Hansen, A. (1996) *Keynote address: Future directions in the study of forced migration*, 5th International Research and Advisory Panel Conference on Forced Migration, 9–12 April 1996, Centre for Refugee Studies, Moi University, Eldoret.

Hansen, P. and Jonsson, S. (2014) *Eurafrica: The Untold Story of European Integration and Colonialism*, London: Bloomsbury.

Hansen, P. and Jonsson, S. (2017) 'Eurafrica incognita: the colonial origins of the European Union', *History of the Present*, 7(1): 1–32.

Hay, T. (2002) *Political Analysis*, Basingstoke: Palgrave.

Jones, A. (ed) (2004) *Genocide, War Crimes & the West: History and Complicity*, London: Zed Books.

Kanji, A., Palumbo-Liu, D. and Bacchetta, P. (2021) 'In solidarity with French academics targeted by the republic', Opinion. *Al Jazeera.* Available from: https://www.aljazeera.com/opinions/2021/4/12/in-solidarity-with-french-academics-targeted-by-the-republic [Accessed 25 July 2021].

Kleist, N. (2019) 'Mobility', *African Diaspora*, 11(1–2): 71–86.

Koh, S.Y. (2015) 'Postcolonial approaches to migration in Asia: reflections and projections', *Geography Compass*, 9(8): 432–44.

Kramer, P. (2002) 'Empires, exceptions, and Anglo-Saxons: race and rule between the British and United States empires, 1880–1910', *The Journal of American History*, 88(4): 1315–53.

Kundrus, B. (2005) 'From the herero to the holocaust? Some remarks on the current debate', *Africa Spectrum*, 40(2): 299–308.

Landau, L. (2012) 'Communities of knowledge or tyrannies of partnership: reflections on North-South research networks and the dual imperative', *Journal of Refugee Studies*, 25(84): 555–70.

Lemberg-Pedersen, M. (2013) 'Private security companies and the European borderscapes', in T. Gammeltoft-Hansen and N. N. Sørensen (eds) *The Migration Industry and the Commercialization of International Migration*, London: Routledge, pp 152–72.

Lemberg-Pedersen, M. (2019) 'Manufacturing displacement: externalization and postcoloniality in European migration control', *Global Affairs*, 5(3): 247–71.

Lemberg-Pedersen, M. (2022) 'The contours of deportation studies', in R. King and K. Kuschminder (eds) *Handbook on Return Migration*, Cheltenham: Edward Elgar.

Lemberg-Pedersen, M. and Haioty, E. (2020) 'Reassembling the surveillable refugee body in the era of data-craving', *Citizenship Studies*, 24(5): 607–24.

Lemberg-Pedersen, M., Hansen, J.R. and Halpern, O.J. (2020) The Political Economy of Entry Governance. ADMIGOV Deliverable 1.3. Copenhagen: Aalborg University.

Long, D. and Schmidt, B. (eds) (2005) *Imperialism and Internationalism in the Discipline of International Relations*, Albany: State University of New York.

Lowe, L. (2015) *The Intimacies of Four Continents*, Durham, NC: Duke University Press.

Lu, C. (2019) 'Decolonizing borders, self-determination, and global justice', in D. Bell (ed) *Empire, Race and Global Justice*, Cambridge: Cambridge University Press, pp 251–72.

Lugones, M. (2007) 'Heterosexualism and the colonial/modern gender system', *Hypatia* 22(1): 186–209.

Lyon, D. (2017) 'Surveillance culture: engagement, exposure, and ethics in digital modernity', *International Journal of Communication*, 11: 824–42.

Madianou, M. (2019) 'Technocolonialism: digital innovation and data practices in the humanitarian response to refugee crises', *Social media + Society*, 5(3): 1–13.

Maldonado-Torres, N. (2007) 'On the coloniality of being: contributions to the development of a concept', *Cultural studies*, 21(2–3), 240–70.

Marcus, G.E. (1995) 'Ethnography in/of the world system: the emergence of multi-sited ethnography', *Annual Review of Anthropology*, 24: 95–117.

Marfleet, P. (2007) 'Refugees and history: why we must address the past', *Refugee Survey Quarterly*, 26(3): 136–48.

Mayblin, L. (2014) 'Colonialism, decolonisation, and the right to be human: Britain and the 1951 Geneva Convention on the Status of Refugees', *Journal of Historical Sociology*, 27(3): 423–41.

Mayblin, L. (2017) *Asylum after Empire. Colonial Legacies in the Politics of Asylum Seeking*, Maryland, USA: Rowman & Littlefield International Ltd.

Mayblin, L. (2019) *Impoverishment and Asylum: Social Policy as Slow Violence*, London: Routledge.

Mayblin, L. and Turner, J. (2021) *Migration Studies and Colonialism*, Cambridge: Polity.

Mbembe, A. (2002) 'The power of the archive and its limits', in C. Hamilton, V. Harris, J. Taylor, M. Pickover, G. Reid and R. Saleh (eds) *Refiguring the Archive*, Dordrecht: Springer.

Mbembe, A. (2003) 'Necropolitics', *Public Culture*, 15(1): 11–40.

McClintock, A. (1992) 'The angel of progress: pitfalls of the term "post-colonialism"', *Social Text* 31/32: 84–98.

Mignolo, W. (2000) *Local Histories/Global Designs*, Chichester: Princeton University Press.

Mignolo, W. (2007) 'Delinking: the rhetoric of modernity, the logic of coloniality and the grammar of de-coloniality', *Cultural Studies*, 21(2): 449–514.

Mignolo, W. (2009) 'Coloniality: the darker side of modernity', in S. Breitwisser (ed.) *Modernologies: Contemporary Artists Researching Modernity and Modernism*, Barcelona: MACBA, pp 39–49.

Mignolo, W. and Tlostanova, M.V. (2006) 'Theorizing from the borders: shifting to geo- and body-politics of knowledge', *European Journal of Social Theory*, 9(2): 205–21.

Moses, D. and Stone, D. (2007) *Colonialism and Genocide*, New York, Routledge.

Nghi Ha, K. (2010) 'Integration as colonial pedagogy of postcolonial immigrants and people of colour: a German case study', in E.G. Rodriguez, M. Boatcă and S. Costa (eds) *Decolonizing European Sociology: Transdisciplinary Approaches*, Surrey: Ashgate, pp 161–78.

Nkrumah, K. (1965) *Neo-colonialism: The Last Stage of Imperialism*, London: Thomas Nelson & Sons, Ltd.

Odhiambo-Abuya, E. (2006) 'Revisiting liberalism and post.colonial theory in the context of asylum applications', *Netherlands Quarterly of Human Rights*, 24(2): 193–227.

O'Reilly, C. (2018) (ed.) *Colonial Policing and the Transnational Legacy: The Global Dynamics of Policing across the Lusophone Community*, New York: Routledge.

Pickering, S. and Weber, L. (eds) (2006) *Borders, Mobility and Technologies of Control*, Dordrecht: Springer.

Picozza, F. (2021) *The Coloniality of Asylum: Mobility, Autonomy and Solidarity in the Wake of Europe's Refugee Crisis*, London: Rowman and Littlefield International.

Proglio, G., Hawthorne, C., Danewid, I., Saucier, P.K., Grimaldi, G., Pesarini, A., Raeymaekers, T., Grechi, G. and Gerrand, V. (eds) (2021) *The Black Mediterranean. Bodies, Borders and Citizenship*, Cham: Palgrave Macmillan.

Quijano, A. and Ennis, M. (2000) 'Coloniality of power, Eurocentrism, and Latin America', *Nepantla: Views from South*, 1(3): 533–80.

Said, E.W. (1978) *Orientalism*, New York: Pantheon Books.

Said, E.W. (1995) *Orientalism: Western Conceptions of the Orient*, London: Penguin.

Seth, S. (ed) (2013) *Postcolonial Theory and International Relations: A Critical Introduction*, New York: Routledge.

Simpson, A. (2004) *Human Rights and the End of Empire: Britain and the Genesis of the European Convention*, Oxford: Oxford University Press.

Spivak, G.C. (1988) 'Can the subaltern speak?', in C. Nelson and L. Grossberg (eds) *Marxism and Interpretation of Culture*, Chicago: University of Illinois Press, pp 271–313.

Spivak, G.C. (1999) *A Critique of Postcolonial Reason: Toward a History of the Vanishing Present*, Boston: Harvard University Press.

Stambøl, E.M. (2021) 'Neo-colonial penality? Travelling penal power and contingent sovereignty', *Punishment & Society*, 23(4), 536–56.

Stoler, A. (2008) 'Imperial debris: reflections on ruins and ruination', *Cultural anthropology*, 23(2): 191–219.

Stoler, A. (2010) *Along the Archival Grain: Epistemic Anxieties and Colonial Common Sense*, Princeton: Princeton University Press.

Stoler, A. (2013) (ed) *Imperial Debris: On Ruins and Ruination*, Durham, NC: Duke University Press.

Tomich, D. (2004) *Through the Prism of Slavery. Labor, Capital, and World Economy*, New York: Rowman and Littlefield Publishers, Inc.

Tuck, E. and Yang, K.W. (2012) 'Decolonization is not a metaphor', *Decolonization: Indigeneity, Education & Society*, 1(1): 1–40.

Tudor, A. (2018) 'Cross-fadings of racialisation and migratisation: the postcolonial turn in Western European gender and migration studies', *Gender, Place & Culture*, 25(7): 1057–72.

Tuhiwai Smith, L. (1999) *Decolonising Methodologies: Research and indigenous peoples*, London: Zed Books.

Vergara-Figueroa, A. (2018) *Afrodescendant Resistance to Deracination in Colombia: Massacre at Bellavista-Bojayá-Chocó*, Basingstoke: Palgrave.

Wallerstein, I. (2004) *World Systems Analysis: An Introduction*, Durham, NC: Duke University Press.

Walters, W. (2015) 'Reflections on migration and governmentality', *Movements: Journal for Critical Migration and Border Regime Studies*, 1(1): 1–25.

Williams, E. (1944) *Capitalism and Slavery*, Chapel Hill: University of North Carolina Press.

Wimmer, A. and Glick Schiller, N. (2002) 'Methodological nationalism and beyond: nation-state building, migration and the social sciences', *Global Networks*, 2(4): 301–34.

Wynter, S. (2003) 'Unsettling the coloniality of being/power/truth/freedom: towards the human, after man, its overrepresentation – and argument', *The New Centennial Review*, 3(3): 257–337.

Zetter, R. (1991) 'Labelling refugees: forming and transforming a bureaucratic identity', *Journal of Refugee Studies*, 4(1): 39–62.

2

Slave Trade Refugees and Imperial Agendas: The Resettlement of 'Liberated Africans' into British West Indian Regiments and Liberian Militias, 1808–60

Laura Rosanne Adderley and Sharla M. Fett

Introduction

In the course of policing the Atlantic slave trade between the first abolition law in 1802 and final decline of the trade in the 1860s, military authorities rescued over 200,000 Africans from illegally operating slave ships. These Africans (termed alternatively *emancipados*, *liberated Africans*, or *recaptured Africans*) became, in effect, slave trade refugees: no longer enslaved, but lacking recognized citizenship, claims of territorial belonging and, in many respects, even basic autonomy (Adderley, 2006; Anderson and Lovejoy, 2020). Treated as an early historical category of 'useful refugee' (see Chapter 3), most ended up consigned to limited terms of indentured labour in agriculture in the Americas or in West Africa. Despite the frequent framing of slave trade suppression policies in humanitarian rhetoric, the governments involved mostly treated African recaptives as exploitable sources of labour that could serve colonial interests. They were a population whose future lives would be shaped and whose labour would be deployed in ways dictated by the governments who directed suppression policies. Governmental and private individuals associated with those policy-making jurisdictions presumed their social imperatives to be more 'civilized' than any other, and in service of the common good. Great Britain led the 19th-century international campaign to end the Atlantic slave trade, and British actors were particularly aggressive in imposing themselves as 'coercive' arbiters of a presumed global common good (Richards, 2020), but Denmark, France, the Netherlands and the United States also conducted notable, although much smaller, slave trade suppression projects. The governments who 'rescued' these captives prevented their enslavement at the hands of private proprietors, mostly in Cuba, Brazil or the United States. But the same governments who carried out such slave ship interceptions presumed for themselves the right to determine the fate of the former captives using racialized logics developed over centuries of colonialism.

A development which particularly betrayed government presumptions about the disposable potential of African recaptive labour as a state resource, was the decision by both Great Britain and the West African colony of Liberia to enlist a number of these people into colonial military forces. Of the roughly 200,000 people taken from illegal slave ships by the British, fewer than 5,000 ended up directed to military service in the British West India Regiments. Meanwhile, of the 6,346 recaptives rescued by the United States, hundreds of men and boys ended up serving in Liberian militia forces. Although the numbers were proportionally small in both cases, the administrative debates around this peculiar military usage of African recaptives illustrate much about the racial, ethnocentric and colonial character of 19th-century anti-slave trade policies. As Jenny Martínez (2012), Maeve Ryan (2022) and others have argued, anti-slavery politics of the 1800s, sometimes rooted in Enlightenment ideas about freedom, citizenship and governance, were an important precursor to more contemporary policies about humanitarian intervention and global regimes related to human rights, and thus also to refugee policies pertaining to the settlement of displaced populations (Candlin, 2009; Simms and Trim, 2011; Everill, 2013).

This chapter takes a selected case study approach to the experience of military labour by African recaptives in the mid-19th century. Specifically, for the case of British colonial policy, the chapter examines responses to an 1837 mutiny in the 1st West India Regiment, reportedly carried out exclusively by recently-enlisted African recaptives. The mutiny provoked a brief but uniquely concentrated mid-century examination of recaptive settlement policies, a moment of administrative reflection on coloniality, that had implications within and beyond recaptive placement in military service. The smaller US case is a counterpoint, highlighting both US displacement of recaptives from North America to West Africa as an early precedent for later externalization policies, and the coloniality of recaptive military service within Liberian Black American settler society.

As historians, our method relies on archival evidence shaped by US and British complicity in the transatlantic slave trade and flawed policies for its suppression. British and US administrative processes for suppression differed dramatically in terms of the scale and scope of archival evidence they generated. Whereas the British developed a detailed system of registration and court documentation for dozens of vessels and tens of thousands of recaptive Africans, the US and then Liberian record of recaptives (often filtered through the American Colonization Society) was much less robust. In both cases though, the viewpoints of administrative officials and other elite observers in the receiving countries or colonies dominate the records. First person narratives of recaptive African experiences with military enlistment were rarely recorded and must be inferred from context and second-hand reports. Furthermore, by the 1830s, the British couched their suppression efforts within the context of a government-sanctioned abolition campaign, whereas Liberia's relationship to US slave trade suppression policies was heavily shaped by the expansion of chattel slavery within the United States. This chapter takes account of diverging political contexts, while at the same time tracking the common ways in which British and Liberian authorities appropriated recaptive military labour for their own purposes, even as recaptives themselves resisted those designs. Imperial and colonial agendas, cloaked in humanitarian rhetoric and saturated in Anglo-American racial hierarchies, informed decisions about the management of 19th-century slave trade refugees in these two case studies. Taken together, they serve as illuminating precedents for coercive policies determining the movements and life chances of displaced refugee populations today (Mayblin, 2018).

Arming slave trade refugees in Caribbean and US/ Liberian contexts

'Forced' military labour and African recaptives in the Caribbean

In the case of British reception of African recaptives into their colonial territories, military enlistment played a significant role from the earliest years after the passage of the abolition law in 1807. The first 22 vessels seized for illegal trading faced legal proceedings in British Vice Admiralty Courts in Caribbean territories between 1807 and 1830. Of these early vessels, more than half saw men and boys directed into military service. This occurred in part because the British army had requested that the abolition law permit such recruitment. As Roger Norman Buckley (1979) explains in his foundational study of the British West India Regiments, colonial authorities sought to recruit both free and enslaved people of African descent into armed forces in the Caribbean in part in pursuit of manpower, and in part in specific pursuit of African men believed to be better suited to the temperature and disease environments of the tropics. The British West India Regiments were formally created in 1795, and enlisted both free and enslaved Black men.

The Army expressed concern that the ending of the Atlantic slave trade in 1807 would dramatically reduce the opportunity to enlist enslaved recruits. According to Buckley (1979: 130–33), it was specifically to address this concern that the Order in Council which laid out guidelines for enforcing the abolition law permitted the recruitment of African recaptives. He notes that emancipated Africans taken directly from slave ships were viewed legally as 'aliens' and permitting their recruitment required a 'special relaxation of the law' which forbade the enlistment of aliens. Thus, roughly 20 per cent of the earliest African recaptives in the British Caribbean were directed into the military. In some cases, this included the direct enlistment of the entire group of captives from a single slave ship. Thus, for example in 1815, in the eastern Caribbean colony of Antigua, all Africans found aboard two captured French slave ships, 512 people in one case and 211 people in the other, were 'taken by His Excellency the Commander of the Forces for his Majesty's service'.[1] This government use of African recaptives occurred at the same time as other recaptives were directed into agricultural, trade and domestic labour with Caribbean employers. In these early years of slave trade suppression, authorities actively debated the most suitable forms of employment for recaptives, noting that the Order in Council strongly suggested that non-agricultural employment should be preferred. Caribbean employers meanwhile seemed to welcome the possibility of any potential workers, but predictably hoped to be able to employ them in whatever form of work local economies demanded. Military service did not exactly compete with these local employment demands, but mass military recruitment marked the recaptive community as more formally at the disposal of the colonial state than either free workers, or even immigrant labourers (see also Brown and Morgan, 2006).

After the 1820s, two notable changes occurred in British slave trade suppression. First, a series of bilateral treaties established Mixed Commission Courts for handling slave trade cases, rather than using the Vice Admiralty Court system. The most important of these courts were the Anglo-Spanish Court in Cuba, the Anglo-Portuguese Court in Freetown, Sierra Leone, and the Anglo-Brazilian Court in Rio de Janeiro. Processing illegal slave ships at these courts moved the bureaucracies of slave trade suppression away from the direct settlement policies which occurred in the Caribbean in the earliest years. Second, after British slave emancipation in 1834, settlement policies shifted overwhelmingly to favour the use of African recaptives as replacement labour in British colonies in the Caribbean and in Sierra Leone. While these policies most directly benefited colonial economic interests, some voices argued that using recaptive labour in this way would benefit the abolitionist cause if British colonies using free labour could compete effectively with non-British territories still relying on slavery. Despite these larger policy shifts, the Army continued to recruit hundreds of African recaptives through the 1860s (Prochnow, 2020). Territorial conflicts had been endemic in the Caribbean in much of the 17th and 18th centuries, but the 19th century proved less territorially competitive in the region. The Army however continuously asserted a right to claim the labour of

African recaptives – and to defend that usage, even in the face of reasonable questioning from within the military itself. In the most comprehensive study of West India Regiment recruitment over time, from the 1790s to the 1860s, Kyle Prochnow argues that the whole process was remarkably exploitative, especially in an age during which British authorities claimed so much credit for anti-slavery policy transformations. Prochnow (2020: 2) emphasizes 'a striking level of cohesion between the pre-and post-abolition enlistment ... [and Britain's] profound dependence on the transatlantic slave trade to provide colonial soldiers' before *and* after 1807.

Recruitment of African recaptives into British military forces occurred alongside a steady expansion of non-military uses of African recaptive labour by British colonial authorities. In addition to people indentured into agricultural labour after being taken from illegal slave ships in the Caribbean during the earliest years of slave trade suppression, the 1840s and 1850s saw the organized transport of almost 40,000 African recaptives from West Africa into British Caribbean territories to serve as a direct replacement labour force after the final emancipation of enslaved populations in 1838. In the mid-1800s Sierra Leone became the main location for the processing of captured slave ships and the settlement of recaptives. In addition to the tens of thousands of recaptives transported to the Caribbean, tens of thousands of others were directed into terms of domestic or agricultural labour with more established settlers in Sierra Leone, including large numbers of employers who were themselves people of African descent (Fyfe, 1962; Asiegbu, 1969; Schuler, 1983; Adderley, 1999; Howard, 2006; Pearson, 2016; Anderson 2020).

Abolitionists reasonably critiqued the transport of African recaptives to indentured agricultural labour in the Caribbean as a scheme alarmingly similar to the Atlantic slave trade itself. They observed that people recently rescued from slave ships had little opportunity to exercise a meaningful choice about entering into supposedly voluntary labour contracts in other British colonies far away. Historians Allen Howard (2006) and Richard Anderson (2020) also emphasize how little choice and how much exploitation was also a part of the recaptive labour contracts executed within Sierra Leone. The labour needs and so-called 'civilizing' designs of colonial actors – both governmental and non-governmental – shaped the fate of recaptives as a matter of course.

Yet, for the whole history of African recaptive military recruitment, some people had questioned the wisdom of recruiting Africans directly from slave ships. Could such Africans be believed to understand 'the obligation of an oath or the nature and extent of engagements consequent on an enlistment for unlimited service'?[2] British authorities continued to use African recaptives as military recruits into the very end of the slave trade suppression campaign in the 1850s and 1860s (Prochnow, 2020). The West India Regiments had initially relied upon the purchase of enslaved men to fill their ranks, so the use of recaptives – although as free people – followed pre-existing colonial presumptions about the exploitability of non-White populations.[3] The second half of the 19th century saw the disbanding and reforming of West India Regiments based on perceived military need in the Caribbean or West Africa. Recruitment in the late 1800s came from the settled population of Sierra Leone, which continued to include African recaptives and their descendants. The West India Regiments were finally disbanded in 1927.[4] Thus, for at least a third of the history of these forces, refugees from illegal slave ships formed the largest portion of their enlisted men. African recaptives in this circumstance appear less as newly free human subjects at the centre of an anti-slavery policy, and more as an unusual exploitable population under presumptive colonial control, control deemed necessary for cultural, social and political reasons.

US externalization of slave trade recaptives to Liberia

In contrast to Britain, with its multilateral treaties and Mixed Commission Courts, the US unilaterally externalized the settlement of slave trade refugees to the newly formed colony of Liberia. In this sense, US recaptive removal policy aligns well with Martin Lemberg-Pedersen's definition of *externalization* as 'processes whereby actors complement policies to control migration across their territorial boundaries with initiatives that manifest such control pre-emptively, through the respatialization, off-shoring or outsourcing of control practices' (2019: 248, on externalization see also Chapters 5, 8 and 13). Liberia became a colony in the early 19th century, intended for the settlement of manumitted African Americans under the auspices of the American Colonization Society (ACS). Here, male recaptives found themselves doing militia duty on behalf of the Black American settler society. Until the very last years of the transatlantic illegal trade, the United States resisted multilateral treaties that would have given Britain the right to search American vessels. At the same time, US White hostility toward the presence of any African-descended person with free status within the United States politicized the distribution of captives seized by US naval patrols (Du Bois, 1970). By 1819, officers of the newly formed ACS – many of whom occupied federal government positions – used the abolitionist-humanitarian premise of establishing a refuge for recaptive Africans to pursue their domestic goal of colonizing free African Americans in West Africa. Supporters of the ACS steered through Congress a bill that shifted jurisdiction over illegally trafficked Africans to federal custody, mandated their removal 'beyond the limits of the United States', and appropriated $100,000 for that purpose. The ACS then drew on US government funding to establish the colony of Liberia with the dual goal of removing not only slave trade refugees but also free Blacks from US society (Sawyer, 1992: 13–42; Clegg, 2004: 29–38;

Burin, 2012; Mills, 2020). Liberia (as well as Sierra Leone under British colonial circumstances) thus offers an important historical precedent for what Lemberg-Pedersen calls 'humanitarianized displacement systems' that impose further forced migration and coercive settlement policies in the name of humane refugee management (2019: 264).

From the 1820s on, the ACS saw recaptives as a strategic resource for the defence of Black American settlements in Liberia. In addition to providing agricultural labour, recaptives also represented a 'buffer people' between Black American emigrants and local African residents. As historian Claude Clegg (2004: 111) observes, the process of creating a Black republic in West Africa 'also constructed a settler society marred by many of the same exclusionary, progressive characteristics common to modern colonial regimes'. The legacy of the Atlantic plantation complex surfaced in the agricultural models of sugar and coffee estates established by wealthier Liberian colonists along St Paul River (Curtin, 1990; Sawyer, 1992: 102–5). Guided by an antislavery mission of Christian uplift and African redemption, and beset by high mortality in a new disease environment, Black American settlers often perceived recaptive Africans as both an abject population in need of 'civilizing' and as potential military labour for conflicts with the indigenes whose lands they occupied (Clegg, 2004: 104–10). Indeed, these two views converged in the idea of military service as a civilizing activity that cultivated the republican potential of future male Liberian citizens. Thus, when almost 800 young traumatized recaptives disembarked in Monrovia in 1845, Liberian settlers received them as both 'fugitive savages' and as a welcome addition to the balance of power between settlers and the 'surrounding tribes'. By 1849, 25 of these recaptives joined with colonial militias to attack nearby indigenous towns engaged in slave trading (Fett, 2017: 164).

When US slave ship interceptions peaked in 1858–61, the policy of externalizing recaptive management to Liberia was already well established. Even after Liberian independence in 1847, the ACS continued to recruit and transport both African-American emigrants and recaptive Africans to Liberia's shores. The US government subsidized Liberian recaptive settlement, directing payments through the ACS and not directly to the Liberian treasury (Younger, 2008; Fett, 2017, Table 5: 167, 168–9). From late 1858 to early 1861, the US government transported over 4,600 recaptive men, women and children to Liberia, whose settler population stood at only around 7,600 at the start of that period (Clegg, 2004: 245). Roughly a quarter had endured a second ocean crossing after being interned in US camps before their removal to Liberia, while three-quarters had been intercepted closer to the West African coast and taken by the US navy directly to Monrovia (Younger, 2008; Fett, 2017). The sudden appearance of thousands of debilitated forced migrants posed an enormous logistical and political challenge to the overwhelmed Liberian government who relied on US appropriations and ACS support to manage recaptives' placement in apprenticeships with Liberian settlers and foreign missionaries. Similar to some British officials in the Caribbean, many White supporters of colonization in the US as well as Liberian officials like Secretary of State John Lewis feared the destabilizing effect of 'wild heathens from various tribes' on the 'civilized' settler population of Liberia (Fett, 2017: 169). Notably, such anxieties did not prevent Liberians from also viewing slave trade refugees as a welcome source of agricultural and military labour, if properly 'managed' and acculturated to settler norms. How recaptives responded to the plans of administrative officials is an entirely different question, however. In moments of collective resistance against the conditions of their new surroundings, it is possible to glimpse recaptive critiques of British and Liberian plans for incorporating recaptives into colonial systems.

African recaptives resist military labour and colonial agendas

Recaptive mutiny in Trinidad: resettlement discontent and anti-colonial rebellion

Beginning on the night of 17 June 1837 and continuing through most of the following day, between 60 and 100 soldiers in the 1st West India Regiment – reportedly all African recaptives – attacked their officers' quarters, seized arms and fled the army barracks in the town of St Joseph in Trinidad. They headed east toward the town of Arima, rather than west toward the capital of Port of Spain.[5] Later accounts would report that rebels hoped to find a means to return to West Africa, but their behaviour during the mutiny itself leaves little clue about detailed plans to carry out that intention (Joseph, 1838; Ellis, 1885). White officers of the regiment successfully escaped injury and raised the alarm. According to local Governor George Hill, older established Black soldiers 'distinguished themselves' in assisting the White British officers in fighting off the mutineers. Over the course of the day on 18 June, militia forces from St Joseph and Arima intimidated, fought off, killed or captured all of the mutineers, including their apparent leader, Dâaga (also known by the English name Douglas Stewart), identified as a recently arrived African recaptive from Dahomey, or the so-called 'Paupau' people.[6]

The 1837 mutiny proves especially illustrative for studying the use of recaptives as military labour because, even in the face of violent rejection of military service by at least some of these unusual recruits, most authorities continued to support the practice of recaptive recruitment, preferring to emphasize the alleged exceptional influence of Dâaga, the leader of the rebellion. Officials also pointed to the supposed special disruptive impact of having a particularly large percentage of newly arrived African recaptive recruits at a single location. According to White Trinidad resident E.L. Joseph who interviewed Dâaga in 1837, the motive for the mutiny arose from general displeasure with their having fallen under the control of Europeans and being displaced to the Caribbean. Dâaga himself had reportedly worked as a middleman between local West African populations and Portuguese slave traders. However, as a result of treachery on the part of Portuguese traders, he and others engaged in the process of selling other African captives were themselves taken prisoner aboard an Atlantic slave ship. Dâaga allegedly promised both his Paupau compatriots and Yoruba people among the captive group that under his leadership they would find a way to fight their way out of European captivity and return to West Africa (Joseph, 1838: 259–62). After British seizure of the Portuguese slave ship for illegal trading, dozens of men from this group found themselves enlisted as soldiers.

In his *History of the First West India Regiment* published in 1885, army Captain A.B. Ellis reported that in the 5 months before the mutiny occurred, over 400 recaptives taken from four illegal slave ships were recruited into this regiment and sent to the barracks at Trinidad (1885: 171). They came collectively from captured slave ships initially brought into port in the nearby islands of Dominica and Grenada. Between September 1836 and May 1837, four slave ships arrived at either Dominica or Grenada having been captured by the British navy. Without any international slave trade Mixed Commission Courts in those islands, British authorities disembarked the rescued Africans in the Caribbean, as emancipated people, while adjudication of all four cases took place months later at a Mixed Commission Court in Sierra Leone.[7]

Ellis identified the large group of recruits from these ships as consisting of people mostly from either the Congo region or from Dahomey, and characterized both regions as being known for 'ultra-barbarism' through most of the 19th century. Of the four vessels from which these recaptive soldiers likely came, two originated from the region around 19th-century Dahomey, one from the Upper Guinea coast (embarked from Gallinhas) and one had no geographic origin recorded. But even more than blaming the uprising on the particular 'barbarism' of its participants, Ellis portrayed the mutiny as the inevitable result of enlisting such a large number of recaptives together, and not taking care to mix them in with other Black soldiers who could presumably have acclimated newcomers to the expectations of colonial military service. Ellis asserted that 'the only result to be anticipated from such wholesale drafting of savages into a regiment was a mutiny'. Like others, he questioned the degree to which these so-called 'savages' could have understood the service into which they had entered, but expresseed a general confidence that more careful supervision and interaction with people experienced in the English language and British military and colonial culture could have prevented the rebellion which occurred. Not unlike slaveholders who interpreted uprisings as exceptional, Ellis's military account dissected the circumstances of these particular recaptive recruits more than questioning the problematic idea of using slave ship survivors as colonial soldiers in the first place.

E.L. Joseph reported that about 40 people, mostly mutineers themselves, died in the course of the uprising, and Dâaga and two other leaders were executed after their court martial a month later. Ellis noted with satisfaction that after this mutiny 'no more wholesale draftings of slaves [from captured ships] into the [1st West India] regiment took place' (1885: 183). But recruitment of recaptives did continue more generally. Absent other significant mutinies led by recaptives, one might accept the judgment of Ellis – himself an army officer in the 1st West India Regiment in the late 1800s – as correct. Over time, most recaptive recruits learned English, followed military rules, did not attack either their officers or local colonial leaders and participated in armed conflicts or local social control as authorities demanded. In sum, the British colonial state extracted a good deal of military labour from men and boys who they 'rescued' from illegally-operating slave ships.

Comparing the fate of recaptives in the West India regiments with the fate of earlier enslaved soldiers in the same armed forces, Joseph wrote: 'Formerly, it was most true that a soldier in a Black regiment was better off than a slave; but certainly a free African in the West Indies now is infinitely in a better situation than a soldier, not only in a pecuniary point of view, but in almost every other respect' (1838: 261–2). Joseph's observation here comports well with Prochnow's (2020: 11) assessment that in conscripting African recaptives, the British Army took advantage of a population 'least able to resist military recruitment'. Joseph highlighted the fact that African recaptive soldiers in Trinidad could directly observe other recaptives in the island living as so-called squatters, or in other words as mostly independent cultivators. He also noted that even recaptives who worked as 'labourers' for private employers often earned more than the soldiers; and most importantly, recaptives outside the military had the liberty to 'wander freely over the country' (1838: 263–4). Joseph (like Governor Hill, and the later military author A.B. Ellis) repeatedly portrayed newly arrived African recaptives as 'savages' more than as either slave trade victims or refugees. Yet even after the dramatic violence of the mutiny, carried out by a culturally foreign population who rejected both military discipline and any possible benefits of Caribbean colonial society, Joseph implied a general confidence (perhaps based on two centuries of European colonial management of subject African populations in the Americas) that British 'civilizing' projects with recaptives (and more generally in the Caribbean and West Africa) would succeed. Whatever else recaptive military service was, it was an integral part of that colonial system and its cultural imperatives.

By emphasizing the apparent imprudence of having a local barracks dominated by *newly arrived* Africans, colonial authorities conceded two important points. First, they viewed enlistment of these African recaptives as soldiers as an acculturation process; a process which would rely on the supervision of White British officers and the presence of longer-colonized Black populations. Second, they understood that this proposed acculturation process might prove difficult, or even fail. Where A.B. Ellis reported that hundreds of African recaptives had joined the 1st West India Regiment in the months leading up to the mutiny, according to local Governor George F. Hill, the so-called 'old soldiers' at the St Joseph barracks when the mutiny broke out numbered only 32 men, perhaps outnumbered by newly-arrived Africans at a ratio of almost ten to one (Ellis, 1885: 171).[8] One note written within the Colonial Office in response to Hill's report of the mutiny specifically contrasted the proportions of 'new savage soldiers' with 'old & civilized' ones. It is worth emphasizing that Hill did not recommend against the continued recruitment of Africans from captured slave ships. On the contrary, he argued that Africans rescued from illegal slave ships would logically expect to be asked to perform some labour in return for their subsistence, and in this context they could willingly and knowingly accept military service as an option.[9]

As already noted, concerns were regularly expressed about the capacity of recaptives – traumatized from their experience aboard slave ships, mostly inexperienced in the English language, and presumed to be culturally unsophisticated – to understand the full meaning of their sworn enlistment. And even Hill himself discussed at some length the nuances or limits of the newly arrived Africans' understanding of the 'comparative difference between doing duty as a Soldier and working for wages as a day labourer'. However, beyond these analyses of the enlistment policy, the underlying narratives about the mutiny circle around colonial insecurities about the civilization project. Authorities had confidence in their right and capacity to manoeuvre subject populations within the colonial worlds that they controlled, but doubt about how societal incorporation would work in those contexts.

Even writing half a century after the mutiny, military author A.B. Ellis stuck to an emphasis on the foreignness of the African mutineers involved, particularly their leader Dâaga and others from Dahomey. E.L. Joseph in his contemporaneous account took a kind of anthropological approach both to Dâaga himself and to the Ewe-Fon peoples of the southeastern Benin region, whom Joseph and other British colonizers called Paupaus. In lengthy descriptions about the mutineers, Joseph ultimately represented rapid, forced, social and cultural incorporation of recaptives as a failure (Joseph, 1838: 259–61). Tellingly, in the manner of an explanatory footnote, Joseph directed his readers to consult the writing of Jamaican planter author Bryan Edwards on the 'character of African negroes' and a similar text focused on French-colonized Martinique (Thibault de Chanvalon, 1763; Edwards, 1798; Joseph, 1838: 262–4). This situated African recaptive management and social perception of these settlers squarely within longer standing colonial discourses about the management of forced, perceived-as-sub-human, captive migrants in Caribbean territories. Even as British colonizers of the mid-19th century often took express pride in their newfound anti-slavery policies, or the potential of African recaptives as soldiers, intellectual and political boundaries between the management of these post-slavery refugees and earlier slave-based colonialism end up blurred. Furthermore, while most recaptive African soldiers did not engage in rebellion, surely more than the 300 men portrayed here wandered away from their places of employment, maintained their own languages and religious beliefs and collectively deconstructed the many coercive qualities of the manner in which they had been 'resettled'. Their experience clearly speaks to more recent conversations about the views of 'refugees' and other displaced people from subaltern populations concerning their own resettlement processes (see Chapter 13).

Liberian colonialism, militia recruitment and resettlement discontent

As in the British Caribbean, Liberian uses for recaptive militia recruits also served colonial military interests, yet the civilizing mission imposed on Liberian militia service had a different point to prove as part of a contradictory national agenda. In 1847, Black American settlers declared the independence of the Republic of Liberia – a Black republic second only to Haiti – whose success thus carried a global burden of racial vindication. In subsequent decades, advocates for Liberia constantly framed the existence of Liberian settler 'citizen soldiers' as proof of the capacity of Black persons for republican citizenship. Composed mostly of male settlers between 16 and 50 years of age, the Liberian militia acquired both material and symbolic importance as a marker of a successful republican government in response to detractors who ridiculed the possibility of Black self-rule (Ralston, 1862: 202; Dillon, 1871: 295; Moses, 1998: 108–9, 220).

Recruitment of recaptives into militia duty performed by all male citizens thus implied the eventual incorporation of recaptives into Liberia's citizenry and the capacity for self-governance. Inclusion of recaptive men and boys in Liberian militias was premised upon both the assumption that they could be assimilated into Liberian society and that such martial structures would have 'civilizing' effects. Much like conversion to Christianity, the adoption of western dress and education in the English language, the display of masculine virtue in militia training vindicated the humanity of recaptive Africans and demonstrated a collective potential for citizenship and nation-building. As Liberian intellectual Alexander Crummell noted in speaking of recaptive military labour, 'There is nothing which does so much for civilizing a man as putting a gun into his hands' (Crummell, 1861b: 276–7; Moses, 2004: 93). In contradictory ways, then, the enlistment of male slave trade refugees both presumed the cultural inferiority of recaptive Africans and asserted their human capacity for republican forms of government, which for Liberian settlers served as proof of the full humanity of African descendants globally.

From the Liberian government and Black American settler perspective, however, the success of this Black republic required indigenous Christian conversion, settler territorial expansion and interference in indigenous economies that local polities often opposed (Holsoe, 1971; Clegg, 2004: 103–11). As a result, Liberian militias aimed to ensure the future of a free-soil refuge for African-descended people, but in the process also defended a settler society deeply imprinted with the 'coloniality of power' inherited from its roots in the 19th-century US, albeit by racially subordinated and formerly enslaved subjects (Moses, 1998: 214; Quijano and Ennis, 2000). At the peak of recaptive arrivals in 1861, Crummell proclaimed to US audiences that 'the Congo additions to our [military] force already staggers and confuses the natives at all our settlements'. Attesting to the history of past settler–indigenous conflict, he went on to predict 'that all our native wars are now at an end' (1861a). From this perspective, a large incoming population of young, male recaptives presented opportunities for holding territory and strengthening the nascent Liberian state. The incorporation of slave trade refugees from other parts of Africa into Liberian towns and militias offers a historical example of situations in which, as Ella Fratantuono notes in Chapter 3, displaced groups sometimes became settlers designated to serve the interests of the state charged with managing their resettlement. Furthermore, the arguments for recaptive incorporation made by Liberian intellectuals like Crummell are part of a complex post-emancipation history of African-descendants deploying colonial rhetoric in the attempt to create territories of Black freedom (Roberts, 2021).

Although ACS and Liberian narratives often depicted recaptives as grateful recipients of Christian benevolence, administrative records actually reveal considerable resistance to conditions of resettlement. Perhaps due to their smaller numbers and distribution across Liberian settler militia units, this resistance centred on protests over physical abuse and other kinds of labour rather than military service. Liberian settler militias suppressed at least two collective uprisings of recaptive shipmates who had been together through several phases of enslavement and forced migration. More often, smaller groups and individual recaptives escaped coercive apprenticeships and even attempted to return to distant homelands. In an echo of US practices with fugitive slaves, most of these 'runaways' were caught and returned to employers (Fett, 2020). Despite the lack of first-person recaptive narratives, clear evidence of resistance in early months of resettlement is an important reminder of the wide gulf between the desires of displaced refugees of the

Atlantic slave trade and the policies intended to incorporate them into Liberian settler society.

Rather than being immediately conscripted into martial units, as Trinidad's recaptives were, Liberian recaptives usually joined settler militias as they grew more accustomed to their new surroundings. Two years following a recaptive uprising in Sinoe County, the Georgia-born Black minister Henry Stewart reported approvingly of the successful integration of 'our recaptives' into the economy and values of the Liberian state. Praising the group for their 'industry and sobriety', Stewart made special note of the 'imposing sight' of roughly 150 recaptives enrolled for the Sinoe County militia near the settlement of Greenville. In one particular company, Stewart observed 'eighty of these once raw heathens under the military command of our Government', and added that 'their deportment and orderly behaviour won the respect of all' (Wiley, 1980: 302–4). The presence of recaptive militia members reinforced the defences of Greenville and surrounding colonial farms in a region with a sparse settler population (Clegg, 2004: 146–7). Moreover, Stewart's account of 'once raw heathens' in admirable military formation conveyed common assumptions about the 'civilizing' capacity of martial service and expectations for the future incorporation of recaptive Africans into Liberia's settler society.

Conclusion

The US settlement of recaptives in Liberia and the height of British slave trade suppression both occurred during a mid-19th century era long recognized as a transitional period in the history of empire and the history of racial slavery in Africa and the Americas. New forms of coloniality emerged in the mid-1800s, especially related to the use of labour from non-European populations and attempts at cultural management of such populations in pursuit of imperial agendas, all constructed as positive steps toward a global modernity, shaped by Western norms, many of which prevail today. British military and civil authorities and US colonizers in Liberia talked around many sides of the challenges and opportunities for using African recaptives as military labour and having that military service contribute to broader colonial and 'civilizing' goals. Dominant though was the reality that, almost from the moment of their celebrated rescue from illegal slave ships, these recaptives became presumed movable and exploitable labour within larger political and cultural projects of which 'humanitarian' slave trade suppression was only a part. Under these circumstances, the recaptive soldiers and militia men in the British Caribbean and in Liberia ended up as hybrid subjects, refugees and immigrants; candidates for civic and cultural tutelage, and literal conscription into 19th-century Westernizing imperial projects, projects which prefigured 20th-century colonial and racial evolutions.

Notes

1 HCCP 1821 (61), Copies of the Several Returns Annually Made by the Collectors of the Customs in the Several West Indian Islands, of the Names, Numbers, State and Condition of All Negroes that have been apprenticed, in pursuance of the directions of the Order in Council, for carrying into effect the Abolition of the Slave Trade:3.

2 Acting Governor of the Bahamas, Colonel Colebrooke to Lord Howick, Secretary at War, 25 August, 1836. Colonial Office and Predecessors, Bahamas Original Correspondence, CO 23/97, National Archives of the United Kingdom (NAUK).

3 The National Army Museum of the United Kingdom emphasizes the radically different terms of recruitment as perhaps the single most distinguishing feature of the West India regiments. See: 'The West India Regiments', National Army Museum. Available from: https://www.nam.ac.uk/explore/slaves-red-coats-west-india-regiment [Accessed 4 January 2021].

4 'Timeline of the West India Regiment', The British Library, Available from: bl.uk/west-india-regiment [Accessed 19 November, 2020].

5 Sir George F. Hill to Lord Glenelg, Principal Secretary of State for the Colonies, 20 June 1837, Colonial Office and Predecessors, Trinidad Original Correspondence, CO 295/37, NAUK.

6 In the era of the Atlantic slave trade, this term, sometimes spelled 'Pawpaw' or 'Popo' usually described Ewe and Fon peoples from a region now located mostly in southeastern Benin, bordering Nigeria. All European descriptions of cultural or geographic backgrounds of African recaptives should be read with caution for multiple reasons but, as in this case, can still provide useful information (see Anderson, 2020: 127–65).

7 See: 'Trans-Atlantic Slave Trade – Database', at slavevoyages.org, voyage numbers: 1483, 1484, 2556, 34697. In 1837 there also arrived at Barbados and then Dominica a Portuguese-flagged slave ship *Don Franciso* which is cited at least once in Colonial Office records as possibly being the ship on which mutiny leader Dâaga had arrived from the port of Ouidah. See: 'Trans-Atlantic Slave Trade – Database', at slavevoyages.org, voyage number: 2555.

8 Hill to Glenelg, 20 June 1837. Trinidad Original Correspondence, CO 295/37, NAUK.

9 Hill to Glenelg, 10 November 1837. Trinidad Original Correspondence, CO 295/37 NAUK.

References

Adderley, L.R. (1999) '"A most useful and valuable people?": cultural, moral and practical dilemmas in the use of Liberated African labour in the nineteenth-century Caribbean', *Slavery and Abolition*, 20(1): 59–80.

Adderley, R.M. (2006) *'New Negroes from Africa': Slave Trade Abolition and Free African Settlement in the Nineteenth-Century Caribbean*, Bloomington: Indiana University Press.

Anderson, R. (2020) *Abolition in Sierra Leone: Re-building Lives and Identities in Nineteenth-Century West Africa*, Cambridge: Cambridge University Press.

Anderson, R. and Lovejoy, H.B. (eds) (2020) *Liberated Africans and the Abolition of the Slave Trade, 1807–1896*, Rochester, New York: University of Rochester Press.

Asiegbu, J.U.J. (1969) *Slavery and the Politics of Liberation, 1787–1861: A Study of Liberated African Emigration and British Anti-Slavery Policy*, London: Longmans, Green and Co. Ltd.

Brown, C.L. and Morgan, P.D. (eds) (2006) *Arming Slaves: From Classical Times to the Modern Age*, New Haven: Yale University Press.

Buckley, R.N. (1979) *Slaves in Red Coats: The British West India Regiments, 1795–1815*, New Haven: Yale University Press.

Burin, E. (2012) 'The Slave Trade Act of 1819: a new look at colonization and the politics of slavery', *American Nineteenth Century History*, 13(1): 1–14.

Candlin, K. (2009) 'The expansion of the idea of the refugee in the early-nineteenth-century Atlantic World', *Slavery and Abolition*, 30(4): 521–44.

Clegg, C.A. III (2004) *The Price of Liberty: African Americans and the Making of Liberia*, Chapel Hill: University of North Carolina Press.

Crummell, A. (1861a) 'Influence of the Congoes', *Public Ledger*, 12 September.

Crummell, A. (1861b) 'Address of Rev. Alexander Crummell', *African Repository*, 37(9): 271–80.

Curtin, P.D. (1990) *The Rise and Fall of the Plantation Complex: Essays in Atlantic History*, New York: Cambridge University Press.

Dillon, T.E. (1871) 'A voice from Africa', *African Repository* 47(10): 291–9.

Du Bois, W.E.B. (1970 [1896]) *The Suppression of the African Slave Trade to the United States of America, 1638–1870*, Mineola, New York: Dover Publications, Harvard University Press.

Edwards, B. (1798) *The History Civil and Commercial of the British Colonies in the West Indies*, London: B. Crosby.

Ellis, A.B. (1885) *History of the First West India Regiment*, London: Chapman & Hall.

Everill, B. (2013) 'Freetown, Frere Town and the Kat River Settlement: nineteenth-century humanitarian intervention and precursors to modern refugee camps', in E. Bronwen and J. Kaplan (eds) *The History and Practice of Humanitarian Intervention and Aid in Africa*, New York: Palgrave and Macmillan, pp 23–42.

Fett, S.M. (2017) *Recaptured Africans: Surviving Slave Ships, Detention, and Dislocation in the Final Years of the Slave Trade*, Chapel Hill: University of North Carolina Press.

Fett, S.M. (2020) '"Fugitive liberated Congoes": recaptive youth and the rejection of Liberian apprenticeships, 1858–61', in R. Anderson and H.B. Lovejoy (eds) *Liberated Africans and the Abolition of the Slave Trade, 1807–1896*, New York: University of Rochester Press, pp 323–44.

Fyfe, C. (1962) *A History of Sierra Leone*, Oxford: Oxford University Press.

Holsoe, S.E. (1971) 'A study of relations between settlers and indigenous peoples in western Liberia, 1821–1847', *African Historical Studies*, 4(2): 331–62.

Howard, A.M. (2006) 'Nineteenth-century coastal slave trading and the British abolition campaign in Sierra Leone', *Slavery and Abolition*, 27(1): 23–49.

Joseph, E.L. (1838) *History of Trinidad*, Trinidad: Henry James Mills.

Lemberg-Pedersen, M. (2019) 'Externalization, postcoloniality and the manufacturing of displacement', *Journal of Global Affairs*, 5(3): 247–71.

Martínez, J.S. (2012) *The Slave Trade and the Origins of International Human Rights Law*, New York: Oxford University Press.

Mayblin, L. (2018) *Asylum after Empire: Colonial Legacies in the Politics of Asylum Seeking*, London: Rowman and Littlefield International.

Mills, B. (2020) *The World Colonization Made: The Racial Geography of Early American Empire*, Philadelphia: University of Pennsylvania Press.

Moses, W.J. (ed) (1998) *Liberian Dreams: Back-to-Africa Narratives from the 1850s*, University Park, PA: Pennsylvania State University Press.

Moses, W.J. (2004) *Creative Conflict in African American Thought: Frederick Douglass, Alexander Crummell, Booker T. Washington, W. E. B. Du Bois, and Marcus Garvey*, New York: Cambridge University Press.

Pearson, A. (2016) *Distant Freedom: Saint Helena and the Abolition of the Slave Trade*, 1840–1872, Liverpool: Liverpool University Press.

Prochnow, K. (2020) '"Saving an extraordinary expense to the nation": African recruitment for the West India regiments in the British Atlantic world', *Atlantic Studies*, 18(2): 149–71.

Quijano, A. and Ennis, M. (2000) 'Coloniality of power, Eurocentrism, and Latin America', *Nepantla: Views from South*, 1(3): 533–80.

Ralston, G. (1862) 'On the Republic of Liberia', *African Repository* 38(7): 193–208.

Richards, J.S. (2020) 'The adjudication of slave ship captures, coercive intervention, and value exchange in comparative Atlantic perspective, ca. 1839–1870,' *Comparative Studies in Society and History*, 62(4): 836–67.

Roberts, A.E. (2021) *I've Been Here All the While: Black Freedom on Native Land*, Philadelphia: University of Pennsylvania Press.

Ryan, M. (2022) *Humanitarian Governance and the British Antislavery World System*, New Haven: Yale University Press.

Sawyer, A. (1992) *The Emergence of Autocracy in Liberia, Tragedy and Challenges*, San Francisco: Institute for Contemporary Studies.

Schuler, M. (1983) *'Alas, Alas Kongo': A Social History of Indentured African Immigration into Jamaica, 1841–1865*, Baltimore: Johns Hopkins University Press.

Simms, B. and Trim, D.J.B. (eds) (2011) *Humanitarian Intervention: A History*, New York: Cambridge University Press.

Thibault de Chanvalon, J. (1763) *Voyage à la Martinique*, Paris: J.B. Bauche.

Wiley, B.I. (ed) (1980) *Slaves No More: Letters from Liberia, 1833–1869*, Lexington: University Press of Kentucky.

Younger, K.F. (December 2008) 'Liberia and the last slave ships', *Civil War History* 54(4): 424–42.

3

Colonization, Territorialization and Displacement in Ottoman Migration Policy, 1856–1918

Ella Fratantuono

Introduction

In January of 1861, *Miralay* (colonel) Nusret Bey, the recently appointed Director of Migrant Settlement in Rumelia (the European territories of the Ottoman Empire) acknowledged the generosity shown by the villages of Gülpınar and Uğurlu in Silistre Province toward the Circassian and Kuban migrants recently settled there. The villagers had provided food for the newcomers and covered the cost of 48 newly constructed houses. Without the villagers' assistance, the immigrants would have remained in temporary housing throughout the harsh Balkan winter. In response to Nusret Bey's note, the Ottoman Prime Minister's office published a brief account recognizing the villagers' kindness and humanity in the *Ceride-i Havadis*, a semi-official newspaper (A.mkt.mhm 205.46, 1861). Publishing news of the villagers' generosity was a matter of policy written into the founding of the Ottoman Migration Commission a year prior; officials hoped to encourage other subjects to respond to the migrants' plight (I.MMS 16.696, 1860).

The Ottoman Empire faced mass migrations from the Crimean War (1853–56) through to its final years after WWI. As a settlement director for the Migration Commission in 1861, Nusret Bey played a role in the empire's first attempt to coordinate centrally large-scale population movements into its territory. Nusret Bey, after acknowledging the assistance he received in finding housing for several hundred migrants, returned to the daunting task of settling some 25,000 to 50,000 other newcomers (I.DH 460.30579, 1860). The migrants entered the empire during the Tanzimat (1839–76), a period of widespread reform. Ottoman officials, facing economic, military and administrative challenges, embarked on an effort to centralize and standardize governance. Large-scale migration presented opportunities to address long-term goals, including widening the tax base, increasing agricultural production and sedentarizing the nomadic pastoralist population.

Nusret Bey's rather mundane note from Silistre highlights fundamental realities of migration in the empire's final decades: that migration and citizenship would be components of reform and that officials remained dependent on subjects to actualize plans. Migrants were agents in social upheaval and, by the end of the empire, wholesale expulsion, but it is worth noting that residents did not always treat migrants as invaders or colonists. Indeed, accompanying the long histories of displacement in the Middle East are long histories of everyday hospitality shown toward those forced to move (Chatty, 2018, compare with the concept of sanctuary, see Chapter 10).

This chapter considers themes of expulsion and colonization within the Ottoman immigration story. The Ottoman Empire does not figure prominently in histories of empire and colonization, yet it offers a specific context to pose questions about forced migrants as tools in empire-building (see also Chapter 2, on this theme). When does a refugee become a settler? How might we understand indigeneity in a multi-ethnic, multi-religious, land-based empire? How do categories of settler, colonist and indigenous persons fluctuate in an empire under threat of displacement? To explore these questions, this chapter will first take a tour through Ottoman immigration policy. This is necessarily a birds-eye view, involving a flattening among individuals and groups that had different encounters with the Ottoman bureaucracy. Next, the chapter considers theoretical frameworks to address those categorization questions. It will conclude by considering what, if anything, is relevant in the Ottoman colonization story to Turkey's treatment of Syrian refugees in the 21st century. In keeping with the insights of this volume, the chapter suggests that historicizing the present reveals patterns of exclusion, assimilation and expulsion across regimes and through time.

Crisis and opportunity

Over the course of seven decades of Ottoman immigration policy, Ottoman officials used migrants to enact large-scale reform. A macro perspective cannot do justice to the complexities and diversity of stories of millions of migrants; nevertheless, such a perspective lends insight into migration policy-making, colonization, social expulsion and ideologies of exclusion across the period. This section limits its focus to how Ottoman officials envisioned using migrants as colonists to revitalize Ottoman agriculture, increase the empire's control over its land, and enact population displacement.

In 1857, the Tanzimat Council issued the Migration Regulations, inviting anyone with capital to relocate to the empire and receive free land. The petition of several hundred Prussian families to settle in the empire prompted the regulations, and the members of the Council embraced the opportunity to divert Europeans headed for the New World to the fertile, supposedly empty terrain of the empire (I.MMS 9.362, 1857). The policy was coeval with similar programs intended to draw colonists from Europe to locations such as Canada, the United States, Brazil and Australia. Though the invitation attracted the attention of entrepreneurs in the United States, Ireland, Prussia and Switzerland, the Ottoman demographic drama of empire building and empire collapse would not feature European transcontinental colonists as its main protagonists. A more urgent immigration issue arose, as several hundred thousand Crimean and Nogai Tatars and more than a million Circassians from the Caucasus began arriving on its territory in the late 1850s and early 1860s. The migrants fled consolidating Russian imperial control, destruction of villages, and threatened population transfer and religious conversion (Karpat, 1985). The arrival of the Tatars and Circassians signalled the beginning of a 70-year period of mass migration into, out of and within the empire, culminating in the expulsion and genocide of Armenians, Assyrians and Greeks during WWI.

Mass migration created multiple crisis moments across the period. In the 1860s, the arrival of hundreds of thousands of Circassians over a few short months left many stranded and subject to starvation. In 1864, the British Consul in Trabzon and Samsun estimated that roughly half of the 220,000 migrants who had arrived in the cities that year had died (FO 195/812, 9/24/1864). Following the 1877–78 Ottoman Russian War, an estimated 1,230,000 migrants arrived from the Balkans, while another half million arrived from the Caucasus (İpek, 1994). Of the 2 million people who left the Russian Empire from 1858 to 1879, 30 per cent died of malnutrition and disease (Karpat, 1985). Following the Balkan Wars of 1912–13, another half million Muslims took refuge in Istanbul and Anatolia (Quataert, 1994). Though most of the migrants were Muslim, they were diverse in terms of resources, languages, sect, cultural ties to the empire, and socio-economic status. Some were former subjects of the Russian Empire; others were Ottoman subjects expelled from newly independent and autonomous states. Many moved multiple times within and across the empire's borders.

Given this diversity, the term 'refugee' is inadequate as a blanket descriptor for all those on the move during this period, though many did flee violence. Migration scholars note that typologies of free and coerced migration fail to capture the complexity of lived experience. Rather than neutral or natural categories, 'refugee' and 'migrant' are labels shaped by historical processes (for example, Malkki, 1995, Zetter, 2007, Long, 2013). Broadening the scope of forces at play in mobility overcomes this definitional problem. Thomas Nail argues that human mobility emerges from expulsion from territorial, political, juridical and economic orders. Various 'figures of the migrant [for example, nomads, vagabonds, refugees, tourists] emerge and coexist throughout history relative to specific sites of expulsion and mobility' (2015: 15). In an Ottoman context, Isa Blumi has encouraged an expansion of the term refugee. In Blumi's depiction, the forces of global finance capitalism across Ottoman society 'created a particular kind of refugee exposed to a form of exploitation that increasingly scoured the earth for cheap labor' (2013: 6). Expulsion from former social orders increased the attractiveness of migrants for Ottoman officials, as it seemed a better guarantee of their loyalty to the state. Ultimately, officials labeled individuals as *muhacir* (migrant) based not on newcomers' reasons for leaving home but rather to signal that they would stay permanently.

The economic, military and administrative challenges the Ottoman Empire faced at the dawn of the 19th century influenced its immigration policy. Widespread upheaval and environmental change in the 17th century and a series of conflicts in the 18th and 19th centuries led to the depopulation of the Anatolian countryside (Özel, 2004). The population only began to recover in earnest beginning in 1830. From the early part of the 19th century to 1914, the empire's population density effectively doubled due to territorial loss and population movements (Quataert, 1994). The Ottoman Empire exercised loose administrative control even in its central regions. Ottoman officials responded with widespread programs intended to centralize and standardize governance, extend control over the provinces, increase tax yields and render nomadic populations sedentary. The interrelated programs were made more complex by the Empire's foreign debt and restricted sovereignty on the international stage.

The era of Ottoman reform spans three periods: Tanzimat (1839–76), Hamidian, named for Sultan Abdülhamid II (1876–1908), and Young Turk (1909–22). Centralizing reforms persisted across the periods. In the midst of reform, officials sought ways to facilitate loyalty among subjects. Ottomanism – an official ideology 'designed by the state to promote and maintain loyalty by national and transnational means' – emerged and changed across the reform era (Akcasu, 2016: 391). The legal framework of the Tanzimat asserted equality under law for all Ottoman subjects. The Hamidian period retained elements of this secular nationality framework while relying on Sunni iconography to appeal to a Muslim domestic majority and a population beyond its borders. The Young Turk period witnessed a return to the rhetoric of legal egalitarianism before more radical nationalists established the one-party rule of the Committee of Union and Progress (CUP) in 1913 (for the contemporaneous imperial war with Italy over Libya, see Chapter 8). Changes in circumstance and ideology created different possibilities of belonging for Ottoman subjects.

The 1857 Migration Regulations were intended to import cultivators and create future tax-payers. Its articles included incentives such as tax and conscription exemptions for 6 to 12 years and stipulations forbidding settlers from selling land for 20 years (HR.ID 24.13, 1864; see also Karpat, 2002). Though their arrival strained Ottoman finances, forced migrants could become the economic colonizers envisioned by the Migration Regulations. As such, personnel, including the army engineers dispatched to survey land; tactics, such as sub-contracting settlement to wealthy migrants who ran agricultural colonies; and policies, such as tax exemption, remained consistent across both groups in the 1860s. Despite these similarities, the Migration Regulations had envisioned welcoming self-sufficient colonists. The Ottoman government thus faced the challenge of turning migrants, many of them impoverished by the circumstances of their flight, into an economically productive, loyal population. Officials developed an aid regime intended to yield this transformation. It had the added benefit of tying migrants more tightly to state institutions.

The principles of the aid regime were established early. In May of 1856, instructions to the Governor of Silistre Province established a 10-year reprieve from the *öşür* agricultural tithe and a 25-year exemption from conscription. Migrants received financial assistance, housing, farming implements, seed and food (Saydam, 1997). Given officials' interest in migrants as colonists, the aid regime relied on categories tied to anticipated productivity. The Migration Commission recorded migrants' age, familial status, occupation, wealth and sex, and differentiated between farmers, artisans, teachers and religious leaders. Officials also relied on categories of unproductivity, including orphans, widowed women, the old and the infirm (Fratantuono, 2017).

The ideal of successful settlement fell short. Migrants remained stuck in temporary housing, and those who received land sometimes found it untenable. Migrants in lowlands died from malaria and other diseases (Gratien, 2017). Dire economic circumstances contributed to migrant participation in illegal activities. In 1880, the British Consul General in Anatolia described migrant illness, death and delayed settlement and remarked that without government rations, migrants had no choice but 'starvation or robbery' (FO 78.3129, 4/12/1880). It is in the space between the vision of self-sufficient colonists and the problems endured by the newcomers that officials developed mechanisms to make the population administratively legible. Officials gathered information to reduce difficulties for locals and migrants and to defray the state's expenditures. Collecting information would hasten migrants' transition to permanent settlement and make it easier to distribute precise amounts of funds and provisions to the newcomers.

Migrant settlement offered a route to increase the legibility of Ottoman territory, too. Officials surveyed land to determine availability and viability for settlement. In 1860, Nusret Bey's job included finding land of high quality;

instructions in 1878 and 1889 reiterated the need for high quality, fertile land (I.DH 460.30579, 1860; Y.PRK.KOM 1.26, 1878; Y.PRK. DH 2.93, 1889). By the 1880s and 1890s, settlement officials described the location of the new villages and provided rough diagrams for settlements, though renewed calls for careful registration and mapping reflected the reality of ongoing problems in the settler project (I.DH 1321.39, 1895; I.DH 1336.29, 1896; I.DH 1336.33, 1896; I.DH 1356.48, 1898). Both the population and the land had to be accounted for in the project of revitalizing the countryside. A year after the Migration Regulations, the Tanzimat Council published the Land Code of 1858. The law was intended to increase taxation and contribute to the sedentarization of nomadic pastoralist tribes. Issuing titles to newly settled migrants contributed to registering land.

Arazi-i haliye (empty land) was key to migrant settlement and land reform. 'Empty land' is a familiar term in histories of empires. In the Ottoman case, cultivation was prioritized in the 'bundle of rights' that constituted land ownership; empty (*hali*) land could be legally conflated with uncultivated (*mahlul*) land (Barakat, 2015: 53). Tying the emptiness of land to its use encouraged officials to envision how rail lines and irrigation works would open vast tracts of underutilized land to new settlers in places like Bursa, Ankara and Malatya (A.Y.PRK.UM 27.104, 1893; Y.MTV 50.5, 1891). Like the 'empty land' of other empires, the emptiness of *arazi-i haliye* was questionable, especially after decades of settlement increased population density in Western Anatolia. Land disputes followed on the heels of migrant settlement.

In what ways and at what moments did migrant settlement become a colonization scheme premised not only on *placing* a productive population but also on *displacing* other Ottoman subjects? The Ottoman government's capacity to provide aid to migrants depended on the participation of residents in the areas migrants settled. Instructions to settlement officials in the 1860s emphasized the importance of intergroup harmony among settlers and the rest of the population (Cuthell, 2005). Even in the 1860s, however, settlement agents used migrants in the larger project of sedentarizing nomads in Eastern Anatolia (Cuthell 2005). Although migrants were tools to undermine the power of the tribes, the Migration Commission differentiated among groups and individuals' social positions within those groups (see also Chapter 9). It welcomed elites in urban centers and diverted non-elites to rural areas. Crimean Tatars, a landed peasantry before arrival, were settled in more developed areas of Rumelia and West Anatolia, whereas formerly nomadic pastoralists such as Nogai Tatars were sent to Central and Eastern Anatolia to compete with existing Kurdish and Turkmen tribes (Cuthell, 2005). The Migration Commission eventually adopted a policy of separation and dispersal to break up the social structure of immigrant groups (Saydam, 1997:123; DH.MKT 1.3, 1861).

Whereas in the 1850s and 1860s regulations welcomed migrants regardless of sect, by the Hamidian period, territorial loss, the specter of nationalism and the threat of European involvement elevated the role of the Muslim migrant in officials' correspondence. Immigrants became tools to engage in demographic engineering throughout Anatolia. The Russo-Ottoman War of 1877–78 and the Treaty of Berlin was a turning point. The treaty established Romanian, Serbian and Montenegrin independence and called for Ottoman reforms for its Armenian population. The empire's loss of some of its most densely populated districts in the Balkans increased the importance of developing Anatolia. Since European backing had influenced independent state making in the Balkans, Ottoman officials interpreted the proposed reforms as a similar threat. The reform plan identified six provinces with large Armenian populations, tying Ottoman sovereignty to demography (Dündar, 2010). From the late 1870s onwards, the state used 'Kurds and other, immigrant Muslims as a weapon in the displacement, terrorization and thinning out of the Armenian population' (Bloxham, 2008: 328). Migrant settlement offered a route to undermine the claims of non-Muslim minorities in Eastern Anatolia and elsewhere.

The promotion of Muslim migrants, especially Balkan Muslims, is clear in sources from the Hamidian period. Officials sent immigrants to strategic regions to shore up Muslim majorities (İpek, 1994). In 1893, an Ankara settlement commissioner observed that placing Muslim migrants near a new rail line would undermine the 'Christian monopoly' on trade in the province (Y.PRK.UM 27.104, 1893). Officials' language of exclusion filtered into land contestations. Yucel Terzibaşoğlu's research on land disputes in Western Anatolia reveals that economic and religious characteristics became components of land claims. By the 1910s, 'the ethnic and religious identity of the title holder had become a criterion for the determination of the rightful owner' of disputed lands (2004: 176). After the Balkan Wars, increasingly radicalized members of the CUP prioritized establishing a Turkish national economy. CUP leaders narrowed their vision of who could be assimilated to the Ottoman state. During the genocide, the CUP appropriated Armenian property; refugee-settlers from the Balkans received houses and lands to create a Turkish bourgeoisie and to prevent Armenian return (Üngör and Polatel, 2011: 81).

Forced migrants are not simply pawns in domestic and international politics; nonetheless, a birds-eye view of Ottoman immigration policy reveals ways in which the 'crisis' of migration offered opportunities for Ottoman reform. Officials used migrants as economic colonizers, as tools in the legibility of land and as material for demographic engineering. Forced migrants were useful, though the ways officials attempted to use them developed alongside changing realities of territorial loss and limited sovereignty.

Social categories in a precarious state

This section assesses whether there is an analytically useful alignment between Ottoman migration policy and concepts in settler colonialism. The goal is not to position the Ottoman state as a settler colonial entity or to make the Ottoman Empire 'like' European empires, but to consider how forced migration and state-building create different modes of social and physical expulsion in a tenuously sovereign state. If settler colonialism as a specific mode of dominance is 'a system defined by unequal relationships (like colonialism) where an exogenous collective aims to locally and permanently replace indigenous ones (unlike colonialism)' (Veracini, 2017: 4), can settler colonial patterns exist in situations that lack coherent 'colonizer-colonized' or 'settler-indigenous' dichotomies? Bloxham argues that Ottoman Anatolia was not a 'colony', given 'its mixture of peoples … and the way that over the centuries they had been more or less absorbed into different levels of the unique Ottoman sociopolitical structure' (2008: 325). From that perspective, the boundary between exogeny and indigeneity is too blurred in the Ottoman Empire to give purchase to either analytical category. Indeed, to apply the framework of imperialism or colonialism to Rumelia and Anatolia incorrectly asserts the presence of bounded collectivities within Ottoman society. Can concepts drawn from settler colonial studies nevertheless shed light on transformations within Anatolia and Rumelia in the 19th century?

In his seminal work in settler colonial studies, Patrick Wolfe describes settler colonialism as premised on a logic of erasing rather than exploiting indigenous peoples. Settler colonialism is inherently territorial, based on claims to land and land use. Territoriality informs a logic of elimination; the logic of elimination, rather than exploitation, distinguishes settler colonialism from other modes of dominance (Wolfe, 2006). The logic of elimination is both assimilative and expulsive, but it is not necessarily ethnic or national in character. It is based on control of territory. The territoriality of the Ottoman migration project suggests an analogy to settler colonialism; the notion of productivity and the concept of empty lands 'justified' expulsion, though the possibilities of belonging to the state shifted across the decades. To claim territory, settler colonial states construct land as 'empty'. The claim of empty land operated differently in different contexts (for the context of Italian settler colonialism in Libya, see Chapter 8). In Australia, the British imagined a nearly uninhabited continent, and saw no need to purchase land from Aborigines, who remained in a 'state of nature', such that they had no legal claim to land (Banner, 2007: 16, 24). In North America before and after US independence, native American dispossession proceeded via treaty and land purchase, though colonists maintained an imaginary of an 'unsettled wilderness' that could be claimed through White settlement (Witgen, 2019: 394).

Indigeneity is not a natural or unchanging category; it is a status shaped by processes of settler colonialism, in which one's right to exist in space is negated. In describing the logic of elimination, Wolfe notes, 'natives are typically represented as unsettled, nomadic, rootless' and 'the reproach of nomadism renders the native removable' (2006: 396). When American Indians were already sedentary agriculturalists, the reproach was one of inefficient land ownership (LaVere, 2000). Emptiness was conflated with underutilized land; the claim to territory emerged from a claim to productivity, in opposition to an indigenous claim of prior existence or ownership. If indigeneity is not a natural, unchanging status, is the same true for 'the settler'? Imperial forms 'produce unstable relationships of colonizer and colonized, of citizen to subject, and unequal struggles over the forms of inclusion and principles of differentiation', yet the distinction between settler and native appears theoretically rigid in settler-colonial societies (Stoler and McGranahan, 2007: 12). According to Lorenzo Veracini, 'everyone is a settler if they are part of a collective and sovereign displacement that moves to stay, that moves to establish a permanent homeland by way of displacement' (2017: 4). Settler colonialism 'is a structure, not an event' (Wolfe, 2006: 388); long-term existence in a territory does not remove settler status. However, histories of 'classic' settler colonial states reveal complexity to the settler/indigenous binary.

Within North America, individuals inhabited different roles across the long history of Indigenous displacement and cultural destruction. As different regimes unfolded in borderlands, indigeneity emerged and retreated. For example, when California shifted from Spanish colony to an outpost of independent Mexico in 1821, second- and third-generation *californios* with indigenous ancestry became 'unequivocally … settler colonists', regardless of their 'racially mixed backgrounds'. American colonization in turn dispossessed the *californios*, though they 'remained firmly on the settler side of the Native/settler divide' (Spear, 2019: 429–30). In other parts of the continent, displaced native Americans adopted the lens of civilized/settled and savage/nomad in their bid to gain land titles and maintain autonomy (LaVere, 2000). In Mexican Texas, displaced eastern tribes formed an Anti-Comanche Union. The Mexican government sought to facilitate land registration for 'civilized' Indians who – as colonizers – could provide a 'buffer' against Comanche incursions (Shuck-Hall, 2003). After the Texas Revolution, nearly all of the anti-Comanche Union were forcibly removed; settler status was tenuous for those excluded from Anglo-American Manifest Destiny.

Historians have described Ottoman colonial techniques in Libya and Yemen as partially defensive, spurred by the European scramble for Africa (Minawi, 2016). In Libya, Ottoman officials brought with them a civilizing mission targeting local inhabitants, though 'colonial Ottomanism' did not stem from the racial anxieties at the heart of other settler colonial projects. Ottoman officials did not codify race or ethnicity into law, and officials balanced the 'politics of difference' with the belief that centralization, standardization and legal equality were key to integrating peripheral regions and saving the Ottoman state (Kuehn, 2011:13). The Ottoman presence in its peripheries was more intuitively imperial than its rule in Rumelia and Anatolia, but in a state with conditional sovereignty, some distinctions between imperial centre and imperial periphery dissolved. In the 1877–78 Russo-Ottoman War, Russian forces halted less than 10 miles from Istanbul, while during the Balkan Wars, Bulgarian troops were within 30 miles of the capital. The 19th-century Ottoman imperial project was one of tenuous sovereignty; thus any space, especially the 'heartland', could be the site of state-building, territoriality and expulsion. In a state of precarity, the centre is subject to a logic of elimination.

The settler retains, at least temporarily, the possibility of being assimilated. Crimean Tatars and Circassians were displaced by Russian policies of removal and replacement. Within the Ottoman Empire, they were targets of assimilation and displacement. Kurdish nomadic pastoralists likewise inhabited the possibility of assimilation, contributed to displacement, and eventually faced expulsion. The refugee was at once indigenous and held the possibility of being a settler; the nomad was indigenous, but could become a tool or victim of displacement. Different axes of expulsion produce new and different conditions of indigeneity.

Discourses of productivity render certain claims to space untenable and shift individuals and groups among positions such as immigrant, indigenous person, nomad and colonizer. The elevation of Anatolia contributed to the narrowing of belonging within Ottoman population policies. Genocide during WWI and the treatment of Kurds in later decades draws attention to the violence of nationalism. Still, as Blumi has noted, historians must avoid narratives of ethno-national incompatibility. Tectonic shifts in capital contributed to the upheaval of which refugees were symptoms and agents (Blumi, 2013). The logic of elimination is both assimilative and expulsive. It targets 'collectivity'; when the collectivity is destroyed, an individual might be allowed to remain (Wolfe, 2006). The plasticity of settler-indigenous status was a fundamental element in Ottoman governance as the state navigated its tenuous existence. Targets of social and physical expulsion changed not because of an underlying ethno-national incompatibility but as they were assigned social categories in competition with Ottomanism.

Useful refugees after Empire

This chapter concludes with a few comments on migration policies and projects in the Republic of Turkey. A meaningful comparison between the late Ottoman Empire and the course of migration policies within the Turkish Republic is beyond the scope of this chapter. Instead, the section examines Turkey's ongoing use of migrants to draw lines of belonging within its population and the persistence of international politics in influencing dis/placement within Anatolia.

The Turkish Republic retained the ethno-nationalism of the final decade of the Ottoman Empire in its migration and citizenship regimes. Ayşe Parla asserts that Turkey is unique in using ethnic status in its legal definition of 'immigrant' (*göçmen*). Thus, as 'ethnic kin', Muslim immigrants from the Balkans retained a privileged position in migration law until 1990 (Parla, 2019). The Turkish government treated Balkan migrants as repatriates rather than refugees, including the 300,000 forced migrants who fled Bulgaria in 1989 following violent assimilation campaigns. After WWI, Balkan Muslims were settled on Armenians' 'abandoned' property; they were tools, as well, in Turkey's relationship to its non-Turkish and non-Sunni populations. Kurds in Turkey have been subject to assimilation and expulsion. Turkish policies have included the banning of Kurdish language and schools, displacement and compulsory settlement. Following Kurdish resistance in 1925, the Turkish National Assembly developed plans to settle 500,000 Balkan Muslims in majority Kurdish areas. The Settlement Law of 1934 maintained this idea, though refugees were settled in Thrace and Western Anatolia instead. In the 1990s, the state forcibly displaced 1.5 to 3 million Kurds from villages in the Southeast (Yeğen, 2009: 600–4).

International conditions affect the drawing of lines of citizenship and reorient the geography of the useful refugee. While Parliament drafted the 1934 law in reference to Kurds, its enactment reflected regional geopolitics. For Turkish leaders, the post-WWI Versailles minority treaties posed a continuing risk of European imperial intervention, threatening the sovereignty of the state. The threat of irredentism and territorial loss determined refugee placement (Öztan, 2020). The themes of refugee utility and international influences in migrant policy are also present in Turkey's response to refugees of the recent Syrian Civil War. As of December 2020, the Turkish Government had registered 3,639,572 Syrian refugees. Aside from the half million registered in Istanbul, a little over half of the total number (1,886,474) are registered in the provinces bordering Syria (T.C. İçişleri Bakanlığı Göç İdaresi Genel Müdürlüğü, 2020). The concentration of Syrians in southeastern Turkey reflects the region's longer history of mobility, refugee movements and cross-border networks (Chatty, 2018).

Turkey retains the geographical limitations written into the 1951 Refugee Convention, which means only individuals fleeing from Europe are eligible to seek asylum. Turkish authorities designate non-European asylum seekers 'conditional refugees'; the UNHCR determines legal refugee status in order to move migrants to third countries. Syrians are not eligible for refugee status in Turkey. Instead, Turkey has granted Syrians 'temporary protection' status. While this status means that Syrians do not need to apply individually for asylum, it leaves them stranded somewhere between refugee and guest, with no clear pathway to citizenship. In 2014, Turkey began offering biometric ID cards to Syrians (on biometrics in migration control, see also Chapters 5 and 6). Registration grants Syrians access to free health care and education, although their access is hampered by informal barriers. Registration does not automatically grant work permits, and many Syrians are trapped in exploitative working conditions (Baban et al, 2017).

The Turkish government's emphasis on the temporary nature of its protective regime distinguishes its treatment of Syrians from its stance toward Balkan Muslims prior to 1990 and the Ottoman expectation of a *muhacir*'s permanent settlement. The utility of the Syrian refugee for the ruling Justice and Development Party [AKP] government was one initially predicated on their return. Turkey's foreign ministry claimed refugees' 'positive feelings' toward Turkey would contribute to its regional role (Memisoğlu and Ilgit, 2017: 327). Turkey has leveraged the refugees in its negotiations with Europe, notably through the 2016 Turkey–EU deal, in which Turkey promised to take back undocumented migrants in exchange for €6 billion, the revival of accession talks, and visa-free travel in the EU for Turkish citizens. It exploited the refugees to gain NATO acceptance of Turkish military operations in Syria. Furthermore, in a bid to undermine Kurdish autonomy, the AKP has proposed repatriating over 2 million refugees to a Turkish-occupied 'safe zone' in northeastern Syria.

The concentration of refugees in the southeast is but one factor that contributes to skepticism among citizens about how the AKP might wield refugees domestically. Syrians face discrimination within Turkey and are blamed for diverting money from Turkish citizens. Recently, representatives of an opposition party criticized the AKP's spending of $40 billion on refugees in comparison to its $15 billion COVID-19 stimulus package (Çetingüleç, 2020). Citizens voice concerns that refugees have easier access to public services, and some Alevi and Kurdish organizations suspect that the AKP is engaging in demographic engineering via refugee settlement. In 2014, they questioned whether the ID cards granted refugees access to vote, with the implication being that they would be loyal AKP supporters (Memisoğlu and Ilgit, 2017).

That states use forced migrants and that they do so with reference to international as well as domestic politics are not new insights in forced migration studies, but this description of Turkey's postcolonial migration policies offers the chance to reflect further on relationships between forced migration and colonization (for the usefulness of recaptured Africans in Liberia and Sierra Leone, see Chapter 2). What factors would lead a Turkish government to welcome Syrians as colonizers in Southeast Anatolia? Who is most prone to the precarity of indigeneity? What does Turkey's migration and asylum regime reveal about current possibilities for inclusion, exclusion and social expulsion? Do structures of settler colonialism and the logic of elimination persist in post-Ottoman states? These are questions that arise from bringing history to bear on the present, and that suggest the potential for many historical sociological analyses in the future.

References

Akcasu, A.E. (2016) 'Migrants to citizens: an evaluation of the expansionist features of Hamidian Ottomanism, 1876–1909', *Die Welt Des Islams*, 56(3): 388–414.

Baban, F., Ilcan, S. and Rygiel, K. (2017) 'Syrian refugees in Turkey: pathways to precarity, differential inclusion, and negotiated citizenship rights', *Journal of Ethnic and Migration Studies*, 43(1): 41–57.

Banner, S. (2007) *Possessing the Pacific: Land, Settlers, and Indigenous People from Australia to Alaska*, Cambridge, MA: Harvard University Press.

Barakat, N. (2015) An Empty Land? Nomads and Property Administration in Hamidian Syria, Doctoral Thesis, Berkeley: University of California.

Bloxham, D. (2008) 'Internal colonization, inter-imperial conflict and the Armenian genocide', in D. Moses (ed) *Empire Colony, Genocide: Conquest, Occupation and Subaltern Resistance in World History*, New York: Berghahn Books, pp 325–42.

Blumi, I. (2013) *Ottoman Refugees, 1878–1939: Migration in a Post-Imperial World*, Oxford: Bloomsbury.

Çetingüleç, M. (2020) 'Syrian refugees villainized as Turkey faces costs of coronavirus', *Al Monitor*, [online] 5 April, Available from: https://www.al-monitor.com/pulse/originals/2020/04/turkey-syria-refugees-blamed-coronavirus-economic-turmoil.html [Accessed 14 December 2020].

Chatty, D. (2018) *Syria: The Making and Unmaking of a Refugee State*, New York: Oxford University Press.

Cuthell, D. (2005) The Muhacirin Komisyonu: An Agent in the Transformation of Ottoman Anatolia, 1860–1866, Doctoral Thesis, New York: Columbia University.

Dündar, F. (2010) *Crime of Numbers: The Role of Statistics in the Armenian Question (1878–1918)*, New Brunswick: Transaction Publishers.

Fratantuono, E. (2017) 'State fears and immigrant tiers: historical analysis as a method in evaluating migration categories', *Middle East Journal of Refugee Studies*, 2(1): 97–115.

Gratien, C. (2017) 'The Ottoman quagmire: malaria, swamps, and settlement in the late Ottoman Mediterranean', *International Journal of Middle East Studies*, 49(4): 583–604.

İpek, N. (1994) *Rumeli'den Anadolu'ya Türk Göçleri, 1877–1890*, Ankara: Türk Tarih Kurumu.

Karpat, K. (1985) *Ottoman Population, 1830–1914: Demographic and Social Characteristics*, Madison: University of Wisconsin Press.

Karpat, K. (2002) 'Ottoman immigration policies and settlement in Palestine', in K. Karpat (ed) *Studies on Ottoman Social and Political History: Selected Articles and Essays*, Leiden: Brill, pp 783–99.

Kuehn, T. (2011) *Empire, Islam, and Politics of Difference: Ottoman Rule in Yemen, 1849–1919*, Leiden: Brill.

LaVere, D. (2000) *Contrary Neighbors: Southern Plains and Removed Indians in Indian Territory*, Norman: University of Oklahoma Press.

Long, K. (2013) 'When refugees stopped being migrants: movement, labour, and humanitarian protection', *Migration Studies*, 1(1): 4–26.

Malkki, L. (1995) 'Refugees and exile: from "refugee studies" to the national order of things', *Annual Review of Anthropology*, 24: 495–523.

Memsioğlu, F. and Ilgıt, A. (2017) 'Syrian refugees in Turkey: multifaceted challenges, diverse players, and ambiguous policies', *Mediterranean Politics*, 22(3): 317–38.

Minawi, M. (2016) *The Ottoman Scramble for Africa: Empire and Diplomacy in the Sahara and the Hijaz*, Stanford: Stanford University Press.

Nail, T. (2015) *The Figure of the Migrant*, Stanford: Stanford University Press.

Özel, O. (2004) 'Population changes in Ottoman Anatolia during the 16th and 17th centuries: the "demographic crisis" reconsidered', *International Journal of Middle East Studies*, 36(2): 183–205.

Öztan, R.H. (2020) 'Settlement law of 1934: Turkish nationalism in the age of revisionism', *Journal of Migration History*, 6(1): 82–103.

Parla, A. (2019) *Precarious Hope: Migration and the Limits of Belonging in Turkey*, Stanford: Stanford University Press.

Quataert, D. (1994) 'Population', in H. İnalcık and D. Quataert (eds) *An Economic and Social History of the Ottoman Empire*, vol. 2. Cambridge: Cambridge University Press, pp 777–97.

Saydam, A. (1997) *Kırım ve Kafkas Göçleri, 1856–1876*, Ankara: Türk Tarih Kurumu.

Shuck-Hall, S.M. (2003) 'Borderlands and identities in imperial Texas: the Alabamas and Coushattas in the Anti-Comanche Union, 1820–1840', *The International History Review*, 25(3): 563–91.

Spear, J. (2019) 'Beyond the native/settler divide in early California', *William and Mary Quarterly*, 76(3): 427–34.

Stoler, A.L. and McGranahan, C. (2007) 'Introduction: reconfiguring imperial terrains', in A.L. Stoler, C. McGranahan and P.C. Perdue (eds) *Imperial Formations*, Sante Fe: School for Advanced Research Press, pp 3–42.

T.C. İçişleri Bakanlığı Göç İdaresi Genel Müdürlüğü (2020) 'Geçici Koruma', [online] 23 December, Available from: https://www.goc.gov.tr/gecici-koruma5638 [Accessed 26 December 2020].

Terzibaşoğlu, Y. (2004) 'Land-disputes and ethno-politics: northwestern Anatolia, 1877–1912', in S. Engerman and J. Metzer (eds) *Land Rights, Ethno-Nationality and Sovereignty in History*, London: Routledge, pp 153–80.
Üngör, U. and Polatel, M. (2011) *Confiscation and Destruction: The Young Turk Seizure of Armenian Property*, London: Bloomsbury.
Veracini, L. (2017) 'Introduction: settler colonialism as a distinct mode of domination', in E. Cavanagh and L. Veracini (eds) *The Routledge Handbook of the History of Settler Colonialism*, London: Routledge.
Witgen, M. (2019) 'A nation of settlers: the early American republic and the colonization of the northwest territory', *The William and Mary Quarterly*, 76(3): 391–8.
Wolfe, P. (2006) 'Settler colonialism and the elimination of the native', *Journal of Genocide Research*, 8(4): 387–409.
Yeğen, M. (2009) '"Prospective Turks" or "pseudo-citizens": Kurds in Turkey', *Middle East Journal*, 63(4): 597–615.
Zetter, R. (2007) 'More labels, fewer refugees: remaking the refugee label in an era of globalization', *Journal of Refugee Studies*, 20(2): 172–92.

Archival Sources

Ottoman Prime Minister's Archive, Istanbul, Turkey
A.MKT.MHM
DH.MKT
HR.ID
I.MMS
I.DH
Y.MTV
Y.PRK.DH
Y.PRK.KOM
Y.PRK.UM

The National Archives, Richmond, United Kingdom
FO 195.812
FO 78.3129

4

Situating the Coloniality of Encampment and Deportation as a Mode of Mobility Governance: Insights from Ceuta and Melilla, Mayotte and Tanzania

Clayton Boeyink, Nina Sahraoui and Elsa Tyszler

Introduction

Bringing together three case-studies differently situated on the colonial–postcolonial continuum, this chapter explores how coloniality, as initially conceptualized by Quijano (2000) and further developed by other decolonial scholars (for example, Gutiérrez Rodriguez, 2018), permeates migration governance in three distinct settings: the Spanish enclaves of Ceuta and Melilla in North Africa, the French overseas department of Mayotte in the Indian Ocean, and Tanzania in East Africa. We are particularly interested in how racialized hierarchies continue to underpin migration policies. These have been central in the organization and control of the mobility of colonized subjects within European colonialism and beyond. Quijano emphasized the continuity of a world order stratified by a model of power revolving around racial categories: 'The racial axis has a colonial origin and character, but it has proven to be more durable and stable than the colonialism in whose matrix it was established' (Quijano, 2000: 533). While European colonialism is not unique in enacting such hierarchies, its implications are particularly relevant today given its recent historicity and scope. Following Gutierrez Rodriguez, we mobilize the notion of 'coloniality of migration', considering that the 'analysis of the connection between transatlantic European migration and racism in the 19th century, and of current migratory movements occurring within the framework of the migration-asylum nexus, requires an analytical framework that reconsiders migration as a metonym of the modernity-coloniality juncture' (Gutiérrez Rodriguez, 2018: 200).

While European colonialism determined migration patterns from the 16th to the early 20th century, migration was only problematized in the late 20th century (Gutiérrez Rodriguez, 2018). Scholars engaging with the coloniality of migration most often analyse how the colonial project is still manifest today in exclusionary and racialized immigration and development policies in Europe and other White settler countries such as the US and Australia (Mayblin, 2017; Gutierrez Rodriguez, 2018; Achiume, 2019; see also Chapter 7). We build on this literature with those exploring how the colonial powers transmuted these practices of mobility control to former and current colonies in Africa (Bakewell, 2008; Brankamp and Daley, 2020). First, in the Spanish enclaves of Ceuta and Melilla, still contested by the Kingdom of Morocco, the genealogies of border fencing, violent push-back and confinement implemented there since the 1990s, notably against Black African migrants, can be traced back to colonial logics specific to their contexts and rooted in their historicity. Second, in the French overseas department of Mayotte in the Indian Ocean, a territory claimed by the Republic of Comoros with the formal support of the General Assembly of the United Nations, Comorians are caught up in restrictive migration policies that simultaneously organize their immobilization – by making regularization very difficult – as well as their forced mobility through on-going massive deportations. Finally, the third case study traces how in spite of a strong anti-colonial rhetoric and policy, the Tanzanian state entrenched racialized hierarchies that hark back to the colonial instrumentalization of tribe identities that aimed at creating borders and controlling the labour force. These three postcolonial settings represent different historic, political and socio-economic contexts. Yet it is striking that in spite of local specificities, the colonial legacies of mobility management appear in all cases in contemporary migration policies. Reviewing mobility related practices such as collective *refoulement*, massive forced removals and strict encampment policies, we aim at debunking the narrative of exceptionalism that is often associated with such policies and oftentimes mobilized to legitimate harsh measures and strict regulations.

Analyses in terms of exceptionality and 'bare lives', referring to the work of Giorgio Agamben (1998) on the relation between sovereign power, law and violence, have provided an important analytical grid for understanding contemporary politics. This literature has identified specific sites where individuals are excluded from fundamental rights. However, this work often fails to recognize the importance of the colonial architectures of power that have been invested in certain places described as exceptional (Gregory, 2006). In contrast to this approach, we argue that the practices of control and repression of undesirable mobilities today are anchored in old colonial practices and inscribed in patterns of continuity rather than exceptionalism. Our comparison indicates that far from constituting ad-hoc solutions to 'exceptional problems' such as unusually high arrivals, these migration policies are imbued with the racialized hierarchies inherited from the colonial governance of these territories. While the space here for substantive comparison is limited, this chapter is an invitation to further explore the striking patterns of coloniality across seemingly disparate geographies and histories in Africa. We see the prevailing continuities of the past Eurocentric and colonial order of the world created across continents in the contemporary management of migrants through their continued racialization.

Defending what remains of the Spanish Empire: about migration control at Ceuta and Melilla borders

> The objective of the Guardia Civil is to save the integrity of the Spanish border and that of Europe. … It is Europe that must go to Africa, not Africa to Europe. They need to be taught how to organize. They must be taught democracy, education, and almost by force if necessary. (Interview with the Colonel of the Guardia civil in Ceuta, 2015, by Tyszler)

Ceuta and Melilla are both coastal towns in northern Morocco which are under Spanish control. As a consequence of their African location and European jurisdiction, both towns have become associated with migrant attempts at clandestine entry into Europe in recent years. It is essential to look back at the long colonial histories of *Sebta* and *Mliliya* – their original names – in order to study the coloniality of the migration control in place today. The contemporary Spanish occupation must be understood initially as the continuation of the struggle against Islam and the *Reconquista*, this time on the other side of the Straits of Gibraltar (Zurlo, 2005). The Portuguese seized Ceuta in 1415. Melilla was conquered in 1497 and became the first Spanish *frontera*. At that time, the term *frontera* referred to a forward military position in enemy territory (Zurlo, 2005). The conquests of Ceuta and Melilla, although not initially considered colonial conquests, heralded the beginning of the era of colonialism.

The offensive aspect of the *fronteras* against Islam and 'barbaric' piracy quickly turned into a defensive situation: the reason for this was that the Spanish and Portuguese were unable to occupy the hinterland and were faced with resistance from the indigenous populations: the Rifains. The following denomination *presidios*, for the two enclaves, designates a prison because very early on the two functions were united, first in Ceuta and later in Melilla (Ferrer-Gallardo and Gabrielli, 2018). In 1889, the enclave of Ceuta officially became a colonial prison or 'penitentiary colony' where

Spanish dissidents from the colonial order were imprisoned, but also from American territories, such as those banished from Cuba, especially freed Black slaves and Criollos and Mulattos (Sánchez, 2018). This is how the history of detention and deportation practices towards certain racialized undesirables in Ceuta and Melilla began.

In the 1860s, Ceuta and Melilla became the bridgeheads of a colonial penetration in Morocco that led, after several bloody wars against the Rifain resistance, to a dual Spanish and French protectorate at the beginning of the 20th century. The enclaves became *plazas de soberanía* (squares of sovereignty) which were then gradually populated by civilians from the Spanish peninsula and Morocco, mostly for economic needs. Apart from a few exceptions of categories of indigenous people useful for the Spanish army or commerce, the Muslim population was banned from the enclaves until the end of the 19th century. After Morocco's independence in 1956, the two cities remained Spanish, becoming in the eyes of Moroccans and until today, occupied territories. Thus, for some, Ceuta and Melilla can be considered the last European colonies in Africa.

Constantly growing, the population of Moroccan origin today raises the fears of some around the loss of 'Spanishness' of the enclave. In a report submitted to the Spanish Ministry of Defence in 2014, the Royal Spanish Institute Elcano warned of a 'Moroccanization process' that could lead in the long term to support for Morocco's demand for sovereignty over the city. Since the 1990s, another invader figure has been proclaimed: that of the migrant from so-called sub-Saharan Africa 'assailing' Ceuta and Melilla border fences (for similar discursive tropes in the Greek/Turkish borderlands, see Chapter 9). The image of 'western islets' in danger of invasion is common in those territories. Much like fears around the threat of invasion by racialized migrants that circulates globally and fuels anti-migration policies in the European context (Huysmans, 2006; Bigo, 2011), the analysis of these cases highlights how it is also embedded in singular colonial stories. Inscribing itself within the current Spanish–European fight against 'illegal migration', the figure of the Black and dangerous immigrant serves to reactivate a violent defence of these remaining territories of the Spanish Empire, notably through practices of 'hot-returns' at the border fences and long-lasting confinement in the enclaves.

The current migration policies implemented in Ceuta and Melilla are often viewed through the prism of their supposed exceptionality (for example, Ferrer-Gallardo and Gabrielli, 2018). However, both colonial history and field research have prompted us to question the rhetoric of exceptionalism, which ultimately tends to endorse an official discourse and obscure the institutionalization of discretionary and violent practices in the name of defending the Spanish–European border. Our research reveals, in concrete ways, how security and militarized devices and imaginaries of colonial genealogies can be found in the context of contemporary anti-migration policies. Beyond the selective permeability emanating from the border regime of Ceuta and Melilla (Ferrer-Gallardo and Gabrielli, 2018), real racial filtering is (re)established at the border. Previously, the Rifain were the invading enemies, today it is mainly the 'Sub-Saharans' from Central and West Africa who are the main target of control at the border. This is based on a racist policy oriented towards tracking down Black skin. In this sense, the fence surrounding the enclaves of Ceuta and Melilla, can be seen as a continuation of the colonial practice of building fortifications in the enclaves against external enemies (Andersson, 2014; Pallister-Wilkins, 2017, for fence-making at the Greek/Turkish border, see Chapter 9). On this border, the official function of the Guardia Civil (military police) is to prevent entry outside the authorized border points and in particular to monitor the fences supposedly separating Ceuta and Melilla from Morocco (and the rest of Africa). However, until March 2015, there was no written protocol specifying how the Guardia Civil agents were to carry out this mission in practice (Tyszler, 2019). It was a matter of carrying out oral orders: intercepting people – generally adult or minor males from Central and West Africa – and systematically carrying out their direct *refoulement* to Morocco by handing them over to the Moroccan militaries, that is, collective *refoulement* prohibited by national and international law.

During these 'hot-returns' carried out at the fence of the enclaves, the undesirable Black bodies can be beaten or even killed, in continuity with colonial and slave regimes. Indeed, migrant people regularly mobilize this analogy. If some people still manage to cross the militarized border, they become indefinitely trapped in so-called 'temporary' stay centres, enclaves then reassigning one of their historical functions. As Sánchez (2018) showed with the example of Ceuta, the colonial prison function of the banished Cubans in the 19th century was replaced by that of a European barrier, 'with the colonial and postcolonial link as a common thread' (Sánchez, 2018: 339, authors' translation). If the forced migrations of the America–Europe banishment are different from the irregularized Africa–Europe migrations, and if they are not located in the same historical temporality, this points to a continuity in the use of the Ceuta enclave, in different modalities, as a 'territory-prison' (Sánchez, 2018) for undesired racialized people.

To deconstruct the dominant discourses, it is necessary to see that the end is in the means. Given the militarized means used to dehumanize or even kill to defend the borders of Ceuta and Melilla, it is necessary to understand what the meaning of this violence is; a violence that is tacitly authorized and perpetuated over time to defend the border, beyond legal and administrative considerations. According to Gurminder K. Bhambra (2016), we must think of colonialism not only as something that states do, but also as something that individuals do. The particular violence inflicted on Black African migrants since the 1990s seems to be aimed at reaffirming a racist but also colonial social order, as illustrated by these remarks of the Guardia civil Colonel: 'The fence symbolizes the failure of many African countries, it is necessary today' (Interview with the Colonel of the Guardia civil in Ceuta, 2015, by Tyszler).

Racial discrimination, first against the Rifains and then more broadly against a population of Moroccan origin, is constitutive and structural in the enclaves and at its borders, and impunity for border guards, yesterday as today, ensures continuity to the violent domination of Africans trying to penetrate these colonial bastions. Violence is intensifying today for people marked by the colour of their skin and their gender (Tyszler, 2019). For some, border violence is necessary to safeguard the Spanish civilization and to continue defending what remains of the Empire. The coloniality of the migration regime at this Euro-African border is striking. But far from being an exception, it must lead us to think in a more global way about the coloniality of the European migration regime. But the everyday attempts (and sometimes successes) of undesired racialized migrants to cross the borders of Ceuta and Melilla, despite all the obstacles imposed on them, also continue a long history of resistance by colonized peoples who shake up the postcolonial order.

Five centuries after the *Reconquista*, the territories of Ceuta and Melilla seem to be returning to their original role, that of outposts for the defence of a Spain, and more broadly of a Europe, that represents itself as White and Christian. The former colonial subjects of the Spanish Empire and other Western colonial empires are treated as outsiders to European nations. Yet, some of the border violence also comes from the Moroccan side, and is redolent of anti-Black racism with pre-colonial roots (El Hamel, 2012). As Ceuta and Melilla sought to regain their strategic status as European outposts in North Africa following increased migrations from West and Central African countries to Europe in the 1990s, similarly Mayotte seems to have also become a strategic borderland which led to a stricter implementation of state borders, notably by imposing a visa in 1995 (widely referred to as the Balladur visa after the name of the Prime Minister who oversaw its adoption). With this second case study we explore yet another example of a strict migration regime that reproduces racialized patterns of exclusion. The recent colonial history and the racialized relations of power it entrenched are too often concealed by a veneer of liberal governance, allegedly freed from its colonial genealogy.

Outside within, the colonial legacy of an 'exceptional' governance of mobilities at the postcolonial periphery of Mayotte

Mayotte is an island under French jurisdiction in the Indian ocean, between Madagascar and Mozambique. This section is concerned with contemporary migration management in the postcolonial periphery of Mayotte, and seeks to situate such practices within a continuum of colonial governance of subaltern mobility. Such historical inscription serves as a key analytical tool that changes the meaning of the observed practices from being construed as exceptional to liberal rule, to appearing as a coherent development in the management of mobility from colonial to postcolonial times. Walters makes that point in his reflections on migration and governmentality: 'The view that illiberal practices are an exception to a liberal norm rather than a measure woven into the way liberal democracy and liberal empire has functioned throughout modernity becomes less tenable the more that we understand the normalcy of illiberal practices within colonial rule' (2015: 15). While the colonial period asserted the right to freedom of movement for White Europeans, the mobility of the colonized was strictly controlled (Cazzato, 2016). The Indian Ocean witnessed in this regard the development of plantation colonies where the abolition of slavery was followed by the arrival of indentured labourers channelled by the British and French empire (for a study of the fate of liberated Africans in the Indian Ocean see Hopper, 2020, see also Chapter 2). Under French rule, an estimated 200,000 indentured labourers were, for instance, brought to The Reunion Island between 1828 and 1933.

After France bought Mayotte from the Malagasy sultan Andriantsoly in 1841 (Denis, 2006), colonial designs for the island also projected agricultural and commercial successes. Yet, colonial administrators were immediately confronted with a shortage of labour to carry out the anticipated colonial undertakings (Martin, 1976). Two years later, to remedy this situation, colonial authorities authorized the recruitment of indentured labourers from the neighbouring Comorian islands and notably the closest one, Anjouan. Yet, contrary to the fate of the Reunion Island, Mayotte did not become a significant destination for labourers. Against this background, years after the official abolition of slavery in Mayotte in 1846, slave trading on French boats was reported to have continued in the Mozambique canal, incentivized by labour shortages (Martin, 1976; on slave trade suppression, see also Chapter 2). While a combination of geographical and political factors hampered Mayotte from becoming the projected plantation colony, attempts to this end demonstrate how mobility was organized to serve this primary colonial interest. Long relatively neglected by the 'metropole', Mayotte achieved symbolic recognition by becoming a French department in 2011, to the satisfaction of the local Mahoran elite.

Yet, similarly to the other two case studies analysed in this chapter, the racial hierarchies upon which colonial domination relied continue to shine through in the multidimensional disenfranchisement of Comorian people in Mayotte. Quoting the American anthropologist Ann Stoler, Davies and Isakjee (2019: 215) argue: 'While it is true that not all forms of social injustice have imperial roots, with European refugee camps, detention centres, and migrant hotspots, it is often possible to "track the tangibilities of empire as effective histories of the present"' (Stoler, 2013: 29).

In this section, we analyse two dimensions of the contemporary migration regime in Mayotte, drawing attention to continuities with colonial modes of governance: the large-scale production of illegality (De Genova, 2002) and the yearly massive deportations (Sahraoui, 2020). The narrative of exceptionality that underpins the justification for practices quite unlike those implemented in the 'metropole' (at least in terms of proportions and scope) conceals the colonial reminiscence of deeply entrenched social inequalities rooted in racialized hierarchies (for metropolian dynamics in Western Africa, and concerning racialized tropes on virulent diseases, see respectively Chapters 5 and 7).

With a population of approximatively 256,500 inhabitants (INSEE, 2019), 48 per cent of the population of Mayotte island fall into the category of 'foreigners' and almost half of them are estimated to be undocumented according to INSEE (the national statistics bureau of France) data. The share of undocumented persons on the island is thus strikingly high. Yet, contrary to dominant media and political narratives that suggest continuous clandestine arrivals to be the cause, a closer look at the trajectories of undocumented women reveals that not only have many resided on the island for long periods of time, they were also afraid to leave out of a fear of being identified, arrested and refused re-entry. In our research, the average length of residence in Mayotte of the 40 women of Comorian origin interviewed was 10.7 years. Comoros is an island nation (that is, not under French jurisdiction) located close to Mayotte in the Indian Ocean. The majority of these women were in an irregular situation and had been living in Mayotte for an average of 6.8 years, a little more than a third had a residency permit, lasting one year in the majority of cases, and some only had a receipt attesting to the submission of their application to the administration, a receipt that was sometimes renewed several times before a response was obtained. Several of the women we met deplored the many barriers to regularization that they faced, such as the complicated access to fair and accurate information, the high cost of these procedures (€340 for a first application for a residence permit), or the many hurdles to even enter the Prefecture building. In 2018, when the services for foreigners were already saturated, the Prefecture closed its doors for several months, making entry literally impossible. As a result, undocumented Comorians in Mayotte are stranded on the island with little prospect for regularization, caught up in the inequalities entrenched by the coloniality of migration governance.

Migrants in Mayotte are also trapped on the island because even when regularized, most types of residency permit delivered in Mayotte are only valid for the island and do not allow travel to metropolitan France. Those holding a residency permit, even though they are legally residing in Mayotte, need to apply for a visa to travel to metropolitan France or to another French overseas department. The difficulties of regularization and the very limited mobility rights it provides testify to a highly hierarchical structure designed to limit not only immigration to Mayotte but also to metropolitan France, while 'metropolitans' are free to visit and work in Mayotte as if it were a fully integrated French territory. Similar to the logic of colonial 'expatriates', the latter are incentivized to settle in Mayotte, at least for a few years, through state financed bonuses and pay rises. The logic of these differentiated rights is intrinsically racialized and facilitates the reproduction of social inequalities with metropolitan 'expatriates' being provided with financial benefits for working in Mayotte while Comorian migrants face significant restrictions in achieving social, administrative and economic security. The local Mahoran population finds itself in a precarious position whereby strengthening the political integration to the French nation seems to translate into increasingly restrictive policies towards Comorians, in spite of the shared linguistic and cultural ties that run across the islands, echoing the examples of anti-Black racism mentioned in the Tanzanian setting, discussed later.

The second dimension of the French migration regime in Mayotte explored here concerns the large-scale forced removals that the French administration carries out. Mayotte breaks French records for the forced removal of people in an irregular situation: in 2017, 25,274 persons were detained in metropolitan France and 17,934 in Mayotte (again for only 256,500 inhabitants), which represents almost 70 per cent of the number of detained persons in metropolitan France for the same year. The vast majority of these persons (94 per cent) were forcibly removed under a regime whereby deportations are accelerated: the average length of stay in the detention centre is only 17 hours, which leaves virtually no room for legally challenging these practices. The coloniality of this system lies in the separation of Mayotte from the general laws and rules that apply in France. As the member of a migrants' rights NGO heard from the director of the detention centre in Mayotte, 'There is the law and there is Mayotte'. This statement demonstrates how the conditions of subalternity are reproduced through the rationale of exceptionalism. Reduced to tools of broader geopolitical concerns, undocumented persons in French postcolonial peripheries become instruments of the politics of numbers, while at the same time being permanently subjected to a hostile climate of potential arrests and deportations. As the Spanish case study equally demonstrates, the racialization of certain categories of migrants underpins the violence they are confronted with at these peripheral borders, while the fundamentally unequal structure of relations between Metropolitan French administrators, Mahoran elites and Comorian migrants are rooted in relations of power entrenched by colonial legacies. In this complex configuration, the Mahoran elite has become a strong advocate for ever harsher migration control, enacting racialized relations between Mahorans and Comorians. The reproduction of divides that have been exacerbated by colonial rule and the drawing of borders also features in the Tanzanian case study.

Tanzania: between expulsion and exploitation of migrants and refugees from colonialism to the present

Tanzania is located in East Africa and has hosted many refugees from other African countries over the decades since independence. A Burundian refugee in Mtendeli camp in north-western Tanzania explained what it is like being Burundian in Tanzania:

> If a Congolese and a Burundian are on a bus and the police stop them, then a Burundian will be taken off and the Congolese can continue on. Burundi has a bad image in Tanzania. The bad image is attached for a long time. Burundians are highly attached to the war from before. All are labelled as bad or dangerous people.[1]

This xenophobia draws from a long racialized history of border control and hierarchization where Burundian migrants were confined to the lowest class rung on colonial plantations (Iliffe, 1979). This resulted in Burundians being seen as 'dirty' (Brankamp and Daley, 2020: 117) or 'tractors', known for menial agricultural labour today (Malkki, 1995; Boeyink, 2020). Unlike the previous two cases, Tanzania is an independent postcolonial state. Moreover, this East African country has a proud history of anti-colonial rhetoric and policy. Yet even in this case, we see patterns of coloniality permeating through mobility control and racialization. Like the Spanish and French-controlled territories described earlier, Tanzania has attempted to seal off its borders and expel huge numbers of the foreign 'other', in this case neighbouring refugees. Moreover, camps hold a similar colonial logic of containment or imprisonment that Ceuta has produced throughout its history.

Central to the colonial project was the extraction of labour and resources, justified and enabled by racist ideology and governance. This was only possible, however, through the containment, control and manipulation of indigenous peoples. To extract labour, people were forcefully conscripted in the worst instances, but were often compelled to move through invasive taxation, which forced labourers to seek wages in plantations, mines, factories and so on (Brankamp and Daley, 2020, on forced labour conscription, see also Chapter 2). Infamously in Apartheid South Africa, and the *kipande* system in British Kenya and Tanganyika, the colonialists created pass laws designed to keep labour circulating between cities or concentrated labour centres and 'native reserves' on the peripheries of territories (Mamdani,

1996). These 'tribal homelands' were a racialized oversimplification of the 'tribe' instrumentalized by colonialists to use chiefs and customary rulers to govern and control 'native' populations (Iliffe, 1979; Mamdani, 1996). This created a racialized territorialization that artificially imposed where categorizations of 'tribes' and nationalities 'belong', which continues today. While this manipulation and containment happened *within* colonies, these controls of mobilities were also present *outside* official borders, as was the case in Tanganyika.

First ruled under Germany until the First World War, followed by the British until independence, both occupiers oscillated between attempts to stop migrant and refugee inflows and actively encouraging neighbouring migrants to meet colonial labour and production demands (Chaulia, 2003; Brankamp and Daley, 2020). Brankamp and Daley sum up this colonial logic in Tanganyika and Kenya: 'Permissions (or denials) to move were issued exclusively at the behest of the colonial government, which always weighed the imagined attributes of certain ethnicized identities as industrious or idle, potential economic burdens or gains, humanitarian responsibilities, and the potential harm caused to the prevailing political order' (2020: 121).

This is a similar rationale demonstrated by the French recruitment of indentured labourers to Mayotte from the nearby Comorian islands. German and British efforts to staunch the migrations and close the borders to neighbours fleeing labour conscriptions, famine and illness were motivated by fear of their own subjects fleeing similarly harsh labour regimes (Chaulia, 2003). The colonialists later changed tack and actively recruited labour from neighbouring colonies following the Great Depression after the 1930s due to labour scarcity within the colony (Brankamp and Daley, 2020).

Tanzania's first President, Julius Nyerere, offered both a radical break and a deep furtherance of the colonial-era mobility controls. On the one hand, Nyerere's Tanzania was a primary driver of anti-colonial and pan-African activities through the Organisation of African Unity (OAU). He openly courted 'freedom fighter' refugees from guerrilla dissidents in neighbouring European White settler colonies. On the other hand, the newly independent state, like many postcolonial states, uncritically adopted colonial borders and continued hostility and exploitations of migrants, refugees and 'foreign' neighbours (Brankamp and Daley, 2020) while maintaining internal migration controls epitomized by colonial pass laws (Bakewell, 2008). Nyerere's nationalizing project largely hardened national borders previously established by the colonialists. These borderlands shared cultural and economic ties and avenues of escape from harsh colonial wage labour. The presence of Rwandan refugees during this time was seen 'as both a developmental opportunity and a security threat' (Rosenthal, 2015: 270). While the 'freedom fighters' were celebrated and seen in Swahili as *wageni* or 'guests' (Rosenthal, 2015), neighbouring Rwandan and Burundian refugees displaced by civil wars were controlled in settlements in the periphery of the country. They were exploited for their labour to clear unproductive agricultural land, cultivate cash crops and build infrastructure through cheap or free labour (Rosenthal, 2015). Any objections or protest by the refugees were dealt with violently (Gasarasi, 1990). Despite Tanzania's history of anti-colonialism since independence, these discriminatory migration hierarchies were the beginnings of xenophobic attitudes and policies, which are presently manifest in Tanzania today, particularly toward Burundians (Boeyink, 2019). These racialized and ethnicized discriminations, as argued by Mamdani and others, have carried over since colonialism:

> Colonizers wrote European race theories and perverted variations on local history into the histories of colonized peoples, making European categories of race and tribe appear local and natural. Thus did colonized peoples learn that they had always been rivals. Colonizers then mapped the colonized using census categories organized according to these histories, reinforcing racial and tribal identification. Finally, by predicating laws and their application on identification with racial and tribal distinctions, colonizers ensured that future political, economic, and social realities would reflect these distinctions. (Mamdani, 2020:12)

Ethnicized xenophobic violence and policing of Somalis in Kenya offer an example of this continuity (Weitzberg, 2017).

In East Africa, the 1990s saw the rise of encampment policies due to the conflagration of economic crises, structural adjustment policies imposed by the World Bank and the International Monetary Fund, which severely curtailed states' capacities to govern, and large-scale civil wars and genocides in DR Congo, Burundi, Rwanda, Somalia and Sudan. This convergence of events led to strict encampment policies forcing refugees to live in camps with no freedom of movement or employment. Most governance in camps is handled by international humanitarian organizations. In Tanzania, this period was marked by massive violent and forced repatriations of Rwandan and Burundian refugees (Chaulia, 2003; Rutinwa, 2005). More recently, since Tanzania's 2015 election of the late President John Magufuli, who was a strident nationalist (Paget, 2020), there have been sustained efforts to reduce refugee numbers and impel refugees to return before they are ready. These efforts include border closures, shutdowns of refugee markets and popular humanitarian interventions such as a World Food Programme cash transfer scheme in Nyarugusu camp, as well as constant admonishments for refugees (particularly Burundians) to leave. While colonial regimes forced movement within their borders through taxation and labour recruitment from neighbouring colonies, inversely, the state since President Magufuli has reignited xenophobic attitudes through a hardening of borders, which has assaulted camp livelihoods in order to cast unwanted refugees out of the country (Boeyink, 2019; 2020).

Conclusion

This chapter has argued that the racialized hierarchies inherited from colonial rule underpin many of the most repressive dimensions of migration control across different postcolonial settings, albeit differently. Borders created under European colonialism as well as former logics of mobility control continue to shine through in the practices of collective *refoulement*, massive deportations and large-scale encampment that characterize these three case-studies. Yet, our case studies also hint that colonial and pre-colonial orders are entangled in the production of contemporary racialized hierarchies and their attached inequalities. At the same time, we recognize that there are myriads of differences in logics and practices of migration control through the *longue durée* and contemporary histories of these brief case studies. The point here is to highlight the patterns and commonalities present in the diverse histories of each colonial occupier and the spaces that they occupied and continue to colonize. While this chapter has limited space to do so, we openly invite more 'odd-pairings' of colonial and postcolonial spaces to elucidate the pervasive continuities of racialized exclusion and exploitation.

Note

1 Clayton Boeyink, Interview, Burundian man, Mtendeli camp, Tanzania, 12 February 2018.

References

Achiume, E. (2019) 'Migration as decolonization', *Stanford Law Review*, 71(6): 1509–74.

Agamben, G. (1998 [1942]) *Homo Sacer: Sovereign Power and Bare Life*, translated by Daniel Heller-Roazen, Stanford: Stanford University Press.

Andersson, R. (2014) *Illegality, Inc.: Clandestine Migration and the Business of Bordering Europe*, Berkeley: University of California Press.

Bakewell, O. (2008) '"Keeping them in their place": the ambivalent relationship between development and migration in Africa', *Third World Quarterly*, 29(7): 1341–58.

Bhambra, G.K. and Narayan, J. (2016) *European Cosmopolitanism: Colonial Histories and Postcolonial Societies*, London: Routledge International Library of Sociology.

Bigo, D. (2011) 'Frontières, territoire, sécurité, souveraineté', *CERISCOPE Frontières*, Available from: http://ceriscope.sciences-po.fr/content/part1/frontieres-territoire-securite-souverainete [Accessed 14 June 2021].

Boeyink, C. (2019) 'The "worthy" refugee: cash as a diagnostic of "xeno-racism" and "bio-legitimacy"', *Refuge*, 35(1): 61–71.

Boeyink, C. (2020) 'Sufficiently visible/invisibly self-sufficient: recognition and displacement agriculture in Western Tanzania', in J. Bjarnesen and S. Turner (eds) *Invisibility in African Displacements: From Marginalization to Strategies*, London: ZED.

Brankamp, H. and Daley, P. (2020) 'Laborers, migrants, refugees: managing belonging, bodies, and mobility in (post)colonial Kenya and Tanzania', *Migration and Society*, 3: 113–29.

Cazzato, L. (2016) 'Mediterranean: coloniality, migration and decolonial practices', *Politics. Rivista di Studi Politics*, 5(1): 1–17.

Chaulia, S. (2003) 'The politics of refugee hosting in Tanzania: from open door to unsustainability, insecurity and receding receptivity', *Journal of Refugee Studies*, 16(2): 147–66.

Davies, T. and Isakjee, A. (2019) 'Ruins of empire: refugees, race and the postcolonial geographies of European migrant camps', *Geoforum*, 102: 214–17.

De Genova, N.P. (2002) 'Migrant "illegality" and deportability in everyday life', *Annual Review of Anthropology*, 31: 419–47.

Denis, I. (2006) 'Les lieux de mémoire à Mayotte', *Outre-mers*, 93(350–51): pp 157–73.

El Hamel, C. (2012) *Black Morocco: A History of Slavery, Race, and Islam*, Cambridge: Cambridge University Press.

Ferrer-Gallardo, X. and Gabrielli, L. (eds) (2018) *Estados de excepción en la excepción del Estado*, Barcelona: Icaria.

Gasarasi, C.P. (1990) 'The mass naturalization and further integration of Rwandan refugees in Tanzania: process, problems and prospects', *Journal of Refugee Studies*, 3(2): 88–109.

Gregory, D. (2006) 'The black flag: Guantánamo Bay and the space of exception', Geografiska Annaler: Series B, *Human Geography*, 88(4): 405–27.

Gutiérrez Rodriguez, E. (2018) 'Conceptualizing the coloniality of migration', in D. Bachmann-Medick and J. Kugele (eds) *Migration: Changing Concepts, Critical Approaches*. Berlin: De Gruyter, pp 192–210.

Hopper, M. (2020) 'Liberated Africans in the Indian Ocean world', in R. Anderson and H. Lovejoy (eds), *Liberated Africans and the Abolition of the Slave Trade, 1807–1896*, Woodbridge: Boydell & Brewer, pp 271–94.

Huysmans, J. (2006) *The Politics of Insecurity: Fear, Migration and Asylum in the EU*, London: Routledge.

Iliffe, J. (1979) *A Modern History of Tanganyika*. Cambridge: Cambridge University Press.

INSEE (2019) 'À Mayotte, près d'un habitant sur deux est de nationalité étrangère', Insee Première, N° 1737, [online] Available from: https://insee.fr/fr/statistiques/3713016 [Accessed 14 June 2021].

Malkki, L. (1995) *Purity and Exile: Violence, Memory and National Cosmology among Hutu Refugees in Tanzania*, Chicago: University of Chicago Press.

Mamdani, M. (1996) *Citizen and Subject: Contemporary Africa and the Legacy of Late Colonialism*, Kampala: Fountain Publishers.

Mamdani, M. (2020) *Neither Settler nor Native: The Making and Unmaking of Permanent Minorities*, Cambridge: Harvard University Press.

Martin, J. (1976) L'affranchissement des esclaves de Mayotte, décembre 1846–juillet 1847. *Cahiers d'Études Africaines*, Vol. 16, Cahier 61/62, Histoire Africaine: Constatations, Contestations: 207–33.

Mayblin, L. (2017) *Asylum after Empire: Colonial Legacies in the Politics of Asylum Seeking*. London: Rowman and Littlefield.

Paget, D. (2020) 'Again, making Tanzania great: Magufuli's restorationist developmental nationalism', *Democratization*, 27(7): 1240–60.

Pallister-Wilkins, P. (2017) 'The tensions of the Ceuta and Melilla border fences', in P. Gaibazzi, S. Dünnwald and A. Bellagamba (eds) *EurAfrican Borders and Migration Management: Political Cultures, Contested Spaces, and Ordinary Lives*, New York: Palgrave Macmillan, pp 63–81.

Quijano, A. (2000) 'Coloniality of power, Eurocentrism, and Latin America', *Nepantla: Views from South*, 1(3): 533–80.

Rosenthal, J. (2015) 'From "migrants" to "refugees": identity, aid, and decolonization in Ngara District, Tanzania', *The Journal of African History*, 56(2): 261–79.

Rutinwa, B. (2005) *Identifying Gaps in Protection Capacity in Tanzania*, Geneva: UNHCR.

Sahraoui, N. (2020) 'Le "nécropouvoir" dans le contrôle migratoire et ses implications genrées dans les périphéries postcoloniales françaises de l'Océan Indien', *Migrations et Sociét*é, 32(182): 21–34.

Sánchez, R. (2018) 'Ceuta: quand la barrière de l'Europe était un bagne colonial', *Mélanges de la Casa de Velázquez*, 48(1): 331–39.

Stoler, A. (2013) (ed) *Imperial Debris: On Ruins and Ruination*, Durham, NC: Duke University Press.

Tyszler, E. (2019) Derrière les barrières de Ceuta & Melilla: Rapports sociaux de sexe, de race et colonialité du contrôle migratoire à la frontière maroco-espagnole [Behind the Fence of Ceuta & Melilla: Social Relations of Gender, Race and Coloniality of Migration Control on the Moroccan–Spanish Border], PhD Thesis, University of Paris.

Walters, W. (2015) 'Reflections on migration and governmentality', *Movements: Journal für kritische Migrations- und Grenzregimeforschung*, 1(1): 1–25.

Weitzberg, K. (2017) *We Do Not Have Borders: Greater Somalia and the Predicaments of Belonging in Kenya*, Athens, OH: Ohio University Press.

Zurlo, Y. (2005) *Ceuta et Melilla: Histoire, représentations et devenir de deux enclaves espagnoles*, Paris: L'Harmattan.

5

Colonial Continuities and the Commodification of Mobility Policing: French Civipol in West Africa

Eva Magdalena Stambøl and Leonie Jegen

Introduction

European control of mobility in and from Africa is becoming progressively commodified, and hybrid public-private companies play a growing role in catering to European security priorities. This claim stems from observations that both authors did during fieldwork in West Africa, which explored the implementation of the EU's security and migration policy towards the region. Stambøl conducted fieldwork in Senegal, Mali and Niger mainly in 2017 and 2018, and Jegen conducted fieldwork in Senegal, Ghana and Niger in 2018 and 2019. During fieldwork, we both frequently came across a French semi-private Agency – Civipol – which has gained a prominent role as implementing partner of EU funds to control mobility, in particular from the EU Emergency Trust Fund for Africa (EUTF). Civipol is the first EU member state Agency dedicated to the training of police and other internal security forces of third countries, in addition to carrying out a variety of security-focused projects. In-depth knowledge on Civipol itself, though, was difficult to attain during fieldwork. This chapter is therefore mainly based on follow-up research of documents and web-content. Our aim here is to historically contextualize EU and French commodified mobility policing in West Africa. We trace historical continuities since early French colonialism to today through consulting secondary historical sources, focusing in particular on two elements: public-private partnerships and policing/surveillance. In doing so, the chapter contributes both to the emerging migration studies literature on public-private partnerships in mobility control (for example Gammeltoft-Hansen and Sørensen, 2013; Lemberg-Pedersen, 2013; Anderson and Franck, 2019) as well as to the criminological literature on state-corporate symbiosis and the commodification of transnational policing (for example O'Reilly, 2010).

The chapter thus investigates how the historical connection between colonialism, corporate interests and policing is mirrored in the current ways that Europe attempts to control mobility from West Africa. We begin by considering the role of public-private relationships and policing during formal French colonization, mainly of West Africa, as well as their continued role after independence in the 1960s. We then go on to introduce Civipol and outline its role in European border externalization to Africa. The final section focuses on one particular type of project that Civipol is implementing in West African countries, that is especially interesting from the perspective of state sovereignty and new trends in the surveillance of mobility, namely the building of biometric civil registries. The chapter argues that we can trace colonial continuities in the ways that migration is currently governed by Europe through crime, security and surveillance in West Africa.

Corporate interests in French colonization

Early French colonialism during the *Ancien Régime* (15th century until the French Revolution in 1789) was essentially commercial and founded to develop the French metropolitan economy (Marzagalli, 2018). This had for some time encompassed the transatlantic slave trade, which was abolished in the first half of the 19th century (Mentan, 2017). French slave trade and plantation colonialism in the West Indies entailed close interconnection between state and private interests: for example, the board of directors of the French Company of the Indies abolished its monopoly over the slave trade to reinstate a system that supported its business model dependent on cooperation with independent traders, thereby making the company's trade in enslaved people, sugar and other plantation products more profitable (Mentan, 2017; for the use of recaptured Africans in Caribbean plantations, see Chapter 2).

In Africa, French colonialism manifested itself as mercantilism for nearly 300 years, dominated by chartered monopolies based on trading posts along the West African coast, with local brokers connecting the coastal trade to the continental interior (Brunschwig, 1970; Thompson and Adloff, 1975). Following mercantilist rules and the Colonial Pact, the colonies could only sell their goods to France, their markets were closed to foreign goods, and only French products could be sold to colonial markets (Marzagalli, 2018). Still, the revenues from this trade did not weigh heavily in the foreign trade balances of the European powers (Brunschwig, 1970). During early colonialism, only a few trading companies profited by their monopolies, while the African colonies were generally unprofitable, placing a financial burden on metropolitan France (Thompson and Adloff, 1975). However, the pure 'commercial colonialism' gradually changed from around 1860 onwards to one that was no longer purely economic, but also political and military intervention, first in Algeria and later in sub-Saharan Africa.

The emergence of the doctrine of French 'imperial colonialism' between 1860 and 1882 comprised three interconnected pillars: economic, political and moral (that is, the civilizing mission) (Charbonneau, 2008: 32). The colonies now became much more important economically to the metropole – not least because it was during this time that France developed its industry which gave an impetus to empire-building, and the colonies contributed to the development of French capitalism and political economy (Thompson and Adloff, 1975; Marseille, 1984). French companies in West Africa engaged in mining, agriculture (including plantations of cotton and ground nuts), forestry, and transportation (rail, river, road) (Ọlọruntimẹhin, 1974). For example, colonial subjects in Western Sudan (today's Mali) were obliged to produce cotton for the French metropolitan textile industry, controlled by the 'partially state-supported but largely privately funded association of metropolitan textile industrialists', the *Association Cotonnière Coloniale (ACC)*, which also built the railway from the interior to the coast to facilitate extraction (Roberts, 1987). In other parts of the empire, such as French Equatorial Africa or the Belgian Congo Free State, engagement in production and extraction was typically done by large private concession companies to which administration was handed over (Roberts, 1987; Manning, 2010). Thus, apart from offering raw materials for French industry, the colonies privileged expansion for French industries because colonial investment offered two major advantages: high profitability and the security provided by direct political domination (Marseille, 1984, on Italian papal and commercial interests in settler colonial extractivism in Libya, see Chapter 8). Charbonneau (2008) argues that colonialism was not only a crucial economic factor in French transition to industrial capitalism, but also foundational for its symbolic nation-building as an empire projecting *grandeur* – something which is still essential to understand French foreign and security policy today. More generally, many have argued that colonialism was constitutive of European state and capitalist systems and, thus, of European modernity (for example, Ọlọruntimẹhin, 1974; Williams, 1994; Mbembe, 2003; Mentan, 2017).

A wide spectrum of private actors (dubbed the '*Parti Colonial*') played a significant role in building public and political support for the French colonial project from the late 19th century until the interwar period (Andrew and Kanya-Forstner, 1971). The extent to which companies played a role in the French colonial project in the late 19th century is unclear; some claim that private corporations played a significant role in supporting the colonial cause (Abrams and Millner, 1976; Marseille, 1984), others argue that nationalist and capitalist interests often diverged in this period (Andrew and Kanya-Forstner, 1976). What seems to be uncontested, however, is that some individuals with strong connections to both politics and business were crucial in building political support for the colonial project – resembling today's 'revolving doors' phenomenon (Lemberg-Pedersen, 2018), which we show in later sections. The *Parti Colonial* constituted an important political pressure group with interests in French colonial expansion. It exerted its influence on both political decision makers and public opinion, with members being journalists, writers, businessmen and politicians (Andrew and Kanya-Forstner, 1971). One important grouping falling under the *Parti Colonial* was the *Union Colonial*, which began as a satellite organization of the French Chamber of Commerce based in Paris in 1893. It maintained connections to important financial institutions while most of its members were small and medium-sized enterprises with vested colonial interests (Andrew and Kanya-Forstner, 1971).

The French private capital invested in the colonies was thus concentrated in trading enterprises whose monopolies were expected to be enforced by the French state. Indeed, until the post-First World War economic depression, 'French trading companies almost completely dominated the African colonies' economy' (Thompson and Adloff, 1975: 131); in particular, these were family-owned firms headquartered in Bourdeaux such as the three limited-liability companies known as the *Grand Comptoirs* which controlled trade, banking and transport business. Importantly, these French companies repatriated their profits made from the colonies (Ọlọruntimẹhin, 1974; Thompson and Adloff, 1975), what we in following sections will refer to as 'revolving credit' (Nkrumah, 1965).

Policing, registration and surveillance in the French Empire

The French imperial loss of Saint Domingue (today's Haiti) following the slave uprising beginning in 1791 was a crucial precursor to militarized French policing of mobility (Ferrer, 2012). In the French African empire, policing was initially mainly a task for the military; civilian administration developed tentatively and experimentally mainly in the 20th century (Manning, 2010). Organization and administration of the colonies was decentralized, with administrators and *commandants de cercle* having high degrees of autonomy and personal control. Gradually, and especially in the areas inhabited by French settlers, policing bodies were created based on models from metropolitan France, such as the *gendarmerie* (that is, military police) and the Paris prefecture of police (Blanchard, 2014). Thomas (2013) argues that the forms and intensity of policing and police repression, especially in the inter-war period, were neatly intertwined with the political economy of the specific colonies as the policing of order was often directly tied to industry and commerce. The police were used by colonial governments to ensure economic extraction from colonized subjects, including tax collection, land appropriation and suppression of worker dissent. They were also assigned, by all the European colonial governments, to assist in maintaining order on plantations, and in processing plants, factories, mines and other forms of extraction, many of which were run by large and powerful European companies.

Blurring state-private relations, policemen were part of 'networks of association' that included administrators, traders and managers: 'At the personal level as much as the structural one, the political priorities and security practices of colonial rule were thereby attuned to its economic organization' (Thomas, 2013: 5). Thomas further argues that due to limited colonial state resources being thinly spread to control vast territories, police repression was concentrated particularly, but not exclusively, around resistance to state as well as private economic exploitation. According to Blanchard (2014), it was also the understaffing and underfunding of the French colonial police which propelled them to use anthropometric and identification techniques, such as carding (forcing people to have an ID) and fingerprinting, techniques that were moreover utilized in vast census and registration projects (on the origins of fingerprinting in British colonial rule in India, see also Chapter 6). Political surveillance and mobility control was, for example, institutionalized through the creation in 1922 in Dakar, Senegal, of the *Service central de police et de sûreté de l'AOF* (Blanchard, 2014: 8). As we later show, identification, registration and census techniques are also an integral part of current French and EU policies to control migration in West Africa.

Pré carré, the blurring of public-private and internal security

After decolonization of the African territories in the 1960s, France maintained close ties to its former colonies and retained its *pré carré*, that is, zone of influence. In fact, it has been argued that 'decolonization did not happen if the term means the transfer of sovereignty or the gaining of independence and autonomy from a former colonial power' (Charbonneau, 2008: 55). The concept of *Françafrique* has been used to describe French relations with its former African colonies, deeply marked by personal relations and patronage (Gegout, 2017). Under Charles de Gaulle, the President's chief adviser on African Affairs, Jacques Foccart – nicknamed *Monsieur Afrique* – was the engineer behind (and the centre of) a personalized network of connections between French and African elites that would serve to perpetuate French patronage through postcolonial 'cooperation' (Charbonneau, 2008). 'Special relationships' were thus a way to entrench, rather than to end, French hegemony (Hansen and Jonsson, 2014). Such cooperation included cultural, political and economic relations (Gegout, 2017, for analysis of parallel Italian-Libyan postcolonial relations, see Chapter 8).

Politically, the Franco-African relationship worked both through formal and informal networks, where especially the latter 'effectively blurred the distinction between private and public' (Charbonneau, 2008: 56). De Gaulle made Africa relations the *domaine réservée* of the President, and Foccart's centralized informal system included business, military, internal security and corporatist networks – such as the Jean-Christophe Mitterrand and Charles Pasqua networks, large businesses like Elf, Bouygues, Bolloré-Rivaud and Castel, secret services, and military elements (Charbonneau, 2008). The networks created systems of dependency that manifested at various levels (institutional, semi-institutional, informal) and through various modalities (cultural cooperation, development aid, the franc zone, the Ministry of Cooperation, personal links and relationships, the President's African cell, Franco-African summits and the networks). France supported political elites and a number of dictators such as Paul Biya in Cameroon; Blaise Compaoré in Burkina Faso; Idriss Deby in Chad; and Denis Sassou Nguesso in Congo (Gegout, 2017). The annual Franco-African summits, which often did not have a published agenda, 'resembled informal family gatherings rather than official intergovernmental meetings' (Chafer, in Charbonneau, 2008: 59).

Economically, *Françafrique* has been marked by close and entrenched relations where France 'focused more on its own economic interests than those of African states' (Gegout, 2017: 141). French asymmetrical economic relations with Francophone Africa have been based on two forms that have maintained the dependency of the former on the latter: the franc zone, and development aid. The CFA franc zone, created in 1945, is still controlled by France and encompasses the West African Economic and Monetary Union (UEMOA), the Central African Economic and Monetary Community (CEMAC) and the Comoros. France has institutional control through the right of veto of French officials on monetary policy within the Central Bank of West African States and the Central Bank of Central African States (Gegout, 2017: 141). Notably, the French treasury centralizes half of the African banks' reserves and invests them so they benefit French citizens. According to Gegout (2017), the interests to African central banks are included in French development aid to these African states, yet France makes the interests conditional upon budgetary restraint by demanding reduction in public spending. Moreover, capital only moves freely between African central banks and France and not between the African states, something which benefits 'French investments in Africa, imports by French companies of natural resources, and the flight of capital from Africa to France' (Gegout, 2017: 142).

French development aid, which has included cultural, economic and technical forms, has, according to Charbonneau, been 'recycled and sent back to France ... through the order books of French companies' (2008: 59). This is precisely what Kwame Nkrumah referred to as 'revolving credit', denoting aid and investments 'paid by the neo-colonial master, passing through the neo-colonial State and returning to the neo-colonial master in the form of increased profits' (1965: xv). As we will see in the following sections, the recycling of aid through French companies and their repatriation to Europe is still happening today – however, no longer only with regard to French development aid but now also with that disbursed by the EU. It should at this point also be remembered that the EU itself has a forcefully forgotten colonial history: the idea of *EurAfrica* was in fact a central part of the debates around the formation of the European Economic Community (ECC) in 1957, to which the French colonized territories were to be associated (Hansen and Jonsson, 2014).

In the security sphere, the literature has focused on military agreements and cooperation (Charbonneau, 2008; Gegout, 2017), which is not surprising given the centrality of these areas for French colonialism and *pré carré*: in particular, French pre-positioned forces, but also military interventions, have been seen as the 'heart and symbol of French power in Africa' (Charbonneau, 2008: 65). Conversely, 'internal security' and French cooperation with African Ministries of Interior and Justice and (secret) police have received much less attention from scholars (though see Blanchard, 2014). Still, it has been mentioned that the French-Africa networks included the French secret police (the SDECE) and the Ministry of Interior (Charbonneau, 2008: 57). As we shall see in the following section, however, French (semi) private actors and corporate interests, such as Civipol, continue to play an important role in European relations with West Africa – including through the EU. Moreover, the objectives of policing and securitization of West African mobility towards Europe has opened new avenues and opportunities for business in the internal security sectors of former French colonies and other African states.

Introducing Civipol and its blurred public-private nature

Created in 2001, Civipol is the technical cooperation operator of the French Ministry of Interior, and has come to play a key role in policing and surveillance of migration in Africa. This Agency implements projects in third countries funded by France or other donors, notably the EU. Its three principal areas of activity are homeland security, civil protection and governance (Civipol, 2017; 2019). Civipol also offers support to French companies when they expand to high risk countries, providing know-how for their establishment (Civipol, 2017). Civipol is a semi-private entity in that it is a private company with the French state as the largest shareholder (40 per cent). Other shareholders include major French security and defence companies such as Thales, Airbus, Morpho and Défense Conseil International (a public-private group linked to the Ministry of Defence). This gives it, in its own words, 'the efficiency of a private company with the power of its public service mission' (Civipol, 2020: np).

Highlighting the relevance of 'revolving doors' for understanding blurred public-private relations – a key characteristic in the growing role of European security companies in spurring EU mobility surveillance (Lemberg-Pedersen, 2013; 2018), Civipol's Chief Executive Officer, Yann Jounot, held the position of national coordinator of intelligence and the fight against terrorism in France prior to his current appointment. The company's blurred public-private nature becomes further evident when considering its key decision making body: the board of directors, which is composed of public actors, such as representatives of the French Ministry of Economy and Finance and the Ministry of Interior, as well as private actors such as Airbus, the Défense Conseil International, Thales International, Idemia Identity and Security France (Civipol, 2017; 2019). A similar composition of public and private actors is found in the company's Audit Committee.

One of Civipol's stated missions is 'promoting the sector of the security industries' (Civipol, 2019: 4). One way in which it does so is through Milipol, which is an event for homeland security organized in Paris, Doha and Singapore, owned 40 per cent by Civipol, alongside other actors such as Protecop, Thales and Visiom (Civipol, 2019). Milipol is managed by Comexposium, itself a subsidiary of the Paris Chamber of Commerce (Bagnoli, 2017), and presided over by Civipol's Chief Executive Officer, Yann Jounot (Civipol, 2019). In another example of 'revolving doors', former Civipol General Director, Pierre de Bousquet de Florian, is currently holding the post of Chief of Staff for Interior Minister Gérald Darmanin. Current chief of staff of French President Emmanuel Macron formerly held a seat at the board of Civipol (Privacy International, 2020).

According to Milipol's website, it is the leading event dedicated to the security profession and 'provides the perfect forum for presenting the latest technological innovations in the area, effectively meeting the needs of the sector as a whole and also addressing current threats and dangers' (Milipol, 2021). Milipol spans a wide variety of security-related sectors, including law enforcement, anti-terrorism, port and airport security and border control. The visitor profile of Milipol Paris 2019 shows a balance between the public sector (46 per cent) and the private sector (54 per cent), where visitors in the former category particularly comprise Ministries of Interior (39 per cent) and administrations of Customs, Defence and Justice (35 per cent) (Milipol, 2020). In 2019, the event welcomed 167 official delegations from 68 countries, and the top ten countries were France, Belgium, Italy, UK, Israel, Germany, Switzerland, the Netherlands, Spain and the USA. Sixty-two per cent of the visitors played an active role in purchasing. While Milipol has stated that it does not promote the sale of 'equipment', 'materials', or 'weapons', investigative journalist Bagnoli (2017) has noted that in May 2016 two exhibitors displayed weapons banned by the European legislation as 'torture arms'. As we shall see in the following section, some of the security technologies developed by Civipol and/or promoted through Milipol are also put to use in the many projects that Civipol manages around the world, and increasingly in Africa.

Civipol's role in European border externalization to Africa

As per 31 December 2018, Civipol was implementing 117 projects across 84 countries, to an annual business volume of €176 million (Civipol, 2020). In 2001, Civipol was mandated by the European Commission as a body to manage its programmes (Civipol, 2017) and has since then developed special know-how in responding to the European Commission's calls for projects (Akkerman, 2018). Moreover, in June 2015 Civipol was chosen as an implementing actor of the French Ministry of Interior's international cooperation actions and projects (Civipol, 2017). Apart from French government departments – most importantly the Ministry of Interior, and other companies (Civipol, 2017), Civipol's main clients in 2018 were the EU (70 per cent), states and cooperation agencies (20 per cent), and the World Bank (5 per cent) (Civipol, 2019). According to Bagnoli (2017), internal security produces almost two thirds of the commissions, one quarter is derived from civil protection projects and the remaining 6 per cent from administrative consultation. Civipol's overall turnover went up significantly from €7.6 million in 2017 to €13.8 million in 2018 (Civipol, 2019) and has been paralleled by an increasingly outward orientation of its project portfolio. This aligns with its motto: 'Those who join us do so with the conviction that internal security is also built externally' (Civipol, 2020).

Civipol has been an agenda-setter on European border policies as it formulated one of the earliest plans for a European Union surveillance system through the 2003 European Commission's feasibility study on the 'Control of the European Union's maritime borders' (Akkerman, 2018). The study framed migration to the EU through a security-focused language denoting immigration as 'migratory pressure' and individuals and networks facilitating irregular migration to the European free movement zone, the Schengen space, as 'transnational crime organisations' (Civipol, 2003;

Lemberg-Pedersen et al, 2020: 46). Further, it proposed to strengthen border surveillance capacity in states at the EU's southern coastline as well as countries of transit and departure. It also introduced the idea of establishing reception areas in third countries and building administrative detention centres in transit countries (Akkerman, 2018; for similar initiatives in Kenya, see Chapter 13; in Ceuta and Melilla, French Mayotte and Tanzania, see Chapter 4). Most importantly, it argued for a technical solution to border control issues, stressing its long-term profitability and suggesting different ways of financing such action. The feasibility study laid the foundation for ongoing measures of border externalization and its proposals were incorporated among others in the European Commission's 2003 Programme of measures to combat illegal immigration across the maritime borders of the European Union or the 2005 Global Approach to Migration (Akkerman, 2018; Lemberg-Pedersen et al, 2020).

Since the mid-2000s, Civipol has concentrated its operational focus and activities towards former French colonies (Bagnoli, 2017). While Civipol's projects in Africa accounted for 51 per cent of its overall activities in 2014, this number rose to 65.7 per cent in 2015, 65.4 per cent in 2016 and 75 per cent in 2018 (Civipol, 2015; 2017; 2019). This may partly be attributable to the fact that Civipol became one of the main implementing partners of the EU's Emergency Trust Fund for Africa (EUTF), but also to a smaller extent that of other EU instruments such as European Neighbourhood Instrument (ENI) and Instrument contributing to Stability and Peace (IcSP). Indeed, Civipol's influence on EU mobility control policies also includes the circulation of personnel – that is, 'revolving doors': a central person administering the EUTF in Brussels encountered by Stambøl turned out to have a long prior career in Civipol.

At the time of writing (September 2020), Civipol was implementing nine EUTF projects to a value of €212 million[1] and between 2015 and 2017 alone Civipol constituted the fourth most funded organization under the EUTF (Bagnoli, 2017). Typically, Civipol is in charge of recruiting (French) law enforcement and security experts to EU projects (for example trainers, attachés, for example to the G5 Sahel Security College in Bamako and G5 Sahel Secretariat in Nouakchott; gendarmerie staff who are training gendarmerie units in all G5 Sahel countries – *Groupes d'Action Rapide - Surveillance et Intervention au Sahel* – GAR-SI). Moreover, its projects encompass the following topics, among many others: border control to fight criminal networks (Guinea); technical support to reinforce customs services; intelligence/information sharing between police/gendarmerie/garde nationale and maintenance of public security in 'remote and transit zones' (Niger); disrupting cross-border criminal organizations profiting from irregular migration, human trafficking and other types of organized crime by focusing on their financial resources (Djibouti, Ethiopia, Kenya, Somalia,

South Sudan, Sudan, Uganda, Yemen and Tanzania); and civil registries (Tunisia, Senegal, Mali, Niger, Cameroon and Cote d'Ivoire). We now turn to take a closer look at civil registries.

Civil registries, biometrization and mobility control

Civipol has been active in numerous capacity building projects in West Africa in the field of civil registration. It has supported the formulation of policies on this topic in Cameroon, Niger and Senegal, and participated in high-level negotiations on the civil registry component in migration agreements in Cameroon, Tunisia and Senegal (European Commission, 2018). Currently, it is also engaged in implementing civil registry projects funded by the EUTF in Cote d'Ivoire, Senegal, and (at least until the recent coup d'état) Mali (on the centralized UNHCR biometric registries for refugees, see Chapter 6).

One of the first civil registry projects was conducted from 2011–2016 in Cameroon and encompassed technical assistance to modernize civil registration systems. The civil registration project in Cameroon brought both legal and institutional changes, and culminated in the establishment of the National Civil Registration Bureau. Implementation was supported through stakeholder workshops and awareness raising campaigns targeting parliamentarians, traditional chiefs and rural populations (Civipol, 2017). Similar tasks were fulfilled by Civipol in Niger where it was contracted under a UNICEF/EU funded project, *Programme d'Appui au Système d'Etat Civil au Niger*, that aimed to modernize the country's civil registries. When asked why the EU is spending such large amounts of money on building biometric civil registries in African countries (each of these projects costs between €25 and €30 million), an EU official interviewed made a clear reference to the migration management objective of EUTF:

> The initial thought [behind these projects is that] if we strengthen the civil registry, it could help the EU to get access and it would be possible to track down who is an irregular migrant. So it has a migration [management] component. The idea is that consulates can monitor, [and choose] to give or not give documents to those people. (Stambøl's interview with EU official, Bamako, 2017)

The political sensitivity of civil registry projects becomes particularly evident in cases such as Senegal, where a reform of civil registries has been ongoing since 1990. Currently, Civipol is the project leader of an ongoing EUTF-funded project to modernize the country's civil registries and establish a national biometric database. This project is a direct continuation of the 2012–16 European Development Fund (EDF) financed project *Projet d'appui à la modernization de l'état civil*, which did not succeed in fulfilling all of its objectives (European Commission, 2018). The project was launched with a 2-year delay in 2018 (Akkerman, 2018; Civipol, 2019), partially caused by the sensitivity of establishing national biometric databases, as a European actor explained:

> So, the project experienced a lot of delay because there was a problem around the appropriation of the project by the Senegalese authorities who in fact were a little afraid of … to consider a little that it was a project that undermined the sovereignty of Senegal. So they had to rework it with the Senegalese authorities on the national formulation. (Jegen's interview with EU member state Agency, Dakar, 2019)

An especially sensitive issue in Senegal has been the question of the extent to which the biometric database is linked to forced returns (on deportations, see also Chapters 4 and 7). The project's document makes this link relatively explicit, stating that in the framework of the project, a legal study will be finalized on the use of the biometric database including 'its use for identification purposes of Senegalese nationals in an irregular situation' (European Commission, 2018: 10, authors' translation). Moreover, these projects have been seen to belong to a 'modular technology', whereby adopting a path will result in a dependency to the ever-evolving system (Frowd, 2018: 127). Similarly, others have argued that in cases of border and migration management being privatized, technical solutions tend to be found before problems have been identified, thereby creating powerful lock-in effects (Lemberg-Pedersen, 2013; Menz, 2013). In this case, the policing of different sovereignties becomes not only an unattainable target but also an endless profit source.

It is timely, then, to ask who is profiting from EU development aid, increasingly channelled to security and mobility control concerns. West African actors have often raised the concern that EU-funded migration projects turn out to be self-serving (Trauner et al, 2019), a criticism backed up by investigative journalism (Vermeulen et al, 2019). Illustratively, an EU official stated that: 'EUTF attracts a lot of interest from EU development agencies: "We get back our money". Now also NGOs want a piece of the cake. We get lots of project proposals. It's very much a politically driven instrument so our margin of management is little' (Stambøl's interview with EU official, Bamako, 2017).

This suggests that the EUTF, and other EU external policy funds, are not only disbursed to control mobility in and from Africa, but also prove useful vehicles for reviving the European development and security industries, seemingly incrementally intertwined, at the same time as allowing for the repatriation of some aid monies – or 'revolving credit' – back to

Europe, and France in particular; just like in the colonial period and after formal decolonization.

Conclusion

The chapter traced colonial continuities in the current ways that Europe attempts to control mobility in and from West Africa. Looking especially at French colonialism, *pré carré* and current EU-French engagement in West Africa, it focused in particular on two aspects: the role of private corporate interests and policing.

Blurred lines between state and private interests are a key colonial continuity that we have identified. French companies have played an important role since the slave trade and plantation economy in the West Indies and throughout the colonization of African territories; blurred public-private networks continued to dominate *Françafrique* after decolonization, and still do so today – Civipol being an illustrative example. Such blurring has encompassed the influence of private corporations on French, and now also on EU policy and law-making, as well as the circulation of personnel between public and private roles (that is, 'revolving doors'). Moreover, French capital has been recycled through, and/or extracted from, the (former) colonies, and ultimately repatriated back to France (that is, 'revolving credit').

Policing, registration and surveillance was an integral part of French formal colonialism, *pré carré*, and it continues to assume a significant role in French and EU policies towards West Africa today (see also Chapter 6). In the colonies, policing was especially attuned to their economic organization and extraction, and French colonial police used 'anthropometric forms of control' such as carding, fingerprinting and various forms of census-taking and registration, including the surveillance of mobility and migrant labour. Civipol's biometric technologies and civil registry databases, with the purpose of controlling the mobility of Africans to Europe, conspicuously mirror these techniques of colonial policing.

The progressive commodification of European mobility control and surveillance in West Africa thus has long historical and colonial roots. Companies like Civipol take advantage of the business opportunities provided by EU aid directed towards mobility control, establishing themselves as providers of technical solutions and know-how. Their defining power in agenda setting and policy development in their home states, at EU level, and in African countries co-shapes the securitization of European engagement in Africa. Problems framed in a security-focused language create new markets for services and solutions, as well as new dependencies (lock-in effects) in beneficiary countries' internal security sectors. Ultimately, development aid, increasingly channelled to security concerns, continues to be recycled and makes its way back to Europe through European companies and agencies.

Note

[1] Completed projects were not included in this count. However, note that the amount of project funds does not go to Civipol alone but is distributed between Civipol and other implementing partners and some channelled as direct budget support to African governments.

References

Abrams, J. and Miller, D.J. (1976) 'Who were the French colonialists? A reassessment of the Parti Colonial, 1890–1914', *The Historical Journal*, 19(3): 685–725.

Akkerman, M. (2018) *Expanding the Fortress*, Amsterdam: Transnational Institute [online], Available from: https://www.tni.org/en/publication/expanding-the-fortress [Accessed 13 September 2019).

Anderson, J.T. and Franck, A.K. (2019) 'The public and the private in guestworker schemes: examples from Malaysia and the U.S.', *Journal of Ethnic and Migration Studies*, 45(7): 1207–23.

Andrew, C.M. and Kanya-Forstner, A.S. (1971) 'The French "Colonial Party": its composition, aims and influence, 1885–1914', *The Historical Journal*, 14(1): 99–128.

Andrew, C.M. and Kanya-Forstner, A.S. (1976) 'French business and the French colonialists', *The Historical Journal*, 19(4): 981–1000.

Bagnoli, L. (2017) 'Civipol, la multinazionale francese che vende sicurezza in Africa – La Stampa', *La Stampa*, [online] 24 May, Available from: https://www.lastampa.it/esteri/2017/05/24/news/civipol-la-multinazionale-francese-che-vende-sicurezza-in-africa-1.36051935 [Accessed 8 December 2019].

Blanchard, E. (2014) 'French colonial police', in G. Bruinsma and D. Weisburd (eds) *Encyclopedia of Criminology and Criminal Justice*, New York: Springer, pp 22–63.

Brunschwig, H. (1970) 'Politique et economie dans l'empire français d'Afrique noire 1870–1914', *Journal of African History*, 11(3): 401–17.

Charbonneau, B. (2008) *France and the New Imperialism: Security Policy in Sub-Saharan Africa* (2nd edn), London and New York: Routledge.

Civipol (2003) Feasibility Study on the Control of the European Union's Maritime Borders – Final Report, Feasibility Study 11490/1/03 REV 1, Brussels: Council of the European Union, Available from: https://web.archive.org/web/20050609105234/http://register.consilium.eu.int/pdf/en/03/st11/st11490-re01en03.pdf [Accessed 19 September 2020].

Civipol (2015) Civipol Activity Report 2014 Outlook 2015, Paris: Civipol. Available from: https://civipol.themecloud.website/wp-content/uploads/2012/06/civipol_rapport_2014_site.pdf [Accessed 8 September 2020].

Civipol (2017) Activity Report 2016 & Outlook 2017, Paris: Civipol. Available from: https://civipol.themecloud.website/wp-content/uploads/2012/06/rapport_civipol_2016-2017.pdf [Accessed 8 September 2020].

Civipol (2019) Rapport d'Activité 2018, Paris: Civipol. Available from: https://www.civipol.fr/sites/default/files/2019-09/Rapport%20d%26%23039%3Bactivit%C3%A9%202018.pdf [Accessed 10 September 2020].

Civipol (2020) 'Civipol: The company', [online] Available from: https://www.civipol.fr/en/civipol/company [Accessed 11 December 2020].

European Commission (2018) 'Programme d'appui au renforcement du système d'information de l'état civil et la création d'un fichier national d'identité biométrique', [online] Available from: https://ec.europa.eu/trustfundforafrica/sites/euetfa/files/t05-eutf-sah-sn-07_etat_civil.pdf [Accessed 16 June 2021].

Ferrer, A. (2012) 'Haiti, free soil, and antislavery in the revolutionary Atlantic', *American Historical Review*, 117(1): 40–66.

Frowd, P.M. (2018) *Security at the Borders: Transnational Practices and Technologies in West Africa*, Cambridge: Cambridge University Press.

Gammeltoft-Hansen, T. and Sørensen, N.N. (eds) (2013) *The Migration Industry and the Commercialization of International Migration*, London: Routledge.

Gegout, C. (2017) *Why Europe Intervenes in Africa: Security, Prestige and the Legacy of Colonialism*, London: Hurst & Co.

Hansen, P. and Jonsson, S. (2014) *Eurafrica: The Untold Story of European Integration and Colonialism*, London: Bloomsbury.

Lemberg-Pedersen, M. (2013) 'Private security companies and the European borderscapes', in T. Gammeltoft-Hansen and N. N. Sørensen (eds) *The Migration Industry and the Commercialization of International Migration*, London: Routledge, pp 152–72.

Lemberg-Pedersen, M. (2018) 'Security, industry and migration in European border control', in A. Weinar, S. Bonjour and L. Zhyznomirska (eds) *The Routledge Handbook of the Politics of Migration in Europe*, London: Routledge, pp 239–50.

Lemberg-Pedersen, M., Hansen, J.R. and Halpern, O.J. (2020) *The Political Economy of Entry Governance*, AdMiGov Deliverable 1.3, Copenhagen [online] Available from: http://admigov.eu/upload/Deliverable_D13_Lemberg-Pedersen_The_Political_Economy_of_Entry_Governance.pdf [Accessed 16 June 2021].

Manning, P. (2010) *Francophone Sub-Saharan Africa 1880–1995* (2nd edn), Cambridge: Cambridge University Press.

Marseille, J. (1984) *Empire Colonial et Capitalisme Français. Histoire d'un Divorce*, Paris: Albin Michel.

Marzagalli, S. (2018) 'French colonial policy, warfare, and eighteenth-century Atlantic trade. Readjustment mechanisms beyond protected markets'. Paper presented at the economic history seminar, Yale, 30 April 2018.

Mbembe, A. (2003) 'Necropolitics', *Public Culture*, 15(1): 11–40.

Mentan, T. (2017) *Africa in the Colonial Ages of Empire: Slavery, Capitalism, Racism, Colonialism, Decolonization, Independence as Recolonization, and Beyond*, Bamenda: Langaa Research & Publishing CIG.

Menz, G. (2013) 'The neoliberalized state and the growth of the migration industry', in T. Gammeltoft-Hansen and N.N. Sørensen (eds) *The Migration Industry and the Commercialization of International Migration*, London: Routledge, pp 108–27.

Milipol (2020) 'Who visits Milipol Paris?', [online] Available from: https://en.milipol.com/Exhibiting/Who-visits-Milipol-Paris [Accessed 11 December 2020].

Milipol (2021) 'About Milipol Paris 2021', [online] Available from: https://en.milipol.com/Milipol-Paris/About-Milipol-Paris-2021 [Accessed 5 May 2021].

Nkrumah, K. (1965) *Neo-colonialism: The Last Stage of Imperialism*, London: Thomas Nelson & Sons, Ltd.

Ọlọruntimẹhin, B.O. (1974) 'The French estate in West Africa, 1890–1918', *Journal of the Historical Society of Nigeria*, 7(3): 447–63.

O'Reilly, C. (2010) 'The transnational security consultancy industry: A case of state–corporate symbiosis', *Theoretical Criminology*, 14(2): 183–210; 1362–4806.

Privacy International (2020) 'Here's how a well-connected security company is quietly building mass biometric databases in West Africa with EU aid funds', [online] 10 November, Available from: http://privacyinternational.org/news-analysis/4290/heres-how-well-connected-security-company-quietly-building-mass-biometric [Accessed 1 December 2020].

Roberts, R. (1987) 'French colonialism, imported technology, and the handicraft textile industry in the Western Sudan, 1898–1918', *Journal of Economic History*, 47(2): 461–72.

Thomas, M. (2013) *Violence and Colonial Order. Police, Workers and Protest in the European Colonial Empires, 1918–1940*, Cambridge: Cambridge University Press.

Thompson, V. and Adloff, R. (1975) 'French economic policy in tropical Africa', in P. Duignan and L.H. Gann (eds) *Colonialism in Africa 1870–1960. Vol 4: The Economics of Colonialism*, Cambridge: Cambridge University Press, pp 127–64.

Trauner, F., Jegen, L., Adam, I. and Roos, C. (2019) 'The International Organization for Migration in West Africa: why its role is getting more contested', UNU-CRIS [Policy Brief PB-2019/3]. Available from: http://cris.unu.edu/international-organization-migration-west-africa-why-its-role-getting-more-contested [Accessed 13 September 2019].

Vermeulen, M., Tromp, R., Zandonini, G. and Amzat, A. (2019) 'A breakdown of Europe's €1.5bn migration spending in Nigeria', *The Correspondent*, 9 December. Available at: https://thecorrespondent.com/150/a-breakdown-of-europes-eur1-5bn-migration-spending-in-nigeria/19837235550-e86e62a5 [Accessed 7 July 2021].

Williams, E. (1994) *Capitalism & Slavery*, Chapel Hill: University of North Carolina Press.

6

Displaced, Profiled, Protected? Humanitarian Surveillance and New Approaches to Refugee Protection

Lina Ewert

Introduction

Recent decades have seen a rise in 'surveillance humanitarianism' (Latoreno, 2019) in contexts of displacement. While migration scholars have examined the control and treatment of refugees in camp settings for decades, recent decentralized urban approaches to hosting refugees and partnerships with the tech industry have led to an increase in data driven forms of governance and surveillance that warrant close scholarly attention. Since 2000, the UN Refugee Agency (UNHCR) has sought to collect the biometric data of millions of refugees worldwide. This is despite the fact that the storing of citizens' biometric information in a central registry is a contentious legal issue in many countries. Biometric technologies such as iris scanning use bodily markers as evidence to either identify individuals that have already been enrolled in existing databases or to verify the claimed identity of a person. Jordan has become a testing ground for the use of iris scanning where it is used, for example, as a means for Syrian refugees in Jordan to withdraw money and pay in the supermarket at Zaatari refugee camp (Staton, 2016). As of February 2018, more than 93 per cent of the 657,628 registered Syrian refugees are 'processed biometrically' (UNHCR, 2018a). This chapter seeks to examine the social impact of such surveillance practices, using the case of UNHCR's biometric governance of Syrian urban refugees in Jordan. It does so by conceptually situating iris scanning of refugees in Jordan in relation to a decolonial perspective on surveillance, combining insights from David Lyon's 'surveillance culture' (2017; 2018) and Mirca Madianou's 'technocolonialism' (2019). Such a perspective sharpens the focus for the reproduction of power asymmetries between UNHCR and refugees within a volatile environment that is marked by information poverty, aid dependence and the extraction of data.

The purpose of this chapter, then, is twofold. First, it examines the fast-paced development of biometric identity systems and aid provision within the volatile context of refugee protection in urban settings. Second, it aims at empirically grounding discussions about biometrics and surveillance humanitarianism in the experiences of those targeted, by documenting the perspectives of Syrians living as urban refugees in Amman, the Jordanian capital. The majority of refugees in the country do not live in designated camps, yet in the academic literature little ethnographic attention had been paid to their perspectives on iris scanning. The chapter draws on ten semi-structured interviews that were conducted with Syrian refugees living in Amman in 2018. My aim with this exploratory research was to start filling the gap of ethnographic accounts that centre on refugees, which were almost absent at the time of research. To do so, I collaborated with Rana, who is a Syrian refugee herself. With her language skills and in-depth knowledge of the field, Rana contributed invaluably by translating and contextualizing participants' statements during interviewing. I also collaborated with Mohamad, a Syrian refugee in Germany, to verify that questions and responses of interesting interview sections were translated and understood correctly. With this two-tier approach, I aspire to diversify the narratives of digital humanitarianism and epistemologies more broadly that shape histories in the making (Bhambra, 2014; Tilley, 2017).

The first section briefly introduces the concepts of 'surveillance culture' coined by sociologist David Lyon (2017; 2018) as well as 'technocolonialism' by Mirca Madianou (2019). It thus situates surveillance and biometrics in a decolonial research frame, pointing to technologies' historical genesis and power asymmetries through data extraction. Rather than assessing how well surveillance is understood, the concepts allow us to focus on power asymmetries and guiding logics, asking what those involved believe to be true and to trace how such assumptions impact their lives. It further explains the characteristics that make biometrics an intrusive technology and examines what is at stake when introducing it into volatile contexts. To understand where the assumed need for biometric technologies in the context of refugee protection comes from, the second section traces the humanitarian imaginaries that shape the UNHCR's approach to refugee protection from encampment to urban settlement. The third section teases out three themes that shape the imaginaries of Syrian refugees about the use of iris scanning by UNHCR: a normalization of the technology as mere procedure, the gateway function to services and privileges, and lastly the accompanying policies.

I argue that while the use of iris scanning per se is not perceived as posing immediate harm to refugees, it does not provide significant benefits compared to other, less intrusive methods of authentication. The chapter concludes by questioning whether and how meaningful consent can be established in volatile contexts in which refugees are concerned with fundamental needs rather than data protection. It reinforces the call of other scholars and civil society advocates for careful consideration of refugee needs and local contexts before implementing ambiguous surveillance technology.

Surveillance culture, techno-colonialism and the ambiguity of biometric technology

Surveillance is often associated with the realm of security agencies and law enforcement. However, the Canadian sociologist David Lyon defines surveillance more broadly as: 'any systematic and routine attention to personal details, whether specific or aggregate, for a defined purpose. That purpose, the intention of the surveillance practice, may be to protect, understand, care for, ensure entitlement, control, manage or influence individuals or groups' (Lyon, 2015: 3).

While surveillance can be perceived as malevolent or benevolent depending on the subject position and context (Raab, 2015), it is never inherently good or bad. Yet, as a relational practice it is never neutral either but deeply enmeshed in power relations (Foucault, 1995; Lyon, 2018). With his concept of surveillance culture, Lyon invites us to look beyond technological affordances and take the experiences of the surveilled subjects into account, bearing in mind contextual power relations (Lyon, 2017). Understanding surveillance as an integral part of many cultures, Lyon identifies a key question in why certain populations and individuals choose to participate in surveillance and where the norms that guide their behaviour come from (Lyon, 2018). He does so by building on the concept of social imaginaries (Taylor, 2004), defining surveillance imaginaries as 'shared understandings about certain aspects of visibility in daily life, and in social relationships, expectations and normative commitments' (Lyon, 2018: 41). For imaginaries to inform practices, they require a certain awareness of, and exposure to, surveillance by those targeted (Lyon, 2018).

Lyon's work on surveillance culture in the early 21st century has been very much informed by observations from North America and Europe. What Lyon neglects are power relations beyond nations and citizens, and particularly postcolonial power imbalances across multi status populations. In short: surveillance of those with insecure immigration or citizenship status, often from the global South, by those of secure status, often from the global North. It is productive, then, to take a decolonial perspective, asking how people subjected to humanitarian surveillance as refugees experience the extraction of their biometric and other personal data, whether they are aware of it and how their perception is negotiated within aid dependency relationships (on the need to acknowledge the agency and experience of refugees in political theory, see also Chapter 11).

In undertaking such a conceptional broadening, I draw on Mirca Madianou's analysis of what she terms 'technocolonialism' (2019). Technocolonialism as a concept looks at the power asymmetries between 'Western "saviours"' (Madianou, 2019: 3) and their subjects of care with a specific view towards their constitution through data-driven means. Sharpening the view for colonial reminiscences of dependency, Madianou points to the extraction of value from data generated by refugees for the benefit of stakeholders (Madianou, 2019). She identifies five complementary logics of technocolonialism: accountability, audit, capitalism, solutionism and securitization. Taking a relational understanding of power, we see that only accountability and securitization describe the relationship between humanitarian actors and their subjects of care. While Madianou did not base her case studies on first-hand accounts of refugees, the concept nonetheless carves out space for the lived experiences of subjects of humanitarian care, which will be explored in this chapter. A decolonial perspective on contemporary forms of biometric surveillance also acknowledges the colonial past of biometric technologies, which have historically been tested in colonized countries before being implemented in colonizing countries. For example, Mark Maguire (2012) reminds us that fingerprints were tested as means of identification with marginalized colonial subjects during British colonial rule in India, before they were subsequently introduced to criminal justice systems in the colonizing countries (Maguire, 2012, for fingerprinting in French colonial rule, see Chapter 5). In a similar vein, Simone Browne points to the involuntary role that Black enslaved people have played historically in testing early forms of identification through bodily markers such as branding to govern their mobility (2010; 2015). As 'digital epidermalization', contemporary biometric technologies such as iris scans and fingerprints reproduce the privileging of 'prototypical Whiteness', thus contributing to the differential treatment of non-White people based on race (Browne, 2015: 118, see also Chapters 2 and 4).

While the use of biometrics for border control purposes and underlying logics of securitization have been well-researched (see for instance Amoore, 2006; Epstein, 2007; FRA, 2018), research into forms of digital humanitarianism (Duffield, 2016), and specifically biometric registration of refugees, is still emerging as a focus area (Franke, 2009; Hosein, 2011; Hosein and Nyst, 2014; Jacobsen, 2015a; b; Jacobsen and Sandvik, 2018; The Engine Room, 2018; 2020; Kaurin, 2019; Latoreno et al, 2019; Madianou, 2019; Cheesman, 2022; Lemberg-Pedersen and Haioty, 2020). The emerging body of work has identified a number of risks associated with the use of biometrics in humanitarian contexts. As biometric identifiers are understood not to change dramatically over the course of a lifetime, their 'non-revocability' (The Engine Room, 2018: 5) renders their validity theoretically endless and their value priceless. Such an infinite life cycle necessitates the anticipation of future risks that may seem dystopian under current circumstances but that may become a reality, considering technological advancements and the interoperability of formerly unconnected databases. Harm may stem from remote identification without consent or social sorting and discrimination based on social markers such as ethnicity or gender (Privacy International, n.d.; the Engine Room, 2018). Further, biometric identification also allows for the tracking of individuals across borders and contexts while the underlying databases facilitate cross-checking and linking of information (Hosein and Nyst, 2014: 16). As in the case of the Holocaust or Rwandan genocide, the delicate alliance of biometrics with data storage in population registries risks misuse for social exclusion and mass atrocities (Rhaman, 2016). Biometric data gathered in humanitarian contexts could also become of interest to national governments who seek to deter migrants from seeking asylum under the guise of combatting terrorism (Corrigan, 2019; Madianou, 2019; see also Stambøl and Jegen, this volume).

From encampment to urban settlement – changing humanitarian imaginaries of refugee protection

In spite of accounts that locate the emergence of refugees and refugee camps in Europe after the First and Second World War (Agamben, 1995; Malkkii, 1995), refugee camps were already used in the 1860s in the United States of America when 500,000 enslaved people self-emancipated following the civil war (Du Bois, 1998 [1935]). As a technology of power, the camp enables the monitoring and controlling of inhabitants, often through spatial confinement, and renders inhabitants accessible and knowable as objects of knowledge production (Malkki, 1995; Agier, 2011). The humanitarian imaginary guiding the asymmetrical power relationship between humanitarian actors and refugees is premised on the assumption that aid is a gift awarded within a one-sided relationship of care 'since it is assumed that they [refugees] can only receive' (Fassin, 2012: 202). This sheds light on a sixth logic preceding the logics mentioned in Madianou's concept of technocolonialism, namely the logics of (White) saviourism (see also Chapter 7). Camps therefore represent the care/control nexus where refugees are both cared for and their lives and mobilities tightly controlled (Agier, 2011). In this section I outline the process whereby encampment gave way to a preference for urban refugee hosting within both the UNHCR as an institution and within Jordan as a host country. Zooming in on biometric surveillance, I will show how the care/control nexus played out within this volatile environment (see also Chapters 9 and 13).

According to Jeff Crisp (2017), a former UNHCR employee involved in developing the Agency's urban refugee approach in 2009, camp inhabitants were kept both somewhat separate from hosting societies as well as dependent upon assistance. Protection thus followed a paternalistic humanitarian imaginary in which refugees were passive objects of care, temporarily controlled via the means of confinement in camps. According to Crisp, encampment as an approach was problematized in the 1990s when it became apparent that refugees lived in camps for years on end without repatriation as a viable option (on the coloniality of encampment, see Chapter 4). In countries such as Jordan, refugees increasingly used their agency to move into cities (Crisp, 2017). The first official UNHCR policy regarding 'urban refugees' was established in 1997. As Crisp states, the urban refugee policy was strongly influenced by donors who were concerned about aid accountability, unauthorized cross-country movements and at times violent resistance against UNHCR policies. Crisp observes that many UNHCR staff members and donors diagnosed urban refugees with a 'dependency syndrome' understood as an 'unwarranted sense of entitlement' (2017: 89). Such expressions suggest that the narrow focus of the humanitarian imaginary regarding refugees shifted from expectations of high degrees of aid dependence to expectations of significant self-sufficiency (see also Ilcan and Rygiel, 2015; Duffield, 2016).

The same allegation of reliance on aid that was fostered by long term care in the camps was thus held against refugees in urban settings. With the advent of mobile and spatially dispersed urban refugees, the policy also problematized mobility control. As Michel Agier notes, care is premised on control (Agier, 2011) and since confinement in camps facilitated direct access to, and monitoring of, refugees, other means of keeping track and surveillance were sought. It is here that the five logics of technocolonialism (accountability, audit, capitalism, solutionism and securitization) come into play. Problematizing mobility, assistance fraud and lack of reliable identity documentation, the Executive Committee of UNHCR proposed setting up a standardized global biometric identification system and endorsed sharing data with national governments in October 2001 (ExCom, 2001). While efforts to establish central repositories for biometric data of millions of refugees and ecosystems for digital identities were set up at a later stage in 2013 and 2018 (UNHCR, n.d.; Accenture, 2015; UNHCR, 2018b; c), biometric technologies and their promise of individual identification already played a crucial role in the fine-grained governance of cash-based assistance (CBA).

The increasing marketization and competition for funding within the humanitarian sector creates a push towards innovative, tech-based approaches (Madianou, 2019, see also Hammerstad, 2014). Although the Refugee Agency had used iris scanning already in the early 2000s in Afghanistan

(Jacobsen 2015a; b), it was in Jordan that the technology became central, not only to registration but also to cash based assistance. In many respects, Jordan can therefore be considered a laboratory for a new urban and data-driven approach in which the UNHCR experimented with new ways of delivering aid to a dispersed population, including by using iris scanning (Duffield, 2016; Lemberg-Pedersen and Haioty, 2020). The Jordanian approach to cash-based assistance was first initiated for Iraqi refugees in 2008. At this time refugees were provided with bank cards as tokens of authentication. In 2012 Syrian refugees were added to the programme (ODI, 2017). The regional office of UNHCR started collaborating with the Jordanian company IrisGuard, one of the forerunners in the area of iris recognition, to set up a biometric database, and has registered refugees since 2013 (UNHCR, 2013). To implement its iris-enabled CBA programme, UNHCR made use of Cairo Amman Bank's already existing customer iris scan infrastructure. The Eyebank is linked to the Eyecloud, a platform that allows for checking of registration data against iris scans at ATMs (Gilert and Austin, 2017).

The CBA scheme is shaped by certain policies such as the 'one cash collector policy'. UNHCR therefore only registered the biometrics of one family representative, usually a nominated or assigned 'head of household'. According to research participants at the time of fieldwork, this person is granted approximately 10 days to collect the money. An assessment of the programme states that 'beneficiaries' are expected to register another person in cases where the designated person is unavailable. However, the authors remained agnostic about the extent to which this rule was understood by refugees (Gilert and Austin, 2017). The humanitarian imaginary underlying these data driven approaches to refugee protection merges its two predecessors: refugees are seen as both potentially self-sufficient and as vulnerable objects of care in need of assistance if (undisclosed) assessment criteria of UNHCR are met. Yet, they were also seen as potentially deceiving, monetizing aid or registering in multiple countries to gain more assistance (Gilert and Austin, 2017). With this set-up, Jordan becomes another example of the outsourcing of risks to refugees within technocolonialism, raising questions of accountability and humanitarian principles to do no harm (Madianou, 2019). What is missing from this picture so far, however, is the experiences of refugees themselves.

Syrians' imaginaries of humanitarian surveillance in Jordan

This section takes a closer look at how Syrians living in Jordan as refugees, current or former 'beneficiaries' of CBA, experience the data-driven approach to protection, and in particular the iris scanning technology. The section draws on the semi-structured interviews with Syrians living as urban refugees in Amman. Most of the participants had not critically questioned the use of biometric technologies or data protection prior to the interview. Initial biometric registration is experienced as a normal part of becoming a refugee. As Ahmad stated: 'I expect that they took this iris scan to know that I am here. … Because I am here in Jordan, I should have [an] iris scan. [It is] only to know me'. While not considering these functions as intrusive or threatening, his statement aptly captures the essence of the purpose of biometric technologies, that is, to make refugees knowable and locatable. The scanning and providing of information upon registration was framed by interviewees as a bureaucratic procedure, in which only the person to be registered had to provide information, not the other way around. As Rana summarized the testimony of Maryam: 'the [UNHCR] interviewer made her understood "we should know everything about you. You should give us all the information about you" … When she ask[s] them, they say to [her] this is only procedure'.

This inequality is not unique to Jordan, but has also been pointed out by Madianou (2019) in her discussion of the biometric registration of Rohingya by UNHCR in Bangladesh. The Eurocentric concept of transparency is thus translated into the problematization of fraud prevention by UNHCR in an unequal exchange of information.

While informed consent presupposes a certain level of information, none of the participants recalled being provided with information about how their data would be used and shared. It is noteworthy that most of the participants did not feel the need to ask questions and to actively gather more information. Madianou and others have pointed to the conditions of consent in which refusal is not a valid option in the face of aid dependency (Hosein, 2011; Madianou, 2019). The same holds true for Jordan where several women stated that they had other, more pressing needs than data protection to worry about. Others stated that they had nothing to hide and therefore nothing to fear, a phrase commonly mentioned in relation to surveillance practices (Lyon, 2018).

However, this does not mean that participants did not care about what information was known about them. Kalil stated that he had deliberately restrained himself in making political remarks: 'Because I am not talking anything against the Syrian government or against the Jordanian government. So, I can easily tell my name right now'. His statement shows that, far from being unconcerned, he withheld specific information such as political opinions that he himself deemed potentially harmful in the future. Whether it was based on his own experiences with the Syrian regime or rumours, assumptions about how certain personal information could be turned against him guided his behaviour in Jordan.

Mohamad, the Syrian translator with whom I worked together at a later research state, explained that caution in sharing political views is expressed by many Syrians, who fear potential retaliation upon return to Syria (see also Davis, 2012). The surveillance imaginary at play is thus shaped by expectations of penalizing state power enabled through specific information. However, this imaginary did not extend to the UNHCR – similar assumptions casting doubt on the refugee Agency's handling of data were absent among participants. They mostly trusted UNHCR with their data and did not fear negative impacts if the data was shared with other organizations or European governments. These findings support Lyon's contention that awareness is key to developing and adjusting surveillance imaginaries. In order to perceive technology as potentially invasive, refugees would have to be fully informed about what data is shared with whom and for what purposes. In situations marked by information poverty this is rarely the case.

With regard to iris scanning, the participants of this study generally did not expect harmful consequences. Jacobsen and Sandvik note that refugees in Lebanon have been deterred from seeking protection because biometric registration was mandatory (Jacobsen and Sandvik, 2018). The Syrians interviewed for this study did not choose to refuse, nor were they aware of any such cases in their social networks. On the contrary, many believed iris scanning to enable access to privileges and services. For example, Jalila explained: 'I think this is only procedures. They should take [the iris scan]. After that I understand. … [T]hey took this iris scan to give me a salary'. In fact, the technology is so much associated with CBA that participants would routinely use the Arabic term for iris scan (نيعلا ةمصب) to refer to CBA. Azima stated that she assumed the iris scanning was for travelling, as her iris had already been scanned at the air border with Jordan when she entered the country. Thus, she assumed travelling was enabled and not restricted by biometric registration. This stands in stark contrast with accounts by migrants in the EU who experience the restrictive effect of the biometric components of the Dublin system (Schuster, 2011; Kaurin, 2019). These statements suggest that the emerging surveillance imaginary surrounding the biometric technology is by no means one of privacy intrusion or restrictive disciplining but rather seen positively as a gatekeeper. This also became apparent when participants shared concerns about assistance fraud and associated fraud prevention as a beneficial effect of the technology (see also ODI, 2017).

The positive associations with the technology do not necessarily mean that refugees fully support iris scanning as a means to receive cash assistance. In fact, the majority of participants would prefer to use a transferable token of identification such as a bank card. This is due to long queues in front of ATMs and the occasional need to let a relative collect the money instead of the head of household. While participants did not feel stigmatized when waiting in line, queueing is especially burdensome for already marginalized groups such as the elderly, people with disabilities or illnesses and single parents.

Regarding the 'one cash collector only' policy, interview statements suggest that some participants did not know about the possibility of registering another person on the account, while others did contact UNHCR in a case of hospitalization but were not provided with a timely solution to their problem. According to an assessment of the CBA programme, the need for quick solutions for emergency cases had been identified, yet still not been implemented in early 2018 (Gilert and Austin, 2017).

While participants generally trusted UNHCR with their data, that trust did not extend to handling complaints. Firas stated, for example, that he had severe problems with the iris scan once. While the details of the case cannot be confirmed, he was left with the impression that UNHCR did not help him sufficiently enough in his efforts to retrieve the allowance for that month. Similarly, Saba related the story of a close family member who had made a complaint and found themselves cut off from assistance soon after. Regardless of whether these events were in fact related, the story shaped her imaginary about UNHCR and filled a void left by a lack of knowledge about institutional norms and opportunities regarding complaints. A study conducted by the Oversees Development Institute supports these anecdotal findings, stating that approximately 17 per cent of urban refugees participating in the study refrained from complaining due to fear of retaliation or losing their eligibility for assistance (ODI, 2017: 114).

This demonstrates that the effect of a surveillance technology is highly dependent upon the policy context guiding its implementation. The surveillance imaginaries depend on the information provided as well as past and current experiences. The affordances of biometric technologies are not apparent when one is exposed to an iris scanner. Rather covertly, their capacity to enable tracking of individuals is linked to databases that are at a distance from the lived experiences of refugees. While the awareness of and exposure to surveillance is necessary for imaginaries to be formed, background knowledge is equally important for the imaginary to guide practices of refugees meaningfully. Due to a lack of background information and pressing fundamental needs, the surveillance imaginary held by participants about iris scanning is shaped by their direct experiences and therefore rather embracing and positive.

Conclusion

This chapter traced how humanitarian imaginaries guiding the protection and aid provision of refugees by UNHCR have changed with the advent of mobile urban refugees in Jordan and the shift from encampment to urban settlement. It demonstrated that tropes of vulnerability and aid dependence have remained at the core of the humanitarian imaginary. Yet without the spatial confinement offered by camps, the unpredictability of mobile refugees fending for themselves has rendered the imaginary more complex. Two imaginaries about the agency of refugees therefore oppose each other: on the one hand, refugee potential for self-sufficiency and socio-economic integration is emphasized in the urban refugee policy. On the other hand, refugees' potential to deceive through assistance and identity fraud as well as their moving towards other countries of asylum has been emphasized in the urban refugee policy and used by UNHCR to legitimize the introduction of biometric technologies since the early 2000s. The surveillance imaginary constructed around refugees thus problematizes issues that biometric technology is seemingly ideally placed to solve in virtue of its capacity to uniquely identify individuals.

In contrast to migrants in the EU, most of the Syrians participating in this study did not associate the technology with control or restriction. Indeed, it appears that participants did not critically question the technology and generally trusted UNHCR with the data it collected. Interviews reveal a lack of information regarding the processing and sharing of data by UNHCR as well as with regard to the affordances of biometric technology in conjunction with large scale databases. Instead, the surveillance imaginaries of participants are based on direct experiences in Jordan, rumours as well as knowledge about the potential harm of sharing personal information in volatile contexts such as Syria. However, the lack of information was not problematized since data protection was of a lesser concern in comparison to more immediate basic needs. Iris scanning was strongly and positively associated with accessing aid. Rather than problematizing the technology itself, the interviewed Syrians were concerned with the policies guiding its implementation. In particular, the transferability of tokens and the need to authorize more than one family member to withdraw cash assistance were emphasized. As the preference for bank cards shows, support for iris scanning stems mostly from the aid it provides rather than a comprehensive, fully informed weighting of the costs and benefits of the technology.

Due to the small scope of the research conducted for this chapter, the insights cannot be generalized. However, the chapter does demonstrate that the impact of biometric technologies is ambiguous and heavily dependent on accompanying policies. Humanitarian actors such as UNHCR base data collection and use of biometrics on the principle of informed consent, yet the interviews show that information is provided in such a way that refugees do not fully understand the procedures they are supposed to consent to. This speaks to Lyon's assertion that surveillance imaginaries presuppose a certain level of awareness in order to meaningfully impact the lives of those surveilled. From a decolonial perspective, it becomes evident that the power relationship between UNHCR and refugees is shaped by the reproduction of power asymmetries and the outsourcing of risks to ill-informed subjects of care, as identified within technocolonialism by Madianou (2019). These findings add to the strand of literature that questions informed consent as an appropriate mechanism to balance out power asymmetries and safeguard rights of refugees (Hosein and Nyst, 2014; Raymond, 2017). Consent places the burden of assessing a complex situation on individuals who are struggling to begin life anew under dire conditions.

This begs the question: if powerful humanitarian actors such as UNHCR chose to collect highly sensitive data such as biometrics, how can they ethically ensure consent within volatile contexts when refugees do not have the capacity to comprehend complex data processing landscapes? How can alternative means of safeguarding rights and ensuring accountability be designed to take the needs of people in search of protection into account? This is a challenge beyond the realm of humanitarian aid, relevant in all contexts marked by information poverty and data-driven service provision. Yet, even before questions of consent come to into play, the decision for implementing biometrics and collecting data needs to be undertaken cautiously. In keeping with a growing chorus of scholars and civil society actors, this chapter calls for careful consideration of necessity and proportionality, especially in contexts that lack clear legal frameworks (Jacobsen, 2015a, b; Jacobsen and Sandvik, 2018; The Engine Room, 2018; 2020; Latoreno et al, 2019). While donor funding for emerging technologies in search of grounds to test their scalability may be abundant, ambiguous surveillance technologies are not necessarily the best answer to local challenges. While biometric identification may serve the needs of refugees in other contexts, for the urban refugees participating in this study, it is not the affordances of biometrics that makes a difference to their lives.

Acknowledgements

I would like to thank Rana for her invaluable support in conducting the research for this chapter. It would not have been the same without her. Further, I would like to thank Mohamad, Leonie Hoffmann, Özgür Özvatan and Philine Seydel for their valuable feedback. I am eternally grateful to my mother for her guidance, support and love. You will be missed.

References

Accenture (2015) 'UNHCR – innovative identity management system uses biometrics to better serve refugees', *Accenture*, [online] Available from: https://www.accenture.com/t20161026T063323__w__/us-en/_acnmedia/Accenture/Conversion-Assets/DotCom/Documents/Global/PDF/Dualpub_15/Accenture-Unhcr-Innovative-Identity-Management-System.pdf [Accessed 18 June 2021].

Agamben, G. (1995) 'We refugees', *Symposium: A Quarterly Journal in Modern Literatures*, 49(2): 114–119.

Agier, M. (2011) *Managing the Undesirables: Refugee Camps and Humanitarian Government*, Cambridge: Polity Press.

Amoore, L. (2006) 'Biometric borders: governing mobilities in the war on terror', *Political Geography*, 25: 336–51.

Bhambra, G.K. (2014) *Connected Sociologies*, London: Bloomsbury Academic.

Browne, S. (2010) 'Digital epidermalization: race, identity and biometrics', *Critical Sociology*, 36(1): 131–50.

Browne, S. (2015) *Dark Matters: On the Surveillance of Blackness*, Durham, NC: Duke University Press.

Cheesman, M. (2022) 'Self-sovereignty for refugees? The contested horizons of digital identity', *Geopolitics*, 27(1): 134–59.

Corrigan, J. (2019) 'DHS is collecting biometrics on thousands of refugees who will never enter the US', *Nextgov*, [online] 20 November, Available from: https://www.nextgov.com/emerging-tech/2019/08/dhs-collecting-biometrics-thousands-refugees-who-will-never-enter-us/159310/ [Accessed 18 June 2021].

Crisp, J. (2017) 'Finding space for protection: an inside account of the evolution of UNHCR's urban refugee policy', *Refuge*, 33(1): 87–96.

Davis, R. (2012) 'Syrian refugees: lessons from other conflicts and possible policies', *Viewpoint*, 4, Middle East Program, Woodrow Wilson International Centre for Scholars, [online] August, Available from: http://www.jadaliyya.com/pages/index/6499/syrian-refugees_lessons-from-other-conflicts-and-p [Accessed 18 June 2021].

Du Bois, W.E.B. (1998 [1935]) *Black Reconstruction in America, 1860–1880*. New York: The Free Press.

Duffield, M. (2016) 'The resilience of the ruins: towards a critique of digital humanitarianism', *Resilience*, 4(3): 147–165.

The Engine Room (2018) 'Biometrics in the humanitarian sector', *The Engine Room*, [online] March, Available from: https://www.theengineroom.org/wp-content/uploads/2018/03/Engine-Room-Oxfam-Biometrics-Review.pdf [Accessed 18 June 2021].

The Engine Room (2020) 'Understanding the lived effects of digital ID: a multi-country study', *The Engine Room*, [online] January, Available from: https://digitalid.theengineroom.org/assets/pdfs/200128_FINAL_TER_Digital_ID_Report+Annexes_English_Interactive_Edit1.pdf [Accessed 18 June 2021].

Epstein, C. (2007) 'Guilty bodies, productive bodies, destructive bodies: crossing the biometric borders', *International Political Sociology*, 1: 149–64.

Executive Committee of the High Commissioner's Programme [ExCom] (2001) 'Conclusion on registration of refugees and asylum-seekers, No. 91 (LII) – 2001', *UNHCR*, [online] 5 October, Available from: http://www.unhcr.org/excom/exconc/3bd3e1d44/conclusion-registration-refugees-asylum-seekers.html [Accessed 18 June 2021].

Fassin, D. (2012) *Humanitarian Reason: A Moral History of the Present.* Berkley: University of California Press.

Foucault, M. (1995) *Discipline and Punish: The Birth of the Prison.* New York: Vintage Books.

Franke, M.F.N. (2009) 'Refugee registration as foreclosure of the freedom to move: the virtualisation of refugees' rights within maps of international protection', *Environment and Planning D: Society and Space*, 27: 352–69.

Fundamental Rights Agency (2018) 'Under watchful eyes: biometrics, EU IT systems and fundamental rights', Luxembourg: Publications Office of the European Union.

Gilert, H. and Austin, L. (2017) 'Review of the common cash facility approach in Jordan', Cash Learning, October, Available from: http://www.cashlearning.org/downloads/calp-ccf-jordan-web.pdf [Accessed 18 June 2021].

Hammerstad, A. (2014) *The Rise and Decline of a Global Security Actor: UNHCR, Refugee Protection and Security*, Oxford: Oxford University Press.

Hosein, G. (2011) 'Why we work on refugee privacy', Privacy International, [online] 8 July, Available from: https://www.privacyinternational.org/node/300 [Accessed 18 June 2021].

Hosein, G. and Nyst, C. (2014) 'Aiding surveillance: an exploration of how development and humanitarian aid initiatives are enabling surveillance in developing countries', Privacy International, [online], Available from: https://privacyinternational.org/sites/default/files/2017-12/Aiding%20Surveillance.pdf [Accessed 22 June 2021].

Ilcan, S. and Rygiel, K. (2015) '"Resiliency humanitarianism": responsibilizing refugees through humanitarian emergency governance in the camp', *International Political Sociology*, 9: 333–51.

Jacobsen, K.L. (2015a) *The Politics of Humanitarian Technology: Good Intentions, Unintended Consequences and Insecurity*, London: Routledge.

Jacobsen, K.L. (2015b) 'Experimentation in humanitarian locations: UNHCR and biometric registration of afghan refugees', *Security Dialogue*, 46(2): 144–64.

Jacobsen, K.L. and Sandvik, K.B. (2018) 'UNHCR and the pursuit of international protection – accountability through technology?', *Third World Quarterly*, 39(8): 1508–24.

Kaurin, D. (2019) 'Data protection and digital agency for refugees', Research Paper No. 12, World Refugee and Migration Council, [online], Available from: https://wrmcouncil.org/publications/research-paper/data-protection-and-digital-agency-for-refugees-research-paper-no-12/ [Accessed 23 March 2022].

Latoreno, M. (2019) 'Stop surveillance humanitarianism', *New York Times*, [online] 11 July, Available from: https://www.nytimes.com/2019/07/11/opinion/data-humanitarian-aid.html [Accessed 18 June 2021].

Latonero, M., Hiatt, K., Antonella, N., Clericetti, G. and Penagos, M. (2019) 'Digital identity in the migration and refugee context: Italy case study', Data & Society, [online report] Available from: https://datasociety.net/wp-content/uploads/2019/04/DataSociety_DigitalIdentity.pdf [Accessed 22 June 2021].

Lemberg-Pedersen, M. and Haioty, E. (2020) 'Re-assembling the surveillable refugee body in the era of data-craving', *Citizenship Studies*, 24(5): 607–24.

Lyon, D. (2015) *Surveillance after Snowden*, Cambridge: Polity.

Lyon, D. (2017) 'Surveillance culture: engagement, exposure, and ethics in digital modernity', *International Journal of Communication*, 11: 824–42.

Lyon, D. (2018) *The Culture of Surveillance*, Cambridge: Polity.

Madianou, M. (2019) 'Technocolonialism – digital innovation and data practices in the humanitarian response to refugee crises', *Social Media and Society*, July–September: 1–13.

Maguire, M. (2012) 'Biopower, racialization and new security technology', *Social Identities*, 18(5): 593–607.

Malkki, L. (1995) 'Refugees and exile – from "refugee studies" to the national order of things', *Annual Review of Anthropology*, 24: 495–523.

Overseas Development Institute [ODI] (2017) 'A Promise of tomorrow: the effects of UNHCR and UNICEF cash assistance on Syrian refugees in Jordan', London: ODI.

Privacy International (n.d.) 'Biometrics', Privacy International, [online] Available from: https://www.privacyinternational.org/topics/biometrics [Accessed 18 June 2021].

Raab, C. (2015) 'Effects of surveillance on civil liberties and fundamental rights in Europe', in D. Wright and R. Kreissl (eds) *Surveillance in Europe*, London: Routledge: 259–67.

Raymond, N. (2017) 'Beyond "do no harm" and individual consent – reckoning with the emerging ethical challenges of civil society's use of data', in L. Taylor, L. Floridi and B. van der Sloot (eds) *Group Privacy – New Challenges of Data Technologies*, Cham: Springer, pp 67–82.

Rhaman, Z. (2016) 'Dangerous data: the role of data collection in genocides', *The Engine Room*, [online] 21 November, Available from: https://www.theengineroom.org/dangerous-data-the-role-of-data-collection-in-genocides/ [Accessed 18 June 2021].

Schuster, L. (2011) 'Dublin II and Eurodac: examining the (un)intended(?) consequences', *Gender, Place and Culture*, 18(3): 401–16.

Staton, B. (2016) 'Eye spy: biometric aid system trials in Jordan', *Irinnews*, [online] 18 May, Available from: http://www.irinnews.org/analysis/2016/05/18/eye-spy-biometric-aid-system-trials-jordan [Accessed 18 June 2021].

Taylor, C. (2004) *Modern Social Imaginaries*, London: Duke University Press.

Tilley, L. (2017) 'Resisting piratic method by doing research otherwise', *Sociology*, 51(1): 27–42.

UNHCR (n.d.) 'Biometric identity management system: enhancing registration and data management', *UNHCR*, [online] Available from: http://www.unhcr.org/550c304c9.pdf [Accessed 18 June 2021].

UNHCR (2013) 'UNHCR slashes waiting time, clears backlog of Syrian registrations in Jordan', *UNHCR*, [online] 3 October, Available from: https://www.unhcr.org/news/makingdifference/2013/10/524d5e4b6/unhcr-slashes-waiting-time-clears-backlog-syrian-registrations-jordan.html [Accessed 18 June 2021].

UNHCR (2018a) 'Jordan: fact sheet', *UNHCR*, [online] 22 February, Available from: https://reliefweb.int/report/jordan/unhcr-jordan-factsheet-february-2018 [Accessed on 18 June 2021].

UNHCR (2018b) 'PRIMES', *UNHCR*, [online] Available from: http://www.unhcr.org/primes [Accessed 18 June 2021].

UNHCR (2018c) 'UNHCR strategy on digital identity and inclusion', *UNHCR*, [online] Available from: http://www.unhcr.org/blogs/wp-content/uploads/sites/48/2018/03/2018-02-Digital-Identity_02.pdf [Accessed 18 June 2021].

7

Of the Mobile and the Immobilized: COVID-19 and the Uneven Geographies of Disease Transmission

Lucy Mayblin

Introduction

This chapter explores the intersection of three vectors: (im)mobility, postcolonial inequality and disease. For decades, the international community has problematized what has been represented as the excessive and dangerous mobility of people originating in the symbolic geography of what is sometimes termed the 'Third World' (which is in this context interchangeable with the global South) moving to the 'First World' (the global North, or 'the West') (see Mayblin and Turner, 2021 for a discussion of these terms). This excessive mobility has been widely viewed by politicians, publics and even academic researchers, as a threat to communities and nation-states in the First World. People who are seeking asylum have paid a heavy price; efforts to quarantine them outside of the global North have intensified with every passing year (Mayblin, 2017). Part of the sense of threat from Third World migrants over at least the past century has been a generalized concern with hygiene, and the bringing of diseases into host countries. This is a theme which recurs in research across a range of times and locations (Kraut, 1994).

This chapter seeks to upend such assumptions through discussing the historical and contemporary disease spreading activities of those usually construed as 'host' communities. It suggests that it is the excessive mobility of those whose border crossing is rarely problematized or curtailed, often from the First World, that has the potential to be a greater threat to communities, societies and nation-states around the world. This is done through focusing on disease, particularly air borne diseases, and discussing the role of international travel in spreading air borne diseases. The chapter first discusses the question of whose mobility is perceived to be a problem, before exploring the emergence of ideas of migrants as disease spreaders. The next section discusses the disease spreading impact of European colonialism from the 15th century onwards in order to establish an inverse analysis of 'whose mobility is a problem'. The final section explores the implications of the COVID-19 pandemic for migrants immobilized by migration governance regimes in camps and detention centres. Immobilized because of a perception that their mobility was dangerous, they now, ironically, find themselves victims of the consequences of the excessive mobility of their wealthier counterparts. Overall, this chapter situates the COVID-19 pandemic within the context of regimes of mobility and immobility and embeds these in histories of colonialism.

To some extent the argument will entail generalizations across two groups – the mobile and the immobilized. This binary distinction is not intended to encompass all peoples in the world or to identify victims and perpetrators. Rather, the binary is used as an analytical device to highlight tendencies in international migration regimes, and ultimately to argue for more just approaches to border governance. My aim is to highlight some of the ways in which the almost unfettered mobilities of the world's wealthier inhabitants might in fact be dangerous (rather than benign, if not positive, as it is often portrayed); and to contrast that with the vast and expensive architecture of control erected to prevent or contain Third World mobilities. In recognizing these uneven geographies of fear and control we might then argue for more just mobility regimes which overcome the embedded racist logics which currently dominate.

Whose mobility is a problem?

Migration and mobility – the permanent or temporary movement of people across sovereign national borders – has been a site of increased scholarly, political and public concern in the First World over the past 70 years. The mobility of some people became a focus of concern in the period following the Second World War because for the first time in living memory increasing numbers of people were seeking to move from former colonies in what became known as the 'global South' to former metropoles or settler colonies in the 'global North'. I say 'move' because many of these people were not migrating between sovereign states but were exercising their rights to mobility *within* empires. For example, until 1981 there was no British citizenship which referred only to the Islands of the British Isles, there was only citizenship of the British Empire and Commonwealth (Bhambra,

2017). This type of migration – South to North – has been problematized as dangerous, or challenging, in a variety of ways (see Chapters 4 and 9). Mobile subjects, often construed as immigrants, have been subject to racism and general hostility in the street, the workplace, the media, and among politicians and policymakers. They have been the subject of concerns around their economic impact, their impact on housing, on schooling, on healthcare and welfare systems; and their ability to 'cohere' or 'integrate' with communities and societies. Equally, there have been, across different societies and 'immigrant groups', repeated concerns around hygiene and diseases which these mobile subjects might bring to their unsuspecting hosts. This is, we might say, a reccurring trope.

Such concerns have, of course, been the subject of extensive academic research to test, prove or disprove the veracity of this range of concerns. Whether legitimate or not, politicians and policymakers have also then sought to govern mobile subjects in ways which might control migrants' (imagined or real) impacts on so called 'host' societies. Part of this project of governing mobility has been a significant effort at simply preventing people from arriving at all, even when demographic analysis of birth and death rates indicates an urgent need for increasing the size of the working population (Hansen and Jonsson, 2014). A vast architecture of control has thus been put in place in all countries in the First World which seeks to prevent, as far as possible, the entry of people from the Third World (with the exception of the very wealthy). Such efforts are even oriented to forced migrants who should be specially protected from arbitrary barriers to sanctuary under international law (Mayblin, 2017; 2019; see also Chapter 10).

Policies to protect against South–North mobility include walls, fences, strict visa regimes, high visa fees, time restricted visas, salary thresholds for or complete bans on family reunification, carrier sanctions, the proliferation of immigration detention facilities – increasingly offshore; and deportation orders, limitations on economic rights around welfare and work, interception at sea, and advertising campaigns discouraging migration. In the UK even *citizens* of global South heritage have themselves been subject to deportation in what has come to be known as the 'Windrush scandal' (de Noronha, 2020). Mau et al (2015) have analysed data on visa agreements and found that since 1969 the opportunities for visa free travel have expanded for citizens of OECD countries while they have stagnated or declined for citizens of African countries. In this way, it is relatively easy for someone with a French, British, or Australian passport to travel around the world almost unfettered. Visa fees will be minimal, interrogations in airports rare. Meanwhile, someone with a Libyan, Guatemalan, or Nigerian passport will be subject to a barrage of checks, costs, barriers and en route interrogations which make moving across borders slow, difficult, expensive, or impossible. This architecture of control aims at preventing South–North mobility, and to quarantine Third World citizens outside of the First world (Achiume, 2019). I discuss encampment as a technology for quarantining forced migrants later in the chapter, but first I will discuss the specific issue of disease as one legitimating factor for the proliferation of such projects of immobilization.

Migrants as disease spreaders

Within this context of enabling the mobility of some people and disabling the mobility of others, the trope of disease control is a reoccurring one. Alan M. Kraut calls this the 'double helix of health and fear' (1994: 1). This 'double helix' originates in colonial ideas of racial hierarchy in which some bodies (White bodies) are superior to other (brown and Black) bodies. As Stuart Hall so eloquently articulated, racism has two registers: biology and culture (Hall, 2000). Thus, the cultural extension of ideas of Black and brown *biological* inferiority also extended to the sense that people racialized as such inhabit *cultures* of poor hygiene, ill health and disease proliferation. In part, this was assumed to be associated with their lack of rationality and an intellectual deficiency which prevented proper bodily hygiene and the adoption of modern medical knowledges and techniques. Colonized people, therefore, came to be thought of as diseased as an extension of being mentally irrational and physically weak (Reitmanova et al, 2015). Such ideas do not map neatly on to contemporary ideas of 'Whiteness' or ethnicity in that groups of people now considered 'White' such as Irish nationals, were racialized as inferior in the same way as other groups of colonized and subjugated people into the early 20th century (Ignatiev, 1995). At the same time, scientific racism and social Darwinism also incorporated poor Whites into racial schemas connoting physical and intellectual inferiority, which naturally extended to the realms of hygiene and disease (Bonnett, 1998).

It is in colonial ideology that we find the origins of ideas of 'immigrants' as bringers of disease. The word immigrants itself is a highly racialized category rarely today associated with those classified as 'White', who tend to be represented as ex-pats, emigres, highly skilled migrants, or travellers. 'Immigrants', then, becomes a category which semantically crosses over with the symbolic geographies of the colonized and racialized world – postcolonial, developing countries, low income, the Third World, the global South. Whatever the label, we find in both representations of South–North immigrants as diseased, and colonized subjects as diseased, the colonial time-space imaginary (Reitmanova et al, 2015). That is, the idea that some places in the world (and therefore the people who live there) are ahead in time while others are behind and must catch up (Bhabha, 2005 [1994]; Bhambra, 2007). To be ahead means that one has discovered rationality, scientific reason, modern medicine and rigorous hygiene. Places which exist in the past embody a dark age in which hygiene and sanitation are poor, and impoverished and irrational people seek superstitious solutions to bodily disease (Ong, 1995; Briggs, 2005). Briggs observes that:

> individuals deemed to possess modern medical understandings of the body, health, and illness, practice hygiene, and depend on doctors and nurses when they are sick. … People who are judged to be incapable of adopting this modern medical relationship to the body, hygiene, illness, and healing – or who refuse to do so – become unsanitary subjects. (Briggs, 2005: 272)

The 'Orient', then, came to be imagined as 'ravaged by virulent, disgusting diseases' (Ward, 2002: 7). Such people and places live in a state of chaos, and bring dirt, disease and irrationality into the calm cleanliness of modernity when they arrive in a First World host state (Ong, 1995; Ward, 2002).

We can see, then, a consistent line from colonial ideas of racial threat articulated in terms of disease, and contemporary articulations of the immigrant threat across a range of postcolonial 'Western' societies, mainly White settler colonies and former colonial metropoles (Kraut, 1994; Bashford, 1998; Ward, 2002). Kraut (1994: 3) observes in the US that 'the entire group is stigmatized by medicalized nativism, each newcomer being reduced [to the diseased group]. … Thus, there is a fear of contamination from the foreign-born'. Contemporary examples are, then, continuous with historical examples from the 19th century or earlier. Kraut (1994) observes that after the 1832 cholera epidemic in the US, there became a common view that:

> the Irish were inherently diseased … merely filthy and unmindful of public hygiene, and therefore, were culpable for epidemic diseases. By contrast, Germans, who arrived in large numbers at the same time as the Irish, were either omitted from blame, or praised for their clean homes and orderly life habits. (p 4)

He suggests that by 1900 scientific medicine had become 'a weapon that White Anglo-Saxon Protestant civilization could use to defend itself against the intrusion of those regarded as of inferior breed' (p 5). In New Zealand, Lawrence et al (2008: 733) find that while it was settlers who originally brought Tuberculosis (TB) to the country, by the 21st century it had become popularly labelled a 'Third World disease' and Third World immigrants were thus cast as the major source of TB in the country.

Asylum seekers specifically have been represented as 'uncontrolled' immigrants bringing the double threat of disease and crime. Indeed, TB is a common focus for 'Third World threat' narratives in a range of countries

(Bell, 2006; Reitmanova et al, 2015). It is therefore clear that an association between disease and South–North migration has been a reccurring trope over several centuries, and that this follows the logics of colonial/modern ideas of racial hierarchy. As with many such examples of prejudice and stereotyping, a large body of academic research has thus followed which problematizes these logics. Part of the contribution of this work has been to highlight the fallacies of the assumption that migrants bring diseases to 'global North' countries. And yet the trope remains resilient against critique in the popular imagination and is one of a range of justifications for controlling South–North mobilities (another key one being economic threat).

Colonialism, mobility, disease, genocide

As noted previously, while there is a plethora of literature which challenges the disease spreading potential of racialized migrants, there is a much smaller literature on the dangerous disease spreading mobilities of First World actors in the contemporary period. There is, however, a well-established literature, particularly in the discipline of history, which describes the impact of European colonial exploration and conquest on indigenous societies from the 15th century onwards. With first contact, colonial explorers and settlers alike brought new diseases to which existing communities had no pre-existing immunity. There are many reports of whole populations being wiped out within very short spaces of time. For example, Columbus found a densely populated Hispaniola (the Caribbean island divided in the present day between Haiti and the Dominican Republic) in 1492 but within half a century 'the paradise Columbus described upon returning to Europe from the first voyage was transformed into a graveyard for most Caribbean natives' (Cook, 1993: 213). Virtually none of the indigenous population, the Taino, remained. This was a result of a variety of factors, including the use of violence by colonizers, but disease played its part across the entire Americas. The first major smallpox outbreak was recorded in 1518 and killed a large proportion of what remained of the population according to Cook (1993). While colonial mobilities and migrations were explicitly violent, then, and sought to subjugate, control, enslave and at times kill local populations, disease also presented an invisible unintended threat to them.

It is unlikely that TB existed in New Zealand before the arrival of Europeans in the 19th century, but it was described as endemic within both European settler and (by then depleted) Maori populations by the second half of the 19th century (Lawrence et al, 2008). Many settlers suffering from TB had come from Britain to the colony specifically in the hope that the milder climate might cure them, but instead they merely spread it in new territories (Bryder, 1996). The Aboriginal population of what is now Australia also declined drastically after the arrival of the British.

Death occurred in all areas soon after contact with Europeans for a number of reasons but was primarily disease related (Moses, 2007). Typically, the decline of American Indian populations by contact, direct or indirect, with Europeans included exposure to smallpox, measles, the bubonic plague, cholera, typhoid, pleurisy, scarlet fever, diphtheria, mumps, whooping cough, colds, gonorrhoea, chancroid, pneumonia, typhus and syphilis, according to Stiffarm and Lane Jr (1992). This killing (whether it constitutes 'genocide' or not is a matter of ongoing debate) through disease was not always intentional, though there is evidence that disease spreading was used as a form of early biological warfare (Mann, 2009). It also pre-empted later purposeful massacres as colonialism took hold. With or without intent, diseases were very effective at decreasing native populations, which was central to settler colonialism (Byrd, 2011).

Thus, while violence was central to colonization, many more indigenous people died from disease, malnutrition and starvation. Ostler (2015: 24) argues that in the case of the Caribbean only a small percentage of the indigenous population died from so called 'virgin soil' epidemics, where diseases are spread at the moment of initial contact. In fact, disease became the largest killer later on, flourishing under conditions the Spanish created as they colonized the islands. Military strategies of destroying the indigenous agricultural base across the Americas 'served to impose starvation conditions upon entire peoples, dramatically lowering their resistance to disease and increasing their susceptibility to epidemics' (Stiffarm and Lane Jr, 1992: 33). Forced relocation or concentration of peoples also had an impact on susceptibility to disease (on racialized disease tropes concerning recaptured formerly enslaved people in the Caribbean, Liberia and Sierra Leone, see also Chapter 2).

The intersection of disease and violence is a common thread through research on colonialism and has been associated with the dramatic decline in indigenous populations around the world from the 15th century onwards. This is not simply about 'first contact' and exposure to new diseases, it is also about a wide range of colonial economic, social and political practices which Europeans introduced, as noted earlier. Colonists forged new 'epidemiological links', 'either by relaying diseases (like smallpox and measles) long present in Europe or by establishing ties between parts of the world that had previously had few (if any) such connections with each other' (Arnold, 1988: 5). At the same time, 'European trade and transportation helped the spread of disease vectors, the mosquitoes, fleas and lice by which epidemics were communicated' (Arnold, 1988). Some diseases required more long-term intimate contact in order to reach epidemic levels. Syphilis, for example (which was known in India in the 16th and 17th centuries as 'the European disease') was communicated via sexual contact with Europeans (Arnold, 1988).

We might imagine that movement around the globe in the contemporary moment is completely different to that in the 16th, 17th, 18th and 19th centuries. While of course travel is much faster and is accessible to a much broader range of the population today thanks to the advent of international air travel, some aspects are remarkably similar. Diseases continue to be silent travellers brought on human bodies from one part of the world to another, and some human bodies are more internationally mobile than other bodies. In fact, those who are the most internationally mobile today are still those coming from the former metropoles of colonizing empires (to be discussed later). In the next section I jump forward to the contemporary period, and highlight the commonalities between these colonial histories and the management of mobilities in the COVID-19 pandemic.

Mobility, immobility and COVID-19

Like other epidemics, COVID-19 spread along circuits of mobility. And since wealthier citizens of the world are more mobile than others, it has been those with relative privilege that took the virus to every populous continent in the world. Having (at the time of writing thought to have) jumped from animal to human in the city of Wuhan in China, the COVID-19 virus first left China with an infected Chinese tourist who was visiting Thailand in January 2019. The virus was first officially identified by the World Health Organization on the 16 January. Within 4 months there were over 1.3m confirmed cases, and over 75,000 deaths worldwide. By December 2021, just under 2 years later) there had been 275 million cases and 5.35 million deaths globally (WHO, 2021). Research to date finds a common thread among those who bring the virus to new countries or create new externally precipitated outbreaks: they are people with the privileges of international mobility. They are international students, tourists, business travellers and aid workers. It should not be a surprise, then, that Europe and North America had outbreaks before South America, and that Africa's outbreaks came later. In researching this chapter I have not found a single report of an irregular migrant being the source of an outbreak.

Global dissemination of COVID-19, according to Frutos et al, writing in *Frontiers in Medicine* (2020: 2) occurred 'due to intensive international mobility and global international trade'. Oztig and Askin (2020) found that countries which have a higher number of airports are associated with a higher number of COVID-19 cases, and those with more internationally mobile populations also had more COVID-19 cases. They explain that the scale of the movement of people today is unprecedented, making the spread of diseases globally much faster than previously. Back in 2006, Tatem and colleagues observed that 'Air, sea and land transport networks continue to expand in reach, speed of travel and volume of passengers and goods carried.

Pathogens and their vectors can now move further, faster and in greater numbers than ever before' (Tatem et al, 2006: 293). Their warning was that this increased global mobility and interconnection was going to increase the risk of large scale outbreaks such as COVID-19.

What such contemporary studies miss are two key historical and sociological facts. First, that while the speed of epidemic spread has increased, sea and land transport in support of colonialism as well as war and trade have very long histories, as outlined earlier in this chapter. And second, that we must not allow the idea of 'globalized' mobility flows to blind us to the fact that the mobility of some groups of people globally, not just for migration, but frequent and repeated mobilities around the globe for tourism and business, is far in excess of the mobility of others (Mau et al, 2015). There were some restrictions on international travel through the pandemic which amounted to inconveniences for highly mobile people with passports that allow almost unrestricted international travel, such as an obligation to quarantine upon return from holidays. But for refugees, already wrapped up in a web of immobilization, it is their very immobility that has exposed them to the virus. I will explain what I mean by this with reference to refugee camps as a specific technology of immobilization.

As part of efforts to regionally quarantine refugees in the Third World, First World states support and fund the UNHCR and host state governments to set up large, often semi-permanent, camps for refugees in locations either on the edge of the First World (for example Greek islands, see Chapter 9) or in the Third World (for example Jordan, Kenya; see Chapter 13). These camps aim to contain, control and segregate refugees from host communities, and are characterized by contradictory imperatives: care/control, compassion/ repression (McConnachie, 2016; see also Chapter 4). Encampment is in part rooted in concern about the impact of refugees on those states that might host them, including the diseases that they may bring, and in a hierarchy of humanity consonant with colonial logics. But it is refugees whose health is damaged by such measures.

Kluge et al (2020: 1238) note that camps 'provide inadequate and overcrowded living arrangements that present a severe health risk to inhabitants and host populations'. They further note the 'absence of basic amenities, such as clean running water and soap, insufficient medical personnel, and poor access to adequate health information are major problems in these settings' (2020: 1238). This is true also for the squalid camps set up on the edges of Europe to contain and segregate refugees. For example, Moria camp on the Greek island of Lesbos was Europe's largest refugee camp before it burned down in July 2020. Twenty thousand refugees were living long term in a camp designed for the temporary accommodation of 3,000 and there was an 'absence of basic amenities, poor sanitary conditions and insufficient medical personnel, equipment and pharmaceuticals' (Vonen et al, 2021). Recent evidence suggests that children's health is worsening over time in Greek camps, though that is also the case for refugee children in other settings (Vonen et al, 2021; De Montgomery et al, 2019).

Poor hygiene in refugee camps and a lack of medication to manage chronic diseases are 'important factors that increase the risk (and spread) of infectious disease outbreaks and emergency cases among refugees (Vonen et al, 2021: np). In the COVID-19 context, then, 'social distancing, hand hygiene and self-isolation, will be almost impossible to implement in any refugee camp' (Vonen et al, 2020: np). There is little data on COVID-19 infection rates in refugee camps in general at the time of writing but Kamal et al (2020) and Lopez Pena et al (2020) have undertaken detailed analysis of the Cox's Bazaar camp which accommodates Rohingya refugees in Bangladesh. Both were pessimistic about a COVID-19 outbreak in the camp owing to overcrowding, lack of testing, lack of public health trained staff, poor access to sanitation, widespread misinformation about how the disease is spread and low literacy levels among camp inhabitants who speak a range of different languages. Poor control of previous disease outbreaks had not led to improvements (Kamal et al 2020). Lopez-Pena et al (2020) found in a phone-based survey of 909 households in 2020 that 24.6 per cent of camp residents compared to 13.4 per cent of those in host communities reported at least one common symptom of COVID-19, and that camp residents were more likely to attend religious or social gatherings, being unaware that this increased the likelihood of contracting the disease. Kamal et al (2020) found that the COVID-19 death rate was higher among the Rohingya refugees (8.04 per cent) compared to the host community (1.66 per cent). In part this was because there was only one testing centre in the camp for a population of 1 million, only one institutional quarantine centre, no Intensive Care Unit (ICU) or ventilator capacity in the camp and no transportation to ICUs outside of the camp, which are only for host state communities (Kamal et al, 2020).

A WHO report on the European region in 2018 explained that the evidence shows that there 'is a very low risk of transmitting communicable diseases from the refugee and migrant population to the host population' (WHO, 2018: ix). Prevalence of longstanding diseases such as TB is present in refugee communities at around the same rate as prevalence among host societies. The same is true for HIV and in fact 'a significant proportion of those refugees and migrants who are HIV positive acquire infection after they have arrived in the [European] Region, and they are more likely to be diagnosed later in their HIV infections' (WHO, 2018: ix). They explain that health systems in European host states are 'well equipped and experienced in diagnosing and managing common infectious diseases' and that the arrival of refugees and migrants does 'not pose additional health security threats to host communities' (WHO, 2018: 80). Yet because of the hostile environments in which refugees in Europe often find themselves, refugees who are not encamped nevertheless 'typically face administrative, financial, legal, and language barriers to access the [host state] health system' (Kluge et al, 2020: np), even where the healthcare system is 'well equipped' to support the population in general. This is sometimes referred to as the 'healthy immigrant effect', whereby migrants tend to be healthier than the general population upon arrival but in worse health than the general population a few years post arrival, owing to socio-economic disadvantage (Kennedy et al, 2015). The evidence suggests, then, that rather than refugees posing a health threat to host communities which must be addressed with stricter border controls, it is anti-migrant border controls and barriers to accessing basic services and resources which threaten the health of refugees – before and in the context of COVID-19.

It should not surprise us then that COVID-19 has led to more restrictions on the rights of refugees to seek asylum and that this has been introduced under the guise of protecting host communities. This is aptly theorized in relation to Achille Mbembe's (2003) work on necropolitical abandonment – letting surplus populations die through inaction. During the pandemic, Sabi Ardalan (2020) suggested in a blog for the University of New South Wales' Kaldor Centre on the impact of COVID-19 on refugees and migrants globally, that border closures implemented in response to COVID-19 have 'effectively suspended the right of people to seek asylum in many countries around the world'. The pandemic and the associated risks 'allegedly posed by the arrival of foreigners may provide the perfect alibi for governments and politicians determined to close their borders and exclude or expel refugees', argued Crisp (2020, np). Border closures have involved people seeking asylum being turned back at sea and on land, even when this will leave them trapped in conflict zones or dangerous transit countries.

In the Aegean Sea, Greece used a tactic of rescuing drowning migrants and then forcing them into life rafts which are left to drift into Turkish waters (Keady-Tabbal and Mann, 2020). Malta refused entry to people seeking asylum rescued on private vessels (Ardalan, 2020), and thousands of Rohingya refugees were left stranded and starving in the Bay of Bengal because, according to the UN, of COVID-19 fears (United Nations, 2020). Meanwhile, the United States (US) introduced summary deportations of people within 2 hours of entry, denying the right to claim asylum, justified on the basis of public health (Department of Health and Human Services, 2020). This was part of a concerted effort by president Trump to 'establish the disease as foreign to the US national body, locating it in Other geographies and bodies', using 'racialized labels emphasizing the virus as foreign or exogenous', for example referring to COVID-19 as *the Chinese virus* and *the kung flu* (Gross-Wyrtzen, 2020: 3).

At the start of the pandemic, search and rescue operations in the central Mediterranean led to the immediate quarantine of migrants in reception centres in spite of the fact that at that time there was not a single confirmed case of COVID-19 on the continent of Africa. Indeed, many refugees and migrants arriving in Europe at this time were 'travelling from countries not yet substantially affected by COVID-19 and entering countries with increasing numbers of COVID-19 cases', leading Kluge et al (2020, np) to conclude that 'this vulnerable population has a low risk of transmitting communicable diseases to host populations in general'. On the contrary, 'refugees and migrants are potentially at increased risk of contracting diseases, including COVID-19, because they typically live in overcrowded conditions without access to basic sanitation'. Once national lockdowns were introduced in Europe, rescues were then suspended, apparently because of logistical difficulties created by COVID-19 (Kluge et al, 2020). This will certainly have led to loss of life in the Mediterranean Sea; weeks-long disembarkation refusals have led to at least six suicide attempts on one humanitarian vessel alone (Gross-Wyrtzen, 2020). In summary then, COVID-19 has posed life threatening risks to refugees as a direct consequence of efforts to exclude them from First World territories at the same time as being disproportionately transmitted internationally by the worlds most privileged people.

Conclusion

This chapter has explored the intersection of three vectors: (im)mobility, postcolonial inequality and disease. It has described the emergence of an international regime of immobilization over recent decades which has in part drawn on longstanding ideas of Third World migrants as disease spreading threats. This regime of immobilization has placed refugees at significantly increased risk before and during the COVID-19 pandemic in spite of the sense of threat commonly being located in the Third World immigrant body. These ideas of disease bearing threat have their origins in colonial (racial) ideas of biological and cultural inferiority. And yet, as the chapter has shown, history tells us that it is colonialism and the mobilities caused by it, as well as the excessive mobilities of colonizers, which have long presented a threat to communities and nations from air borne disease.

In building this argument, I hope to have shown how uneven geographies of disease related to fear and control are both misplaced and actively endanger refugee and irregular migrants who find themselves entangled in regimes of immobilization. Drawing on this, we might then argue for more just mobility regimes which overcome the embedded racist logics which currently dominate. Indeed, through equalizing rights of mobility we might not only decrease the risks to all humans from air borne disease, and protect the world's most vulnerable and in need from the consequences of excessive privileged mobility. Relentless and proliferating circular mobilities – tourism, business trips, backpacking and so forth, might then give way to safe and legal one way mobilities for those in actual need of sanctuary and protection. Colonial histories, then, give us the tools to not only correct misplaced anxieties, but also to imagine more just regimes of mobility and immobility moving forward.

References

Achiume, E.T. (2019) 'Migration as decolonisation', *Stanford Law Review*, 71(6): 1509–74.

Ardalan, S. (2020) 'The Trump Administration, COVID-19, and the continuing assault on the rights of asylum seekers and refugees', Kaldor Centre Covid 19-Watch [blog] 11 May, Available from: https://www.kaldorcentre.unsw.edu.au/publication/trump-administration-covid-19-and-continuing-assault-rights-asylum-seekers-and-refugees [Accessed 13 June 2021].

Arnold, D. (1988) *Imperial Medicine and Indigenous Societies*, Manchester: Manchester University Press.

Bashford, A. (1998) 'Quarantine and the imagining of the Australian nation', *Health*, 2(4): 387–402.

Bell, M., Brown, T. and Faire, L. (2006) 'Germs, genes and postcolonial geographies: reading the return of tuberculosis to Leicester, UK, 2001', *Cultural Geographies*, 13(4): 577–99.

Bhabha, H.K. (2005 [1994]) *The Location of Culture*, London: Routledge.

Bhambra, G.K. (2007) *Rethinking Modernity: Postcolonialism and the Sociological Imagination*, Basingstoke: Palgrave Macmillan.

Bhambra, G.K. (2017) 'Brexit, Trump, and "methodological whiteness": on the misrecognition of race and class', *British Journal of Sociology*, 68(S1): 214–32.

Bonnett, A. (1998) 'How the British working class became white: the symbolic (re)formation of racialized capitalism', *Journal of Historical Sociology*, 11(3): 316–40.

Briggs, C.L. (2005) 'Communicability, racial discourse, and disease', *Annual Review of Anthropology*, 34(1): 269–91.

Bryder, L. (1996) 'A health resort for consumptives: tuberculosis and immigration to New Zealand, 1880–1914', *Medical History*, 40(4): 453–71.

Byrd, J.A. (2011) *The Transit of Empire: Indigenous Critiques of Colonialism*, Minnesota: University of Minnesota Press.

Cook, N.D. (1993) 'Disease and the depopulation of Hispaniola, 1492–1518', *Colonial Latin American Review*, 2(1–2): 213–45.

Crisp, J. (2020) 'UNHCR at 70: an uncertain future for the international refugee regime', *Global Governance: A Review of Multilateralism and International Organizations*, 26(3): 359–68.

de Montgomery, C.J., Stathopoulou, T. and Eikemo, T.A. (2020) 'Asylum-seeking parents' reports of health deterioration in their children since fleeing their home country', *Journal of Refugee Studies*, 32(1): 52–62.

de Noronha, L. (2020) *Deporting Black Britons: Portraits of Deportation to Jamaica*, Manchester: Manchester University Press.

Department of Health and Human Services, C. f. D. C. a. P., (2020) 'Notice of order under Sections 362 and 365 of the Public Health Service Act suspending introduction of certain persons from countries where a communicable disease exists', *Federal Register*, 85(59) [online] Available from: https://www.govinfo.gov/content/pkg/FR-2020-03-26/pdf/2020-06327.pdf [Accessed 13 June 2021].

Frutos, R., Lopez Roig, M., Serra-Cobo, J. and Devaux, C.A. (2020) 'COVID-19: the conjunction of events leading to the coronavirus pandemic and lessons to learn for future threats', *Frontiers in Medicine*, 7(223): 1–5.

Gross-Wyrtzen, L. (2020) 'Policing the virus: race, risk, and the politics of containment in Morocco and the United States', Roundtable on Borders and the State in Light of COVID-19, Arab Council for the Social Sciences & Security in Context, Available from: www.securityincontext.com/publications/borders-roundtable-policing-the-virus [Accessed 11 April 2022].

Hall, S. (2000) 'Conclusion: the multicultural question', in B. Hesse (ed), *Unsettled Multiculturalisms: Diasporas, Entanglements, Transruptions*, London: Zed Books: 209–41.

Hansen, P. and Jonsson, S. (2014) *Eurafrica: The Untold History of European Integration and Colonialism*. London: Bloomsbury.

Ignatiev, N. (1995) *How the Irish Became White*. New York: Routledge.

Kamal, A.-H.M., Huda, N., Dell, C.A., Hossain, S.Z. and Ahmed, S.S. (2020) 'Translational strategies to control and prevent spread of COVID-19 in the Rohiynga refugee camps in Bangladesh', *Global Biosecurity*, 1(4). DOI: http://doi.org/10.31646/gbio.77

Keady-Tabbal, N. and Mann, I. (2020) 'Tents at sea: how Greek officials use rescue equipment for illegal deportations', Just Security [blog] 22 May, Available from: https://www.justsecurity.org/70309/tents-at-sea-how-greek-officials-use-rescue-equipment-for-illegal-deportations/ [Accessed 13 June 2021].

Kennedy, S., Kidd, M.P., McDonald, J.T. and Biddle, N. (2015) 'The healthy immigrant effect: patterns and evidence from four countries', *Journal of International Migration and Integration*, 16(2): 317–32.

Kluge, H.H.P., Jakab, Z., Bartovic, J., D'Anna, V. and Severoni, S. (2020) 'Refugee and migrant health in the COVID-19 response', *The Lancet*, 395: 1237–39.

Kraut, A.M. (1994) *Silent Travelers: Germs, Genes, and the "Immigrant Menace"*, Baltimore: Johns Hopkins University Press.

Lawrence, J., Kearns, R.A., Park, J., Bryder, L. and Worth, H. (2008) 'Discourses of disease: representations of tuberculosis within New Zealand newspapers 2002–2004', *Social Science & Medicine*, 66(3): 727–39.

Lopez-Pena, P., Austin Davis, C., Mushfiq Mobarak, A. and Raihan, S. (2020) 'Prevalence of COVID-19 symptoms, risk factors, and health behaviors in host and refugee communities in Cox's Bazar: a representative panel study', [Preprint] *Bulletin World Health Organisation*, E-pub: 11.

Mann, B.A. (2009) *The Tainted Gift: The Disease Method of Frontier Expansion*, Santa Barbara: ABC-CLIO.

Mau, S., Gülzau, F., Laube, L. and Zaun, N. (2015) 'The global mobility divide: how visa policies have evolved over time', *Journal of Ethnic and Migration Studies*, 41(8): 1192–1213.

Mayblin, L. (2017) *Asylum After Empire: Colonial Legacies in the Politics of Asylum Seeking*, London: Rowman and Littlefield International.

Mayblin, L. (2019) *Impoverishment and Asylum: Social Policy as Slow Violence*, London: Routledge.

Mayblin, L. and Turner, J. (2021) *Migration Studies and Colonialism*, Cambridge: Polity.

Mbembe, A. (2003) 'Necropolitics', *Public Culture*, 15(1): 11–40.

McConnachie, K. (2016) 'Camps of containment: a genealogy of the refugee camp', *Humanity: An International Journal of Human Rights, Humanitarianism, and Development*, 7(3): 397–412.

Moses, D. and Stone, D. (2007) *Colonialism and Genocide*, New York: Routledge.

Ong, A. (1995) 'Making the biopolitical subject: Cambodian immigrants, refugee medicine and cultural citizenship in California', *Social Science and Medicine*, 40(9): 1243–57.

Ostler, J. (2015) *Genocide and American Indian History. Oxford Research Encyclopedia of American History*, Oxford: Oxford University Press.

Oztig, L.I. and Askin, O.E. (2020) 'Human mobility and coronavirus disease 2019 (COVID-19): a negativebinomial regression analysis', *Public Health*, 185: 364–67.

Reitmanova, S., Gustafson, D.L. and Ahmed, A. (2015) '"Immigrants can be deadly": critical discourse analysis of racialization of immigrant health in the Canadian press and public Health Policies', *Canadian Journal of Communication*, 40(3): 471–87.

Stiffarm, L.A. and Lane Jr, P. (1992) 'The demography of native North America: a question of American Indian survival', in M.A. Jaimes (ed), *The State of Native America: Genocide, Colonization, and Resistance*, Boston: South End Press.

Tatem, A.J., Rogers, D.J. and Hay, S.I. (2006) 'Global transport networks and infectious disease spread', *Advances in Parasitology*, 62: 293–343.

United Nations (2020) 'Amid COVID-19 pandemic, thousands stranded in Bay of Bengal "unable to come ashore"'. UN News [online], 6 May, Available from: https://news.un.org/en/story/2020/05/1063402 [Accessed 13 June 2021].

Vonen, H.D., Olsen, M.L., Eriksen, S.S., Jervelund, S.S. and Eikemo, T.A. (2021) 'Refugee camps and COVID-19: can we prevent a humanitarian crisis?' *Scandinavian Journal of Public Health*, 49(1): 27–8.

Ward, P.M. (2002) *White Canada Forever: Popular Attitudes and Public Policy Toward Orientals in British Columbia*, Montréal: McGill-Queen's University Press.

World Health Organization (2018) *Report on the Health of Refugees and Migrants in the WHO European Region: No Public Health without Refugee and Migrant Health*, Copenhagen: WHO Regional Office for Europe.

World Health Organization (2021) WHO Coronavirus (COVID-19) Dashboard, https://covid19.who.int [Accessed 20 December 2021].

8

The Long-term Influence of a Short-lived Colony: Postcoloniality and Geopolitics of Energy and Migration Control in Libya

Mathias Hatleskog Tjønn and Martin Lemberg-Pedersen

Introduction

In the summer of 2019, two dramatic events took place on the coastline of northern Libya which illustrate how postcolonial constellations shape politics of energy and displacement in the country. First, on 10 June, Turkish-controlled militias supporting the Government of National Accord (GNA) attacked the Greenstream Pipeline in Western Libya, a key infrastructural site for the transport of natural gas to Italy and Europe. Less than a month later, on 2 July 2019, an airstrike hit the Tajoura migration detention centre in Tripoli, killing at least 53 and wounding 130 people inside (BBC, 4 July 2019). Both events were part of an intensifying Libyan civil war, between the power centres in Tripoli and Tobruk, which also saw the two former imperial colonizers of Libyan territory, Italy and Turkey, pitted against one another.

What does it mean to apply a postcolonial gaze to Libya? Certainly, the country has been central to discussions of European migration control across media and scholarship in recent years. However, this focus has often reproduced an ahistorical and Eurocentric gaze similar to that advanced by policymakers, carrying with it flawed assumptions about power relations in the region. Libya is often represented as a failed 'transit state' mired in humanitarian crisis leading to European-bound immigration, and migration control as a necessary means to impose order upon such crises. By contrast, this chapter's postcolonial approach recognizes that colonial infrastructures and matrices of power did not end when colonized countries gained independence, but can be identified also in the country's forced migration dynamics today (Lemberg-Pedersen, 2019; Mayblin and Turner, 2021). We understand postcoloniality not as a page turned on history, nor as part of a historical trajectory towards progress, but as still unfolding, contingent power matrices. In this chapter, we show how a *longue durée* of migration control practices, and competing imperial and geopolitical interests in energy, have shaped displacement in Libya over a century.

Our way of examining postcolonialty aims to avoid the pitfall of applying generic assumptions about the character and function of colonialism which disregards the different times, spaces and actors of colonial encounters. Of course, colonial empires themselves were notoriously eager to generalize, compare, criticize and placate practices between them, and inter-imperial networks also circulated and mutated shared policies, practices and ideas. Still, the centuries-long colonial era was characterized by *multiple colonial encounters*, with different contexts and different postcolonial trajectories leading to today. Our focus is therefore trained on the particular context of current-day Libya, and more specifically on how the Ottoman and the Italian Empires have been related to Libyan politics on energy and forced migration, during and after colonial encounters.

Italian and Ottoman/Turkish imperialism have been relegated to the periphery in both colonial and postcolonial studies (though see Distretti, 2021; Hom, 2019). For the latter, one reason is Eurocentrism in the postcolonial gaze, combined with the differences between the Ottoman Empire and European and Western powers, regarding geography, the dynamics of settler colonialism and slavery, and governance structures (Chatty, 2010; see also Chapter 3). For the former, Libya's 'double marginalization' in Italian and colonial studies (Ben-Ghiat and Fuller, 2005) is linked to the belated and limited role of Italian colonialism, as well as the policing of, and erasures in, Italian colonial archives. For decades, this left only oral traditions of certain communities in Eastern Libya to preserve witness accounts of the brutality unfolded during Italian colonialism (Ahmida, 2020; on the political power of oral tradition see also Chapter 12). Furthermore, the centuries-long decentralized Ottoman Empire also differed from the short-lived Italian colonization campaigns of maritime possession and settler colonialism of Albania, Libya and Abyssinia. Uncovering the impact of these two empires on forced migration politics in Libya today thus offers an intriguing new case for postcolonial migration studies.

Our chapter begins with the dramatic context where the interests of the two empires became inextricably imbricated in one another, after the 1911 Italo-Turkish war that transformed the Ottoman provinces of Cyrenaica, Tripolitania and Fezzan into the Italian colony of Libya. We centre our analysis around energy and forced migration politics and their connection to imperial and economic interests. These are traced through events and strategic appeals to colonialism and decoloniality in various actors' discourses from the 1930s fascist re-colonization efforts, through Italian energy companies' navigation of the post-Second World War situation, and into Libyan nationalization in the 1970s. We argue that these developments are crucial for understanding the 2000s Italian and EU ambitions for externalization of migration control, complementing the management of migration across national boundaries, with the exercise of such control extraterritorially, in Libya. Towards the end, we relate these politico-discursive postcolonial arcs to the reappearance of Turkish interests in Libya, through the Turkish-GNA Treaty concluded amidst discourses of neo-Ottomanism.

Methodologically, our post-1911 focus means that we have used Italian archives as primary source material, namely the Italian *Archivio Centrale dello Stato* (ACS), and the *Archivio Storico dell'ENI* (ASENI), both in Rome. For the inter-imperial context, we complement this primary material with secondary literature about Ottoman and later Turkish geopolitics. Substantiating how the events detailed in this historical material link to ongoing postcolonial dynamics related to Libya, we use a series of Italian, EU and Turkish policy documents and treaty texts as prime sources to observe strategic discourses, coupled with secondary material in the form of Italian, Turkish and European news coverage.

The next section identifies an ensemble of forced migration practices, which were developed during the violent Italian colonization of current-day Libya.

Reimagining Rome on the fourth shore: forced displacement and settler colonialism

The Italo-Turkish war commenced on 3 October 1911 when Italian war ships attacked the Ottoman navy in the Eastern Mediterranean and the Ottoman provinces of Tripolitania and Cyrenaica in northern Africa. In line with imperial-nationalistic Ottoman politics, insurgents, including Mustafa Kemal (later Atatürk) were sent to Cyrenaica through the British colony of Egypt to co-organize an anti-colonial guerrilla campaign through *Teshkilat-I mahsuas* groups formed with local Senussi and Arab tribes (Gawrych, 2013; McCollum, 2017). Hostilities between Italy and the Ottoman Empire officially ended with the Treaty of Ouchy in 1912, but Senussi resistance only ceased in 1931, 8 years after Mussolini launched another military campaign aiming at a settler colonial, racial and imperial-capitalist colonization of Libya. Here, territory and land use were especially coveted for water resources, as these were necessary to support the export of Italian agricultural settlers into the desert land (on colonial schemes of mass movement of populations from the global North, see Chapter 7). Italy's colonization of Libya laid the groundwork for unbalanced exchanges between the two countries running through the 20th century.

The settler colonial campaign required cleansing the lands of local nomadic pasture and Bedouin populations (Wolfe, 2006). Moreover, Italian elites dominated by political-industrial powers and papal financial networks perceived the colonial 1884–85 Berlin Conference as having left Italy as a minor colonial power, with territories only in Somalia and Ethiopia. France, by comparison, had expanded its colonial sphere to Algeria, Tunisia and Morocco. And while defeated within the newborn Italian state, papal financial circles had a strong strategic interest in imperial Italian expansion into Ottoman peripheral territories. At the time, this strategy was referred to as 'peaceful penetration' and facilitated by actors such as the Italian *Banco de Roma*. However, peace turned to war, when Ottoman hindrances to these economic activities quickly morphed into an Italian argument for militarized colonization (Conte, 2021). Nocentini (2016) has therefore argued that in 1911, an oligarchical Italian state was co-opted by otherwise rivalling elites, who coalesced around opening new colonial markets in Libya. From the 1920s onwards, the colonization of Libya became enmeshed in fascist discourses portraying Libya as Italy's *quarta sponda* ('fourth shore'), and making the Central Mediterranean Italy's *mare nostrum* ('our sea'). These discourses were deeply embedded in a racially hierarchized geostrategy designating Libya as a *spazio vitale* ('living space') for Italians, similar to German National Socialist visions of *lebensraum* (see Rodogno, 2006).

The capitalist dynamics of Italian colonization of Libya can also be interpreted as a form of settler capitalism. That is, settler colonies thoroughly imbricated in capitalist trade and finance networks with colonial metropoles as well as internationally (Denoon, 1979: 515). The literature on settler capitalism has tended to write out indigenous people's presence, and sustained resistance to these activities (Veracini, 2013: 323; on a discussion of settler colonialism in the Ottoman Empire, see also Chapter 3). Yet, a dual focus on both colonial capitalism and indigenous dispossession proves highly relevant for analysis of forced migration dynamics during and after Italian colonization of Libya. National and commercial-industrial Italian actors were very much part of the new colonial markets in Libya.

In order to support Italian settler colonial ambitions, exploratory drilling for underground water resources was undertaken immediately, and water was found in 1914 south of Tripoli, by the *Scuola d'Agricoltura* [Italian School of Agriculture]. Notably, this was alongside the first traces of petroleum and methane gas (ACS, *Ricerche di petrolio,* 1923). The first dedicated AGIP petroleum exploration well, led by the geologist Ardito Desio, was dug on 13 April 1938, near Tripoli and the 1914 findings. In May 1939, Desio suggested searching further east in Cyrenaica's favourable geological conditions, near the Egyptian border (ASENI, 1939), and the year after, he tried, unsuccessfully due to the war, to move AGIP's search to the Gulf of Sirte – an area where the American company Esso would strike black gold in

1959 (ASENI, 1940). Illustrating the intergenerational and postcolonial ties in Libyan geopolitics, the Desio family would return for oil exploration in the 1960s, where Gianluca Desio, son of Ardito, conducted ENI exploration missions in the same areas. Today the area is dotted with rigs and oil facilities from a variety of transnational oil companies, including ENI (Di Gregorio, 2015). But the history of Libyan oil reserves, now estimated as the largest in Africa, started with the search for water coveted for the Italian settler colonial designs.

After 1911, the Italian industrial actors expanding into Libya also included the energy company *Azienda Generale Italiana Petroli* (AGIP) (founded in 1926, now part of ENI), and the two military-industrial companies *Fabbrica Italiana Automobili Torino* (FIAT) (founded in 1899) and Gio, Ansaldo & Co. (founded in 1853, now part of Leonardo). All three companies also played parts in the markets of decolonized Libya, and have continued to do so today when it comes to Libyan contracts for transport (FIAT), energy (ENI) and control systems to manage displaced populations (Ansaldo) (for similar commercial designs in the French colonial empire, see Chapter 5).

It was the energy explorations and the industrial-capitalist underpinnings of the Italian colonization project, which provided the incentives and material infrastructures used to displace civilian populations in the new colony. Thus, in July and August 1930, the Italian army displaced 100,000 civilians from the Libyan coastal town Cyrenaica and moved them to 16 concentration camps along the coastline, from the Bay of Sirte in the west, to Marmarica in the east (Di Sante and Sury, 2009). Entire villages were emptied and left deserted as columns of several thousand people were forced to march days on end to the camps (Holmboe and Pelt, 2011), stretching over 1,000 kilometres, leaving in their desert trails around 10,000 dead. Exemplifying the colonial practice of *policing others by others*, marches were patrolled by colonial Askari and Quadi troops drafted from present-day Eritrea and Somalia (Morone, 2015). When the camp system was dismantled in September 1933, around 60,000 had died from diseases and starvation. Others perished as oasis water wells were poisoned or sealed off by Italian forces, or their livestock destroyed to make it impossible for the civilian population to return to the best agricultural areas now reserved for Italian settler colonialists (Del Boca, 2011; Morone, 2011). Libyans were instead made into a sedentary and dependable workforce for the civilizing colonial agents of Italy (Ballinger, 2016; see also Chapter 3). The new governor of colonial Libya, Italo Balbo initiated a mass transfer of Italian colonists (Segré, 1972) into ethnically cleansed agricultural land, where settlements, ports and roads, such as the *Via Balbia* Northern coastal highway, were constructed in record time.

While Italian and European discourses almost immediately shrouded the Italian displacement politics in silence, and only as part of harsh, but necessary societal improvement of Libya, Ottoman and Arab media discussions differed. In April 1931, Amir Shakib Arslan published the booklet *The Italian cruelties in Tripolitiania*, alongside many critical articles in the Egyptian daily *al-Mu'ayyad* and Geneve-based *La Nation Arabe*. That same year brought with it anti-colonial consumer boycotts of Italian goods across the Arab world, and a League of Nations report was also produced by 100 Egyptian intellectuals and politicians concerning Italy's destructive policy in Libya. Still, without international sanction, the Italian colonization solidified for a time. After the outbreak of the Second World War, Tripoli fell to Allied forces on 23 January 1943, but the racialized repression, deprivation and traumatization of the displaced populations lasted for generations (Ahmida, 2020). After the war, the resource-rich Libyan territories were divided among the Allied powers: Western Tripolitania and eastern Cyrenaica were placed under British administration, while the Southern province of Fezzan was placed under French administration. The colonial practices of displacement, control and encampment constitute a terrifying historical backdrop to today's migrant detention camps in Libya, many of which are located in the same areas, such as al-Abiar, Ajdabiya, Ganfouda/Benghazi and Shahat/Apollinia (Labanca, 2005; UNHCR Flash Update Libya, 27 July to 3 August 2018).

This section has detailed the complex, inter-imperial situation that precipitated the Italian colonization of Libya, and how its unfolding was tied to settler colonial visions, which coincidentally also led to the first petroleum finds. Moreover, it has argued that the control, mass displacement and brutal erasure of indigenous populations that ensued must be seen as facilitated by a particular fusion of racialized and industrial-capitalist logics. These would form threads into the future of Libyan politics.

ENI and strategic appeals to postcoloniality in postwar Libyan politics

After Libyan independence in 1951 and the country's first Petroleum Law of 1955, the arrival of the world's largest oil companies changed the landscape for Italian economic and oil explorative ambitions in the ex-colony. This led to a rupture towards a new, strategic discourse on decoloniality from both the Italian state and Italian companies, as well as the soon-to-be European Union (EU). In order to better its chances for acquiring oil rights, ENI now highlighted support for decolonization and Libyan independence. For example, in 1957 when ENI lost an oil exploration concession in Fezzan to an Anglo-American cartel, its director Mattei accused Libyan Prime Minister Kubar of putting personal gain over Libyan interests and Third World solidarity. Turning down ENI's bid was tantamount to blocking the country's path to decolonization, he argued (Cricco, 2014). While scholarship has tended to reproduce ENI's self-portrayal as a David facing Anglo-American oil Goliaths and its claim to side with the Third World

(Joesten, 1962), our argument is that ENI's self-image represents a striking attempt to prolong colonial matrices of power by appealing to Third World decolonial solidarity against national and commercial competitors to Italian oil concessions.

ENI's decolonial narrative links to a point raised by Hansen and Jonsson (2014), namely that post-war European integration was intimately tied to colonial economic interests in labour circulation and resource extraction in Africa. Our findings in the historical archives of ENI strongly indicate that the company continued bribery practices towards the Libyan elite. A folder titled 'The Corradi Affair' contains coded correspondence between FIAT's local representative in Libya, AGIP Mineraria's vice-president and Corradi, a mysterious courier receiving undisclosed funds from AGIP, and travelling among a small Libyan elite in 1957 to 'take care of formalities' related to ENI's oil exploration bids' (ASENI, 1957; Pozzi, 2010). There is a strong indication that this was in fact an attempt at bribery and although corruption in itself does not amount to colonial methods, it had certainly been part of the standard colonial stable of practices employed by Italy. The 1957 Fezzan bid did not go ENI's way, but this quote is telling: 'Unfortunately … our hopes of taking care of the question of concessions have come to nothing. The Libyan magnates are smart, too smart. I have to acknowledge that we Europeans are simpletons compared to them' (ASENI, 1957). Two years later, however, the company was given oil explorations rights, ushering in a highly lucrative first decade of petroleum extraction. Yet, despite ENI's public, decolonial narrative, a legal advisor still provided a postcolonial slip, when writing to the Italian Ministry of Foreign Affairs that ENI was successfully exploring and exploiting petroleum resources 'in the colonies' (ASENI, [ca. 1959]).

On 1 September 1969, Muammar Gaddafi seized on a growing popular resentment towards Italian involvement and foreign dominance in the Libyan oil sector, abolished the monarchy and proclaimed the Great Socialist People's Libyan Arab *Jamahiriya* (Seton-Watson, 1980). Shortly after, Libya deported 20,000 Italians, and expropriated Italian businesses and land. Attempts were also made to force oil companies to offer better terms. Unlike British and American petroleum companies who refused the demands, ENI accepted partial nationalization and the renegotiation of royalty contracts (Cricco, 2014), and picked up several competitor oil fields in joint ventures with the new Libyan National Oil Corporation (NOC). Several Turkish companies also began to receive contracts in Libya after 1972. Gaddafi sought to replace the Italian and European workers in the oil, mining and agricultural sectors by enacting large labour migration schemes with sub-Saharan countries. As the final remnants of the Italian settler colonial regime left Libya, a new economic system of joint Italo-Libyan oil extraction followed, built on the preceding financial-colonial domination (van Genugten, 2011). But towards the end of the 20th century, displacement politics and practices reappeared as dominant Italian and European geopolitical interests in Libya. This led to a new phase in the discursive use of the country's colonial history.

Libya, EU's gatekeeper: a Mediterranean migration regime on imperial-colonial undercurrents

The emerging focus on Libya as a locus for European forced migration politics involved the EU making strategic appeals to Libyan postcoloniality. In this period, the European Community has depicted itself as a liberal-egalitarian project distinct from crude imperial powers, and in fact as a supporter of decolonization (Hansen and Jonsson, 2017). However, rather than being an agent for decolonization, four of the six founding member states were colonial powers, their access to resources in colonial territories was a pivotal backbone for the formation of a steel and coal community, and some have continued possession of 'overseas territories' to this day. The free circulation of people and goods within the European Economic Community (EEC) was thus linked to a new geostrategic perspective on resource extraction and labour in Mediterranean and North African territories. But after the 1973 oil crises, European countries abruptly shifted towards restrictions on immigration policies (de Haas et al, 2019), and Libya accordingly shifted to being represented as a zone for externalized EU 'flanking measures'. These externalization practices were designed as migration control perceived as necessary by European politicians to safeguard the internal free movement of Europeans in the Schengen Space, through the prevention of asylum seekers' arrival to European territory (Lemberg-Pedersen, 2017, see also Chapters 4 and 13. For colonial-imperial Anglo-American variants of externalization, see also Chapter 2). Italy's 1990 entry into the Schengen zone was also conditioned on a restrictive approach to European-bound migration (Paoli, 2015). But the lacking EU engagement or even acknowledgment of colonial legacies of geostrategy in Libya illustrates how the Union's positionality has been based on epistemological erasure.

For Italo-Libyan relations, the period witnessed the *politica del buon vicinato* ('good neighborhood policy'). On 4 July 1998, the two countries signed a Joint Communiqué promoting collaboration on petroleum, natural gas and migration management, in exchange for the political recognition of Libya (Coralluzzo, 2008). Notably, the 1998 Communiqué framed the collaboration as a mutual desire to leave behind the negative colonial heritage (Italian Government, 1998). Acknowledgement of colonial brutality was depicted as a barrier to progress, which was in turn symbolized by lucrative energy politics and effective migration control. On 1 October 2004, Berlusconi and Gaddafi inaugurated the 540-kilometre *Greenstream Pipeline* transporting natural gas from western Libya to Italy, built by

AGIP Gas BV, a joint venture between ENI and the Libyan National Oil Company (NOC).

On 20 August 2008, the two countries signed the Treaty on Friendship, Partnership and Cooperation (Italian Government, 2008). Even though the Treaty does not mention Libya's colonial past, its articles on cooperation on energy, migration control and arms exports (Gazzini, 2009) were promoted by Berlusconi in the media as an apology via colonial reparations. Gaddafi stated that it was now possible to 'turn a page' on Libya's tragic colonial past (Dogget, 10 June 2009). Despite the reparations discourse, it is worth noting that the $5 billion to Libyan infrastructure projects, promised by the Treaty, were not given directly to Libya. Instead, they were raised by taxing Italian oil companies, in particular ENI, and then distributed among Italian companies active in Libya (Ronzitti, 2009).

Some benefits did accrue to Libya. For example, Italy successfully lobbied for the EU to lift its arms embargo against the country in 2003 (Commission of the European Communities, 2003), a decision that facilitated a market boom for European defence contractors winning exports for arms and border control equipment to the Libya authorities. Italian Finmeccanica (now Leonardo) and its subsidiaries were uniquely situated in this market, since its largest and third-largest shareowners were, respectively as of 26 September 2011, the state of Italy (32 per cent) and Libya (2 per cent). A flurry of contracts for border control equipment followed with Finmeccanica subsidiary AugustaWestland selling helicopters, Alenia Aeronautica selling maritime patrol aircrafts, Selex Galileo announcing plans for drone sales and Selex-SI winning a contract for an entire C3 (command, control and communication) border security system along the Libyan borders with Niger and Chad (see also Chapter 5 on revolving credits in French postcolonial commercial activity). This provided the technological infrastructure for Italo-Libyan naval push-backs of European-bound boat migrants in the Mediterranean (Lemberg-Pedersen, 2013). Reports have since documented brutal conditions for hundreds of thousands of people in a Libyan migration system refitted from intra-African labour migration, to European-dictated policing and containment of migrants. People are detained and traded as cheap or forced labour in the Libyan oil, mining, construction and agricultural sectors. This exploitative displacement grid is characterized by racism, corruption, torture, rape and murders committed by smugglers, police and military actors (Human Rights Watch, 2009; Moreno-Lax and Lemberg-Pedersen, 2019).

The rising number of EU statements about displacement in Libya appears oblivious to the recent colonial past. Despite encouraging and funding new detention structures and the policing of displacement, references to the colonial experience of deportation, forced migration, internment camps or forced marches through Libyan deserts are nowhere to be found in the

European Commission's 2004 Technical Mission or Frontex's 2007 Technical Mission to the country, nor in any later reports or statements (European Commission, 2004; Frontex, 2007). The EU's deafening postcolonial silence thus stands in stark contrast to recent Italo-Libyan discourses. It illustrates that besides its immense humanitarian consequences, the categories and discourses of EU externalization politics also represent an epistemological erasure of this particular racialized, political economic and societal context where the Union's policies play out (Vergara-Figueroa, 2018).

Yet, Italian and European media uncritically accepted the Treaty's postcolonial discourse. German daily *Süddeutsche Zeitung* lauded Italy's alleged apology and promise of reparation as being 'not only morally but also financially expedient' (De Cesari, 2012). Some scholars praised the Treaty with few reservations (Miranda, 2011; Ronzitti, 2009) or did not address its geostrategic motives (Lombardi, 2011). Others pointed out that while it addressed colonial misdeeds, it never pointed out what these or their damage actually consisted of (De Cesari, 2012; Morone, 2013). The vagueness of the 2008 Treaty on Libya's colonial past does not exactly confirm a colonial amnesia or silence (De Cesari, 2012; Labanca, 2015). Rather, it seems to be a willful inability to reflect upon, or learn from, the striking continuity whereby a string of Italian companies have remained central actors in Libyan politics on energy supply and border controls through several phases: first, discourses of fascist settler colonialism; second, the chase of concessions and contracts through discursive appeals to decoloniality, apology and reparations; and, third, a framing of geostrategies that relegated colonial relevance to the past.

Libya in a postcolonial mix: from an Italian 'mare nostrum' to a Turkish 'blue homeland'?

The so-called Arab Spring arrived in Libya in 2010–11 and the massive geopolitical upheaval that ensued resulted in new alliances, and heralded the return of Turkey to the former Ottoman provinces, thereby reconfiguring the discursive tropes on Libyan postcoloniality. After 2010, at first Berlusconi cautioned against toppling the Gaddafi regime, in order to allow for the continuation of the Italo-Libyan deals on energy, military and border control. Knowing well his European counterparts, Gaddafi, on the other hand, pursued stark racialized discourses about Sub-Saharan migrants. He threatened that Europe would face a 'human tsunami' and 'turn black' without his border controls (Corriere della Serra, 1 April 2011). While Gaddafi was ultimately deposed and killed on 20 October 2011, migrant conditions in Libya deteriorated further. A 2011 IOM Fact Finding Mission discovered desert camps with tens of thousands of people lacking access to sanitation, food or electricity, and being sold as labour on slave-like auctions to actors in the agricultural, oil, mining and construction sectors (IOM, 2011). Although European politicians expressed outrage at the time, the practice was allowed to continue, and resurfaced 7 years later as a mediatized scandal after CNN aired hidden camera recordings from inside similar auctions (CNN Special Edition, 2018).

Between 2013 and 2014, Italy launched the militarized search and rescue operation *mare nostrum*, which allegedly rescued 160,000 boat migrants, but its continuation was halted by EU member states like Denmark and United Kingdom who argued that such rescuing would attract more migrants to Europe. Frontex instead launched Operation Triton in 2014, without a rescue mandate in international and Libyan waters, and later a slightly expanded Operation Triton+ followed. A European Union Border Assistance Mission (EUBAM) was also launched (Council of the European Union, 2013). It was heralded as 'civilian' training of Libyan border police, but the mission could not attract Libyan partners, and quickly faced allegations of arming paramilitaries (Rettman, 2013). During the Libyan civil war erupting in 2014, EUBAM was repeatedly evacuated to Tunisia. True to form, both the Frontex and EUBAM missions remained within the standard depoliticized, ahistorical and generic EU narrative of Libya as a failed-turned-transit state, in dire need of EU support to rebuild its capacity to manage migration from scratch.

A UN-brokered agreement from 17 December 2015 formed the GNA led by Fayez al-Sarraj, but it quickly splintered into two rivalling governments, the Tripoli-based GNA and the Tobruk-based HoR governments. Each was connected to local militias and smugglers, had their own armies and was supported by different international actors. The GNA has been recognized by the EU and UN, while the Tobruk government, supported by the Libyan National Army (LNA) was recognized by Egypt, United Arab Emirates, France, the US and Russia. On 2 February 2017, Italy signed a new Memorandum of Understanding with the GNA reviving the 2008 Treaty's provisions on border control and energy, and establishing migrant detention centres and European-paid patrols against smuggling (Italian and Libyan Governments, 2017).

As regards Turkey, the long summer of migration in 2015 and the mass displacement of Syrians precipitated the controversial 2016 EU-Turkey Statement (Council of the European Union, 2016). This provided the AKP government with a powerful bargaining chip *vis-à-vis* the EU member states wishing to avoid refugees coming to Europe. Concurrently with the growing Turkish role in EU politics, Italy was given more room to manoeuvre as an 'old colonial hand' (Morone, 2015), by promoting EU border externalization to its former colonial territories Libya, and in the Horn of Africa through the Khartoum Process and the EU Emergency Trust Fund for Africa (EUTF). In collaboration with the Italian Ministry of Interior, the EUTF also channelled €318 million to Libyan border control between 2014–2019, including €91.3 million for naval operations. From 2018, this support focused on an Italian-funded Maritime Rescue Coordination Centre (MRCC) and the EU's desire to construct a Libyan Search and Rescue (SAR) zone. Since then, many boat migrants have been intercepted by Libyan patrols before reaching international waters, rescue NGOs and European territory, with 12,000 pulled back in 2020 (InfoMigrants, 2021). Although this has decreased migrant arrivals to Europe via the Central Mediterranean route, it has simultaneously increased the rate of fatalities on the route dramatically.

In April 2019, General Haftar's LNA launched a military campaign from the southern to the western parts of Libya, with Tripoli as the final destination. Several of the largest Libyan oil fields were taken in quick succession, with the LNA assisted by mercenaries, drones and air forces from Russia, UAE, Saudi Arabia, Egypt and France (Wintour, 8 February 2019). Since ENI had investments in several offshore oil fields close to Tripoli, including the Greenstream Pipeline, Italy began informal talks with the LNA, and thus the Tobruk government. This incurred massive rage from the GNA (El-Mahrouki, 2020). And then, on 27 November 2019, Turkey suddenly entered the scene, signing a Maritime Boundary Treaty with the GNA paving the way for energy exploration. Turkey and the GNA portrayed the Treaty as an 'energy corridor' providing progress and development to a Libyan government struggling after the civil war, and abandoned by European countries during the LNA campaign. It was underpinned by a Memorandum of Understanding between the two countries' central banks, and the involvement of Turkish energy companies. This illustrates the expansion of Turkish geopolitical ambitions for the Mediterranean, aligned with the 'blue homeland' doctrine (*mavi vatan*), developed by nationalistic admiral officers in the mid-2000s, and then integrated into the AKP government's geostrategy. In June 2020, a pro-Turkish militia attacked the Greenstream Pipeline complex, leading to fierce Italian condemnation (Hernández, 2020). Shortly thereafter, Turkey launched an unprecedented military campaign sending drones, Turkish troops, navy vessels and thousands of Syrian insurgents into the former Ottoman provinces of Cyrenaica, Tripolitania and Fezzan. Ultimately, the LNA campaign ground to a halt, and a ceasefire was signed on 23 October 2020.

The Turkish-GNA Treaty challenged the privileged Italian position, and has pitted the two former imperial powers against each other. But this has also meant a change in the actors and forms of appeal to Libyan postcoloniality. Thus, the LNA's General Haftar accused Turkey's President Erdogan of reviving Ottoman imperialism in Libya, and calling on the population to take up arms 'against the colonizer' (Naar, 2020). Erdogan, on the other hand, appeals to neo-Ottomanism, framed as a vast and old empire, and has stated that Libya 'has been an important part of the Ottoman Empire for centuries'. He in turn accused Haftar of conducting 'ethnic cleansing' of the minority Köroğlu Turks, and argued for Turkish military intervention since 'protecting ancestral grandchildren is one of our foremost duties' (Bloomberg, 2020). In Italy, the development was cast as undermining of migration control. Disregarding the question of Libyan self-determination, but reflective of the *mare nostrum* logic, Italian media argued that Turkey infiltrated Libyan border control policies, removing Libyan displacement from the sovereign discretion of EU member states. The right-wing Italian political party Brothers of Italy-leader Giorgia Meloni even warned of Turkish intentions to 'explode an unprecedented migration bomb over Italy' (Il Tempo, 2020), and calling for an immediate naval blockade of refugees.

Conclusion

This chapter has shown the relevance of imperial and colonial trajectories for understanding dynamics and practices in current Libyan displacement politics in two ways. First, it has examined how the postcolonial nexus between energy and migration management was interwoven with political-discursive constellations. These strategically instrumentalized the colonial history as cultural-political capital during moments of geopolitical ruptures. Moving from the pre- and pro-colonization discourses over fascist geostrategies and to ENI's allegedly decolonial reconfiguration, the gallery of actors exhibits different approaches. Compared to these, the EU's epistemological erasure of colonialism in Libya stands out in comparison with both Italy's and Turkey's recognition of certain – highly selective – aspects of their respective colonial legacies. This has engendered peculiar differences when it comes to the perception of Libyan energy and displacement dynamics, when comparing these three geopolitical actors. Further nuancing such an analysis, one can also consider Italian criticism of French neocolonialism in Libya. Considering intra-European arguments about ongoing colonial matrices of power, the EU's general preclusion of colonial awareness, and its facilitation of nationalistic and singular understandings of the causes for displacement, becomes no less striking.

Second, the chapter has also examined how, from the beginning, Italian settler colonialism imbricated forced migration control and energy politics with each other, ranging from water to postwar petroleum and gas extraction. After the Second World War, investments in the existing colonial infrastructures along the coastal highway accelerated ENI's access to oil fields and inland/offshore installations. The Italian-EU border externalization agenda, and its many contracts to companies like AGI and Leonardo, all ripe with colonial history, also allowed Gaddafi's regime to use the highway for the practices it was originally built for during Italian colonialism; the transfer of troops from one end of the country to the other in order to police populations. As such, forced migration, deportations and camps concentrating segments of displaced civilian populations are long-spanning practices in Libya. While Italy deployed Abyssinian troops from present-day Eritrea and Somalia for these purposes during fascist colonialism, today, Italy, the EU and increasingly also Turkey, support Libyan police, military and paramilitaries which intern and detain migrants, including Eritreans and Somalis. This instrumentalization of forced displacement and its control constitute a remarkable postcolonial continuity in Libyan geopolitics, whether by reference to an Italian *spazio vitale* and *mare nostrum*, as a flanking measure for an EU Area of Security, Freedom and Justice, or as part of a Turkish 'blue homeland'.

References

Ahmida, A.A. (2020) *Genocide in Libya: Shar, a Hidden Colonial History*, London: Routledge.

Archivio Centrale dello Stato (ACS), Ministero dell'Africa Italiana (MAI), Direzione Generale Affari Economici e Finanziari (1918–1958) (1923), Affari Generali 1918–1953, Miniere e prodotti minerari AGIP (Libia) 1925–1940, b. 206, f. 1, Ricerche di petrolio, Rome, 18 July.

Archivio Storico dell'ENI (ASENI), DESIO (1939) (Ardito 38–42 e Gianluca 61–62) relazioni su Libia, ex Scatola 607, b. 74, f. 48561, Notizie preliminari sulle ricerche geo-petrolifere nella Gefara Tripolina, Milan, 3 May.

Archivio Storico dell'ENI (ASENI), DESIO (1940) (Ardito 38–42 e Gianluca 61–62) relazioni su Libia, ex Scatola 607, b. 74, f. 48565, *letter from Desio to AGIP's Research and Development section*, Milan, 30 January.

Archivio Storico dell'ENI (ASENI) (1957) Libia, "Pratica Corradi", b. 90, f. 2224.

Archivio Storico dell'ENI (ASENI) (1959) Investimenti in Libia da parte ENI tramite la Cori, b. 36, f. 4ABC, *letter from Niutta to Bianchedi*, Rome.

Ballinger, P. (2016) 'Colonial twilight: Italian settlers and the long decolonization of Libya', Journal of Contemporary History, 51(4): 813–38.

BBC (2019) 'Libyan migrants "fired upon after fleeing air strikes"', [online] 4 July, Available from: https://www.bbc.com/news/world-africa-48871430 [Accessed 8 June 2021].

Ben-Ghiat, R. and Fuller, M. (2005) *Italian Colonialism*, New York: Palgrave Macmillan.

Bloomberg (2020) 'Erdoğan: Hafter kaçtı, bundan sonrası Putin'e ait', [online] 14 January, Available from: https://www.bloomberght.com/cumhurbaskani-erdogan-suriye-libya-akdeniz-de-macera-pesinde-degiliz-2244028 [Accessed 9 June 2021].

Chatty, D. (2010) *Displacement and Dispossession in the Modern Middle East*, New York: Cambridge University Press.

CNN Special Edition (2018) 'Migrants being sold as slaves', [online]. Available from: http://edition.cnn.com/videos/world/2017/11/13/libya-migrant-slave-auction-lon-orig-md-ejk.cnn [Accessed on 9 June 2021].

Commission of the European Communities (2003) 'Commission staff working paper: intensified cooperation on the management of migration flows with third countries' (SEC 815), 9 July.

Conte, G. (2021) 'Unholy alliances: disentangling the economic relations between Italy, the Holy See and the Ottoman Empire', *The International History Review*: 43(5):1142–59.

Coralluzzo, V. (2008) 'Italy and the Mediterranean: relations with the Maghreb countries', *Modern Italy*, 13(2): 115–33.

Corriere della Serra (2011) 'Berlusconi: 100 riumpati al giorno apello a Tunisi: "É uno tsunami umano"', [online] 1 April, Available from: https://www.corriere.it/politica/11_aprile_01/immigrazione-piano-cabina-regia_ef3d7c94-5c38-11e0-b06c-b43ad3228bba.shtml [Accessed 9 June 2021].

Council of the European Union (2013) 'Green light for civilian mission to support border security in Libya', 9478/13 PRESSE 189, 22 May.

Council of the European Union (2016) 'EU-Turkey statement', Press Release 144/16. 18 March.

Cricco, M. (2014) 'L'ENI in Libia: dal trattato italo-libico del 1956 ai negoziati degli anni Settanta', *Nuova Rivista Storica*, 98(2): 555–66.

De Cesari, C. (2012) 'The paradoxes of colonial reparation: foreclosing memory and the 2008 Italy – Libya Friendship Treaty', *Memory Studies*, 5(3): 316–26.

de Haas, H., Miller, M.J. and Castles, S. (2019) *The Age of Migration: International Population Movements in the Modern World*, London: Red Globe Press.

Del Boca, A. (2011) 'Cento anni in Libia', *I Sentieri della Ricerca – Rivista di Storia Contemporanea*, 13(1): 7–17.

Denoon, D. (1979) 'Understanding settler societies', *Historical Studies*, 18(73): 511–27.

Di Gregorio, P. (2015) 'Eni: agente speciale della decolonizzazione', *Meridiana*, 83: 195–214.

Di Sante, C. and Sury, S.H. (2009) *The Italian Occupation of Libya: Violence and Colonialism, 1911–1943*, Tripoli: Centre for National Archives and Historical Studies.

Distretti, E. (2021) 'The life cycle of the Libyan Coastal Highway: Italian colonialism, coloniality, and the future of reparative justice in the Mediterranean', *Antipode*, 53(5): 1421–41.

Dogget, G. (2009) 'Gaddafi "turns page on past" in Italy', *The Courier Mail*, [online] 10 June, Available from: https://www.couriermail.com.au/news/gaddafi-turns-page-on-past-in-italy/news-story/d79531b7d040b490909c661e8487c30a?sv=788d7296d72d8945f59e5010ce4b118c [Accessed on 21 June 2021].

El-Mahrouki, M. (2020) 'Turkey's encroachment in western Libya puts Italy's interests at risk', *The Arab Weekly*, [online] 2 June, Available from: https://thearabweekly.com/turkeys-encroachment-western-libya-puts-italys-interests-risk [Accessed on 9 June 2021].

European Commission (2005) *Technical Mission to Libya on Illegal Immigration 27 Nov–6 Dec 2004*. Report. DG H1. 7753/05. Available at: www.statewatch.org/news/2005/may/eu-report-libya-ill-imm.pdf [Accessed 10 April 2022].

Frontex (2007) *Frontex-led EU Illegal Immigration Technical Mission to Libya, 28 May–5 June 2007*. Report. Warsaw.

Gawrych, G. (2013) *The Young Atatürk: From Ottoman Soldier to Statesman of Turkey*, London: Bloomsbury Publishing.

Gazzini, C. (2009) 'Assessing Italy's Grande Gesto to Libya', Middle East Research and Information Project, [online] Available at: https://www.merip.org/mero/mero031609#_3_ [Accessed June 5 2018].

Hansen, P. and Jonsson, S. (2014) *Eurafrica: The Untold History of European Integration and Colonialism*, London: Bloomsbury.

Hansen, P. and Jonsson, S. (2017) 'Eurafrica incognita: the colonial origins of the European Union', *History of the Present*, 7(1): 1–32.

Hernández, H. (2020) 'Pro-Turkish militias attack Italian gas plant in Libya', Atalayar, [online] 10 June, Available from: https://atalayar.com/en/content/pro-turkish-militias-attack-italian-gas-plant-libya [Accessed on 9 June 2021].

Holmboe, K. and Pelt, M. (2011) *Ørkenen brænder: oplevelser blandt Saharas og Libyens beduiner* 2. udg., Copenhagen: Forlaget Vandkunsten KS.

Hom, S.M. (2019) *Empire's Mobius Strip: Historical Echoes in Italy's Crisis of Migration and Detention*, Ithaca: Cornell University Press.

Human Rights Watch (2009) 'Pushed back, pushed around: Italy's forced return of boat migrants and asylum seekers, Libya's mistreatment of migrants and asylum seekers', [online] Available from: https://www.refworld.org/docid/4ab87f022.html [Accessed 9 June 2021].

Il Tempo (2020) 'Allarme dei servizi: ventimila migranti in arrivo. Meloni (Fdi): "Subito blocco navale"', [online] 8 June, Available from: https://www.iltempo.it/politica/2020/06/08/news/allarme-servizi-ventimila-migranti-arrivo-libia-turchia-immigrazione-matteo-salvini-giorgia-meloni-blocco-navale-europa-redi-23172675/ [Accessed 9 June 2021].

InfoMigrants (2021) 'Italy-Libya accord, NGOs call for immediate revocation', [online] 3 February, Available from: https://www.infomigrants.net/en/post/30036/italy-libya-accord-ngos-call-for-immediate-revocation [Accessed on 21 May 2021].

International Organization for Migration (IOM) (2011) 'Assessment mission finds migrants in remote Libyan Town of Al-Kufrah in need of help' [Press release] 16 August. Available at: www.iom.int/news/assessment-mission-finds-migrants-remote-libyan-town-al-kufrah-need-help [Accessed 10 April 2022].

Italian Government (1998) 'Comunicato congiunto (Joint Communiqué)', Available from: https://web.archive.org/ web/20100124055608/http://airl.it/accorditrattati2.php [Accessed 9 June 2021].

Italian Government (2008) 'Trattato di Amicizia, Partenariato e Cooperazione tra la Repubblica Italiana e la Grande Giamahiria Araba Libica Popolare Socialista (The Treaty on Friendship, Partnership and Cooperation)', Available from: http://www.istitutospiov.it/articoli/trattato-di-amicizia-partenariato-e-cooperazione-tra-la-repubblica-italiana-e-la-grande-gia [Accessed 9 June 2021].

Italian and Libyan Governments (2017) 'Memorandum d'intesa sulla cooperazione nel campo dello sviluppo, del contrasto all'immigrazione illegale, al traffico di esseri umani, al contrabbando e sul rafforzamento della sicurezza delle frontiere tra lo Stato della Libia e la Repubblica Italiana (The Valletta Memorandum of Understanding)', Available from: https://eumigrationlawblog.eu/wp- content/uploads/2017/10/MEMORANDUM_translation_finalversion.doc.pdf [Accessed on 9 June 2021].

Joesten, J. (1962) 'ENI: Italy's economic colossus', *Challenge*, 10(7): 24–27.

Labanca, N. (2005) 'Italian colonial internment', in R. Ben-Ghiat and M. Fuller (eds) *Italian Colonialism*, New York: Palgrave Macmillan, pp 27–36.

Labanca, N. (2015) 'Post-colonial Italy – the case of a small and belated empire: from strong emotions to bigger problems', in D. Rothermund (ed) *Memories of Post-Imperial Nations: The Aftermath of Decolonization, 1945–2013*, Delhi: Cambridge University Press, pp 120–49.

Lemberg-Pedersen, M. (2013) 'Private security companies and the EU borderscapes', in N. Nyberg Sørensen and T. Gammeltoft-Hansen (eds) *The Migration Industry and the Commercialization of International Migration*, New York: Routledge, pp 152–71.

Lemberg-Pedersen, M. (2017), 'Effective protection or effective combat? EU border control and North Africa', in P. Gaibazzi, S. Dünnwald and A. Bellagamba (eds) *EurAfrican Borders and Migration Management: Political Cultures, Contested Spaces, and Ordinary Lives*, New York: Palgrave Macmillan US, pp 29–60.

Lemberg-Pedersen, M. (2019) 'Manufacturing displacement: externalization and postcoloniality in European migration control', *Global Affairs*, 5(3): 247–71.

Lombardi, B. (2011) 'The Berlusconi government and intervention in Libya', *The International Spectator*, 46(4): 31–44.

Mayblin, L. and Turner, J. (2021) *Migration Studies and Colonialism*, Cambridge: Polity Press.

McCollum, J. (2017), 'Reimagining Mediterranean spaces: Libya and the Italo-Turkish War, 1911–1912', in S. Saffari, R. Akhbari, K. Abdolmaleki and E. Hamdon (eds) *Unsettling Colonial Modernity in Islamicate Contexts*, Newcastle upon Tyne: Cambridge Scholars Publishing, pp 49–66.

Miranda, V.V. (2011) 'Striking a balance between norms and interests in Italian foreign policy: The Balkans and Libya', IAI Working Paper. Istituto Affari Internazionali (IAI): 1–20.

Moreno-Lax, V. and Lemberg-Pedersen, M. (2019) 'Border-induced displacement: the ethical and legal implications of distance-creation through externalization', *Questions of International Law*, 56: 5–33.

Morone, A.M. (2011) 'Italiani d'Africa, africani d'Italia: da coloni a profughi', *Altreitalie*, 42: 20–35.

Morone, A.M. (2013) 'Asimmetrie postcoloniali: le relazioni italo-libiche tra storia e memoria', in F. Sinopoli (ed) *Postcoloniale Italiano – tra letteratura e storia*, Anzio-Lavinio: Novalogos, pp 174–190.

Morone, A.M. (2015) 'La Libia, crocevia migratorio. Nuove e vecchie dinamiche dal 2011 al 2014', in L. Ciabarri (ed) *I Rifugiati e l'Europa: Tra Crisi Internazionali e Corridoi d'Accesso*, Milan: Edizioni Libreria Cortina, pp 59–78.

Naar, I. (2020) 'Haftar accuses Erdogan of attempting to revive Ottoman legacy in Libya', *Al Arabiya English* [online] 4 January, Available from: https://english.alarabiya.net/en/News/north-africa/2020/01/04/Haftar-accuses-Erdogan-of-attempting-to-revive-Ottoman-legacy-in-Libya-region [Accessed on 9 June 2021].

Nocentini, V. (2016) 'L'Italia della guerra di Libia (1911–1912): un burattinaio contro il potere', *Annali d'Italianistica*, 34: 339–55.

Paoli, S. (2015) 'The Schengen agreements and their impact on Euro-Mediterranean relations: the case of Italy and the Maghreb', *Journal of European Integration History*, 21(1): 125–45.

Pozzi, D. (2010) 'Entrepreneurship and capabilities in a "beginner" oil multinational: the case of ENI', *Business History Review*, 84(2): 253–74.

Rettman, A. (2013) 'EU "civilian" mission training paramilitaries in Libya', *EUObserver* [online] 18 November, Available from: https://euobserver.com/investigations/122134 [Accessed on 9 June 2021].

Rodogno, D. (2006) *Fascism's European Empire: Italian Occupation during the Second World War*, Cambridge: Cambridge University Press.

Ronzitti, N. (2009) 'The treaty on friendship, partnership and cooperation between Italy and Libya: new prospects for cooperation in the Mediterranean?', *Bulletin of Italian Politics*, 1(1): 125–33.

Segré, C.G. (1972) 'Italo Balbo and the Colonization of Libya', *Journal of Contemporary History*, 7(3): 141–55.

Seton-Watson, C. (1980) 'Italy's imperial hangover', *Journal of Contemporary History*, 15(1): 169–79.
UNHCR, (2018) *Flash Update – Libya (27 July – 3 August 2018).* [Operational Data Portal] UNHCR, [online] Available from: https://data2.unhcr.org/en/documents/details/65029 [Accessed 20 February 2019].
van Genugten, S. (2011) 'Libya after Gadhafi', *Survival*, 53(3): 61–74.
Veracini, L. (2013) '"Settler colonialism": career of a concept', *Journal of Imperial and Commonwealth History*, 41(2): 313–33.
Vergara-Figueroa, A. (2018) *Afrodescendant Resistance to Deracination in Colombia: Massacre at Bellavista-Bojayá-Chocó*, New York: Palgrave Macmillan.
Wintour, P. (2019) 'Conflict erupts for control of Libya's largest oil field', *The Guardian*, [online] 8 February, Available from: https://www.theguardian.com/world/2019/feb/08/conflict-erupts-for-control-of-libyas-largest-oil-field [Accessed on 9 June 2021].
Wolfe, P. (2006) 'Settler colonialism and the elimination of the native', *Journal of Genocide Research*, 8(4): 387–409.

9

Echoes of Imperialism: Crisis, Conflict and the (Re)configurations of Otherness in the Evros/Edirne Borderlands

Peter Teunissen and Penny Koutrolikou

Introduction

In February 2020, against the backdrop of the escalating conflict in Syria, the Turkish President Tayyip Erdoğan claimed that Europe had left Turkey alone to deal with the people fleeing hardship and war in Syria. Framing Turkey as the sole bearer of humanity in supporting Syrian people and expressing frustration at the lack of European support for its military operations in Syria, Erdoğan proclaimed what he had long threatened to do: 'We opened the doors'.[1] Within days, thousands of people who aspired to a different life in Europe travelled to the Evros/Edirne border region from where they tried, supported by Turkish authorities, to cross into Greek territory.[2] The Greek Prime Minister Kyriakos Mitsotakis reacted by saying that 'The borders of Greece are the external borders of Europe. We will protect them'.[3] Greek authorities further increased the securitization of the border and on 1 March they suspended all new asylum applications for 1 month (FEK 45A/02-03-2020). People who tried to cross the border were attacked with tear gas, batons, stun grenades, rubber bullets and live ammunition, and violently pushed back to Turkey (Arsis et al, 2020; Forensic Architecture, 2020; Human Rights 360, 2020).

This series of events was highly mediatized, being covered by several European news agencies for days, which reported on clashes between police forces and migrants at the border, while the Greek government announced the transfer of additional military and police personnel to the borderland.

Greek mainstream news agencies described the events through a militarized language of invasions and interceptions, with the migrants being depicted as a threat that was further strengthened by rumours concerning hundreds of thousands of people waiting to cross to the Greek islands from the Turkish shores. From the perspective of the European Union (EU) and the Greek government, this 'spectacle of migration' (DeGenova, 2013) represented a threat posed by the migrants trying to cross the border. Several commentators (including the Greek PM)[4] were quick to classify the people trying to cross the border as 'illegal' (*sic*) migrants ('not Syrians') rather than as potential refugees; predefining the outcome of a possible asylum claim (for example Tzimas, 2020a; b; Newsroom, 2020a; b; Ioannidis, 2020).

In multiple, yet intersecting ways, these discourses on invasions and interceptions echo the complex histories that have shaped the borders of these territories, most notable since the Lausanne Treaty of 1923. The Evros/Edirne border region has been (re)shaped by numerous wars, conflicts, imperial conquests, and shifting conceptions of insiders and outsiders. The notions of us/them are not necessarily something stable but a question of positions. In this fluctuating dance of friends/enemies, migrants are often conceptualized as the 'Other'; a signifier that is operationalized by different external actors. By this we do not wish to argue that migrants have limited agency, but rather to emphasize the way other actors try to operationalize them. Various scholars have noted how these intersecting histories of otherness provide insights into the contemporary working of how states and intra-state organizations control peoples' movement within and across borders (Hage, 2016; Loyd, 2016; Mbembe, 2019, see also Chapter 12, this volume).

The border tensions in February-March 2020 demonstrated how these discourses created and enforced a 'racial trope of non-Europeans' that frame certain groups of people on the move as an invasion and a threat (De Genova, 2018). Taking this series of events as our starting point, this chapter explores the postcolonial spatializations and manifestations of an 'imperial present' (Morrisey, 2013). Rather than trying to interpret past and present events as a linear process of cause and effect, we read them as a conjuncture (Hall and Massey, 2010: 38) in which different processes, antagonisms and significations are condensed in the same moment. Critiques of colonialism and imperialism which pay attention both to their discursive constitution as well as to their material spatialities (Said, 1993; Gregory, 2004; Hage 2016), provide an analytically rich frame for disentangling these conjunctures and help us to observe (and question) shifting imagined geographies and scales as well as the shifting definitions of us/them, and others.

In this chapter we examine the textual, political-institutional and socio-cultural dimensions of the February-March events along with the historical trajectories of the specific region and its emerging materialities. Drawing on critical discourse analysis (CDA) (Fairclough, 2001; Wodak and Meyer, 2009) that examines the social, political and material implications of discourse, we focus on the construction of otherness and of imagined geographies by looking at notions of us/them and inside/outside (on discourses of power, see also Cole, on the silencing of indigenous community voices through sociology of forced migration, see Vergara-Figueroa and Marino, both this volume). Our material is collected from political speeches, statements and press releases made during and immediately after the border tensions in February-March 2020, and of relevant media articles from Greek and Turkish media outlets published at the same time. Following Fairclough, we analyse this material as a three-level process of description (text-level), interpretation (here, by institutions) and explanation (the socio-political level) and by also looking at specific historical dimensions (Reisigl and Wodak, 2009).

The chapter is divided into four parts. First, we will elaborate on the imperial borders of Europe and discuss how the internal opening of the borders of EUrope came together with the hardening of its external borders. Second, our textual analysis focuses on representations of migrants and of the main (state) actors involved in these events, and processes of construction of others. Third, we turn to the EU's expansive border practices achieved through political economy and securitization of spaces through which different states and intrastate alliances mobilize resources to enforce control over mobility. Next, we turn our attention to the Evros/Edirne border and use the events of February-March 2020 to analyse the discursive, material and geographical strategies employed by some of the actors involved and to discern their postcolonial and post-imperial legacies which are inscribed in discourses, territories and people. Here, we look at how the representations of the actions taken place with a particular attention on accusations or declarations of support, and on the images presented to audiences by these texts. In so doing we aim to demonstrate how the borders of the Evros/Edirne region hold traces of an imperial past that continues to influence the EU's border regimes.

The imperial borders of EUrope

The European Union, as we know it today, is a relatively young alliance of states that binds several European nation-states into a bordered space. It is also the coming together of several old imperial and colonial powers. While internally the consolidation of a European political space was premised upon both coercion and consent (Hadjimichalis, 2018), externally imperial modalities of power were recast in a more benevolent language of '"democratization", "reconstruction", "securitization" and "development"' (Morrisey, 2013: 494). The establishment of the EU's project and its gradual internal integration and harmonization accentuated the othering of third countries, often echoing colonial legacies and imperial rivalries. While 'third country nationals' were constructed as others, often along orientalist representations, another category was rapidly becoming the EU's threatening other, namely (particularly Muslim) migrants (Hage, 2016).

The project of constructing a politically and territorially unified space was discursively and spatially underwritten by the implementation of the Schengen regulation and the opening of the internal borders of Europe, while fortifying its external borders (Balibar, 2009). Following Stuart Hall's conceptualization of the West and the Rest, the EU and its Schengen Zone is not just a geographical-political demarcation on a map. We understand it as a political-historical representation of a 'new Europe, fortified by very old and morbid cruelties' of imperialism and colonialism (De Genova, 2017: 18). In this chapter, we therefore henceforth write 'EUrope' in order to accentuate how the European Union is also a discursive construction beyond the spatial demarcation of its borders. The external borders of EUrope are articulated and policed through mobility regimes. They maintain a global order that is deeply informed by intersecting histories of imperialism and colonialism (Walia, 2013, Saucier and Woods, 2014; Sheller, 2018). These racialized (but also gendered) modes of governing territory manage mobilities through coerced mobility and labour exploitation, such as exclusive visa regimes, deportations and short-term working visas, which, as argued by various scholars, are the legacies of imperial practices of othering (Walia, 2013; Sheller, 2018). From a more spatial perspective, in their research on human mobility and US military bases in the Caribbean and the Pacific, Loyd et al (2016) show how both colonial empires and state entities enforce mobility regimes through gradated forms of sovereignty enforced via arcifinious boundaries, such as islands, corridors, enclaves and irregular zones around them. The authors observe a repetition of geographical patterns, including militarization, confinement, exceptionalism and dispossession, through which both colonial empires and governmental entities exercise power over mobility regimes.

Imperial formations at the Greek/Turkish border

In this section, we argue that the Evros/Edirne borderlands have also been mobilized as an 'arcifinious space' (Duncan and Levidis, 2020). According to the CDA framework, this then amounts to an explanation at the socio-political level, where colonial and imperial and geographical patterns and discourses have been continuously reproduced in order to maintain sovereignty over territorial borders. The land border between Greece and Turkey cuts through the territory known as Thrace, which came under Ottoman control in 1263–1364. During the Greek War of Independence (1821), and the two Balkan Wars (1912 and 1913), the borders of the territories changed significantly. After the first Balkan Wars, the Ottoman Empire lost the territories up to the Bosporus, then gained significant territory after the second Balkan War, before ultimately disintegrating amidst the emergence of the Republic of Turkey (see also Chapter 3). After the First World War, the Treaty of Sevres (1920) and the Lausanne Treaty (1923) demarcated the borders between Greece, Bulgaria and Turkey. The Lausanne Treaty negotiations occurred between the delegation of the Turkish Grand National Assembly (*Türkiye Büyük Millet Meclisi*), Greece and the four big imperial and colonial powers of the time: the French Empire, the British Empire, the Kingdom of Italy and the Empire of Japan, that among others, negotiated the borders between Greece and Turkey. In *The Colonial Present* (2004) Gregory demonstrates how the falling apart of the Ottoman Empire in the 1920s, and the (re)bordering of the territories of Iraq, was driven by the extractive interests and ambitions of other empires as well as by Orientalism (for a similar analysis of Ottoman relations to current-day Libya, see also Chapter 8).

The consolidation of the border that came with the Lausanne Treaty brought with it forced migrations in the form of population 'exchanges' and further otherings (internal and external) entangling Turkey and Greece in an antagonistic relationship. In the aftermath of the Treaty, the two countries pursued a 'homogenization' of these territories based on a religiously defined concept of ethnicity (Keyden 2004: 52; see also Chapter 3). In Greece, the Evros province was almost emptied of Muslim-Turks who had to abandon everything and took refuge in Turkey (see Alexandris, 1983), while the incoming Rums were settled in Western Thrace (Oran, 2004). This can be traced back to formal identities in the Ottoman Empire based on religion, so that subjects were administered in communities, the 'millets'. Thus, Orthodox Christians were members of the 'Rum' millet. The term 'Greek', strictly speaking, 'would then refer only to citizens of the Greek state established in 1830 (Hirschon, 2004: xii). This process of enforcing homogeneous space through displacements and discourses of nationalities and citizenship (Sheller, 2018) functions both as 'an instrument for exercising that power and containing perceived threats to that power' (Sardar, 1999: 110). However, while the two states were involved in an antagonistic relationship that partially continues to this day, the lives of many of their residents – particularly at the border regions – entailed far more mixed inter-group relations, and thus otherings, than the essentialized Greece/Turkey dichotomy.

Since then, the land-border between Greece and Turkey has been 206 kilometres long and it mostly follows the Evros/Meriç River which runs with a strong current from the Rila Mountains in Bulgaria towards the Aegean Sea. Here, 'the hostile characteristics of arcifinious boundaries of the Evros/Meriç river were mobilized to enforce and maintain sovereign claims to territory' (Duncan and Levides, 2020: np). These borders became 'the materialization of socio-political relations that mediate the continuous production of the distinction between the putative inside and outside' (De Genova, 2017: 21). This is an illustrative example of how intersecting histories of imperialism, dispossession and state violence, including discourses of otherness, have co-shaped the foundations for the present-day securitization of migration. These echoes of the past resonate with Stoler's description of *Imperial Formations*, that emphasizes the 'mutant, rather than simply hybrid, political forms that endure beyond the formal exclusions that legislate against equal opportunity, commensurate dignities and equal rights' that continue to influence this region (Stoler, 2013: 15).

Reconfigurations of the borders of EUrope

The shifting tides of imperial geopolitical power games in this border region resulted in discursive shifts in tropes of us/them. The Ottoman Empire constituted an 'other' through the imperial eyes of European colonial powers, and the populations of its postcolonial geographies continue to be defined as others until today. At the same time, Greece and several Balkan countries also constituted others, albeit passing through gradated forms (Balibar, 2009). The imagined geography of ancient Greece was partially incorporated into the new nation-state. Broader geopolitical interests of the time also served to bring Greece closer to the perceived European community; something that was further solidified in 1981 when Greece joined the EU, and in 2001 when it joined the Eurozone. These institutional developments had repercussions for how the ensuing discourses surrounding Greek border control can be interpreted along the lines of CDA.

From the 1990s onwards, after the wars and political transformations in the Balkans, Eastern Europe and the Middle East, Greece became more prominent as a migration destination and transit country for people migrating to Europe (Vaiou and Stratigaki, 2008; Frangiskou et al, 2020). By the end of the 2000s, migration routes shifted towards the Greek-Turkish land and sea borders and increased priority was given to securitized border controls. Migration was increasingly gaining ground as a priority issue for the EU, reflected in an intense pressure for greater European integration and harmonization of asylum and border policies (McDonough and Tsourdi, 2012; Angeli et al, 2014; Hess and Kasparek, 2017).

The opening of the internal EU borders and the Europeanization of asylum and border policies through the responsibilities prescribed by the Dublin Agreement moved the border further away from North-Western European countries and towards the South-West and Greece, Italy and Spain, and also to non-EU transit countries, such as North Macedonia, Libya, Morocco and Turkey, through the externalization of border control (Casas-Cortess and Cobarrubias, 2019; Lemberg-Pederson, 2019). Here we observe a triple shift regarding migration and asylum in the EU: first, the strengthening of

EU external borders (Schengen) to aid internal mobility, and the transfer of the EU's asylum responsibilities to the Union's border countries; second, the external dimensions of migration spatialized through partnerships and bilateral agreements with third countries such as Turkey accompanied by discourses of democratization, securitization, development and migration control; and, third, traces of an 'imperial present' (Morrisey, 2013) that follow similar patterns as the spaces we described earlier.

As migration routes shifted eastwards, the presence of the European Border and Coast Guard Agency (Frontex) at the Greek-Turkish borders has been continuously intensified since 2007. In 2010, the Agency mobilized for the first time its Rapid Border Intervention Team whose deployment 'was the first time that an EU member state invoked a situation of emergency and asked for assistance to guard its borders' (Angeli et al, 2014). This Frontex operation at the borders between Greece and Turkey was designed to 'intercept migrants at the border, register and identify them, and assist the Greek authorities with returns and readmissions' (Angeli et al, 2014).

Parallel to this Frontex mission in 2012, two Greek operations were initiated: Operation Aspida and Operation Xenios Zeus (FIDH et al, 2014: 18), the latter concerned solely the Attica and Evros regions, and received strong criticism for racializing migrants and violating their rights (see HRW, 2013). Since the discursive construction of other-ness and its imagined geographies are pivotal imperial strategies, it is interesting to further reflect on discursive elements of these two operations since their legacies echo at the recent border events of February-March 2020. Thus, Aspida ('Shield') describes an object used to provide protection to oneself. It correlates to the sentiment of fear of imminent attack that, as argued by Hage (2016), is a sentiment characterizing settler-colonialism, and also resonates with an image of protecting a body from the external threat. According to Hage (2016), as the European border crisis made headlines in 2015, the idea of EUrope being surrounded by 'barbarians' (sic) gained traction. Through the analytical lens of CDA, the discursive descriptions embedded in the institutionalization of the Frontex Agency's geo-securitized operations in peripheral EU countries can then be seen as a depiction of a national/EUropean body shielded from an alleged migrant/barbarian threat.

Xenios ('Hospitality') Zeus, on the other hand, was assigned the name of the ancient Greek god of guests and friendships (see also Chapter 10) in order to characterize what were stop-and-detain operations targeting migrants in house raids across Athens and in Evros. Here, in symbolic, or perhaps more ironic, terms, the Greek police assumes the role of the benevolent God, by providing hospitality to those legally resident in the country, but also detention to those without a residence permit, thereby securing the national territory. The discursive transformation of hospitality into detention practices represents what border scholars have described as the double-edged sword of care and control forming the continuum of the humanitarian border (Walters, 2011; Pallister-Wilkins, 2015; Lemberg-Pedersen, 2019); a border shaped and enacted by war and humanitarian imperialisms (Bush et al, 2011).

Amidst the Eurozone crisis, rising far-right attitudes and rising numbers of migrant crossings, the Greek government also constructed a 10.3-kilometre fence between Kastanies and Nea Vyssa at Evros. Since EU funding for the fence was rejected, the fence was paid by Greek resources costing €5.5 million. Nevertheless, since the European Commission considered technical equipment and specially equipped vehicles more effective (Angeli et al, 2014) it co-funded 23 thermal vision cameras (Nielsen, 2012). After the February-March 2020 events, the Greek authorities started to further fortify the Evros fence. The construction of the fence, completed in 2021, cost €63 million, and there are plans to extend it. The textual and institutional discourses surrounding the Evros fence can similarly be understood as a continuous shielding of the territory resulting in variegated dimensions of confinement and processes of border externalization and internalization.

The (rather) permanent emergency of migration

The year 2015 became a signifier for what has been termed the EU's 'refugee crisis'; a crisis that in our view to a certain extent challenged aspects of the European establishment's drive for fortification as expressed by the Schengen agreement. An extensive body of research explores EUrope's responses to this so-called crisis in 2015, and it demonstrates how politicians and EUropean policy frame people on the move as a problem to be solved (see, for example: Carrera et al, 2015; Berry et al, 2016; Stern, 2016; Collett and Le Coz, 2018). Here, the words 'crisis' and 'emergency' have been strategically deployed for the 'reconfiguration of tactics and techniques of border policing and migration and asylum law enforcement' (New Keyword Collective, 2016 see Karamanidou 2015) to further materialize EUrope's desire to control and stop so-called irregular movement into its territory. In this, and the following two sections, we show how, at the socio-political level, a CDA-based approach to European, Greek and Turkish discourses on migration control, offer explanatory power for our postcolonial analysis.

Responding to this alleged emergency, several new directives and regulations were introduced within the EU Agenda on Migration in 2015.[5] Featuring prominently among them, at least regarding the scope of this chapter, was the newly introduced 'hotspot approach' concerning Italy and Greece. It signifies an up-scaling of border control initiatives mostly delivered via Frontex, and the revamping of EU partnerships with third countries. Most notable of the latter is the heavily criticized EU-Turkey press statement of 2016 that turned migration into an exchangeable commodity (Neilson, 2018). The EU promised to pay Turkey € six billion to prevent new migration routes to EUrope and host refugees, while people who crossed irregularly from Turkey to the Greek islands would be deported to Turkey. For every Syrian returned to Turkey, it was claimed that another Syrian would be resettled to the EU. Thereby, it *de facto* categorized Turkey as a 'safe third country'.

Although the statement was introduced as a temporary and extraordinary humanitarian solution to the so-called refugee crisis, Ustübici (2019) argues that the technocratic approach of the statement is the coming together of EU's earlier processes of externalizing migration governance to Turkey. Furthermore, as Karadağ (2019) articulates, European borders do not only move outwards from the European centre and then straightforwardly get implemented by the 'passive others'. They are also enacted through transit and destination countries that cooperate with the EU. This has become evident through the ways Turkish authorities instrumentalized migration to push for financial and military support. In this turbulent period, the prevalent crisis-discourse was accompanied by continuous representations of migrants as threatening others. Simultaneously we can observe the pivotal role of geography: Borders become critical territories for deterring asylum seekers from reaching the European heartland and hence an assemblage of security apparatuses is increasingly established there.

(Re)instrumentalization of migration at the Evros/ Edirne border in 2020

From taking office in 2020 the new EU Presidency was quick to announce the preparations for a new Pact on Migration and Asylum as well as to create a new Commissioner position for ensuring the 'European' quality of life. The border tensions in a way condensed the past, present and future EU and national approaches to migration and accelerated their implementation. This becomes discernible when we look at the discourses pertaining the February–March 2020 Evros border tensions.

As already mentioned, these border tensions were initially dealt with through a discourse of double defence from others (migrants) by Greece and Turkey. Turkey employed discourses of humanitarianism to refugees, and of blame of the EU abandoning its responsibility, in order to support an 'open door policy'. Erdoğan said 'we only host 3.7 million Syrians in our country of course we are not in a position to handle a new wave of immigration now'. He also stated 'what did we say months ago? If it goes on like this, we will have to open the doors. They were uncomfortable, they did not believe what we said. And what did we do yesterday? We opened the doors'. According to Erdoğan, 'the European Union must keep its word. ... We are not obliged to look after and feed so many refugees'. In Greece on the other hand, the media employed a clearly militarized discourse of an 'invasion' by 'migrants'. For example in one of the several articles by Tsimas (2020a) writing that 'the aspiring "invaders" stay behind the barbed wire hoping that, at some point, they will attempt to storm, they will break the barbed wires and will force the Greek guards to abate, in order to make the first big step'. Moreover, the Greek PM Mitsotakis accused Turkey of operationalizing refugees and for not adhering to the Press Statement (Hellenic Republic Ministry of Foreign Affairs, 2020).

> It is an asymmetrical threat against Greece's Eastern borders, which are also European borders. The unlawful entry of thousands of people turns into a breach of our sovereign territory, with people of unknown origin and unknown purposes at the forefront, who don't hesitate to blatantly use violence to enter Greek territory.[6]

Border tensions among Greece and Turkey are not uncommon. What is uncommon in this case is the rapid response of High EU officials in discursive, geographical and material manners. All political leaders emphasized different aspects of this border crisis, according to their priorities while declaring their support to Greece; some of them referring back to the 2015 'refugee crisis' as something to be avoided by all means. Charles Michel stated, 'the Greek borders are the European borders and what you are doing is important for Greece, it's crucial as well for the future of the European Union'.

With the exception of the Greek PM, Turkey has been considered a partner to be supported as long as it respects its responsibilities. The Greek PM was quick to impose further categorizations upon the people trying to cross, dividing them between legitimate refugees (namely Syrian) and (non-rightful) migrants living safely in Turkey: 'the tens of thousands of people who tried to enter Greece over the past few days did not come from Idlib. They have been living safely in Turkey for a long period of time; most of them speak Turkish fluently'. What also became apparent, was the external attribution of characteristics and legal designations to the 'legitimate refugees' and the 'illegal migrant'. For example, Kathimerini (Newsroom, 2020a), a Greek newspaper reported that '64% of those arrested at the Greek-Turkish borders comes from Afghanistan, as it evidenced from the data processed by the Greek authorities. The numeric data concern the period from Friday 28 February until today. Only four per cent of those arrested comes from Syria'. Both statements implied that people who come from Afghanistan or who do not come from Idlib cannot be considered legitimate refugees, thus predefining their asylum status. Despite the interplay of national shades of otherness, from the statements it became clear that the ultimate threatening others were the refugees who crossed the border, thus challenging the EU's sovereignty (and territory) not at the border but within its 'core'.

A practice of imperial legacy whereby presenting people as both other and powerless, is used to legitimize violent border management and interventions. The border was evoked in all these statements, both as a guarantee of sovereignty and as a major defence. But the same border bears many meanings extending across varied geographies. The Greek Prime Minister accentuated that the Greek border is the EU border and thus that Greece is Europe's 'shield' against possible threats from the South-East. All European Heads of State echoed in agreement the amalgamation of the Greek and EU border, with the president of the Commission, Ursula von der Leyden, further enhancing the discursive Shield-representation by stating 'our first priority is making sure that order is maintained at the Greek external border, which is also a European border', and thanking 'Greece for being our European shield in these times'.[7]

Similarly, however, Turkey, on the other side of the EU external border, was also represented as the 'external' shield of the Union. The EU-Turkey Press Statement featured prominently in all aforementioned official statements, albeit with different intonations and associations. It became clear that despite differences with Turkey, the press statement was of utmost importance for the EU and something that should be continued; at times implicitly underscoring that Turkey is de facto made into a safe third country. As mentioned by Charles Michel, 'we have an agreement with Turkey on migration and indeed it is very important to implement this agreement'.[8] Yet, in order for Greece and Turkey to continue to be the EU's Shields, both countries required tangible support. Support that was outlined by the European Commission president and was delivered in the border region and beyond.

The material shield started to be implemented rapidly with the deployment of further police and military personnel under Operation Aspida (Shield) and under EU agencies. More manifestly, the Greek authorities started to further fortify the Evros fence. The wall will be supported by watch towers both with and without border guards, and further improvement works will take place in existing border infrastructures. In addition, digital border surveillance will be upgraded. As the Greek Minister of Protection said in the beginning of 2021, '2021 is the year of security. The [COVID-19] vaccine and the fence' (AlphaTVnews, 2020). These varied human, material, digital and discursive features of the border constituted an assemblage established primarily for the prevention of migration and the 'proper' categorization of people crossing it. At the same time, this border apparatus is extended to the interior of Greece and Turkey, at the hotspots, facilities and camps that host numerous refugees in a 'state of injury' (Mbembe, 2003).

The construction of the fence along with Frontex's operation can be understood as an assemblage of power, knowledge and geography employing both discursive and material technologies resembling those employed in order to 'underwrite colonial violence' (Morrisey, 2013). Moreover, the geographic patterns of militarization/securitization, financialization, exceptionalism and dispossession identified by Loyd et al (2016) can also be discerned in present-day migration regimes at the Evros/Edirne region. Despite the well-acknowledged fact of its permanence, the logic of crisis remains a constant reference point for political discourses on migration and thus a legitimation signifier for the promotion of policies. The soaring amounts of funds directed towards the borders, EU peripheries and neighbouring third countries in order to prevent migration reflect some of the financial aspects of migration (Akkerman, 2016).

In these processes, migrants become a negotiating card, an exchangeable commodity for all major actors involved; albeit for different purposes and interests. A constellation of 'shifting others' supports this border apparatus, sustaining variegated and temporal us-and-them categorizations and producing multi-scalar geographies of control, dichotomous geographies such as civilized/barbarous and inside/outside. As Klein points out (1994:5 as cited in Morrisey, 2013) geopolitics 'provide a map for the negotiating of these dichotomies in such a way that Western society always winds up on the "good" … side of the equation'.

Reflections on the borders

As we have argued, historical and contextualized repertoires of imperialism, reproduced in constructions of otherness and 'us and them', are interwoven with practices of migration governance. This takes place in multiple scales and spatialities externally, peripherally and at the core of the EU through mobile, itinerant and dispersed practices (Casas-Cortes and Cobarrubias, 2019). Nevertheless, disentangling such practices in the specific region is not as clear-cut. Our analysis based on Critical Discourse Analysis illustrates that the European, Greek and Turkish discursive construction of others in the Evros/Edirne border region have been aligned and facilitated by shifting colonial-imperial and postcolonial geographies and scales as well as their associated definitions of us/them, and others.

With the internal opening of European borders, the borders of Greece became the borders of Europe. Since then, migration has increasingly been framed as an EU-wide threat. Post-2015, this narrative crucially included the Evros/Meriç border. Through discourses of crisis, threat and shielding, vast financial resources are increasingly directed towards a securitized migration management. This is either through development/humanitarian projects, externalization projects, or material and digital securitization to maintain something of a European b/order (De Genova, 2017: 352). Hence this south-eastern border underwrites the continuation of the EU internal unity while simultaneously becoming a pivotal 'outpost' for ensuring that others remain 'safely' outside Europe.

The February-March 2020 border events make tangible how technologies of imperial rule operate through contested scales of differential access and rights allowing some people to cross freely, while others are illegally pushed back to Turkey. These imperial legacies are inscribed in discursive, material and geographical practices influencing the Evros/Edrine borderlands and people who cross them. These 'imperial eyes' of EUrope discursively construct certain migrants and people on the move as ' "problems," ' while framing other migrants as workers that supply the EUropean economy with its needed workforce' (Bass et al, 2020). This has shaped the EU border and migration arenas, which denotes its borders through fixed centres and imagined periphery. We argue that this operates according to mobile, itinerant and dispersed practices once evident also in imperial sovereignties.

Notes

1 https://www.tccb.gov.tr/konusmalar/353/38794/tugik-genel-kurulunda-yaptiklari-konusma; https://www.tccb.gov.tr/konusmalar/353/116848/istanbul-milletvekilleri-bulusmasinda-yaptiklari-konusma

2 http://gocmendayanisma.com/2020/03/06/pazarkule-evrostan-notlar-altinci-gun-notes-from-pazarkule-evros-sixth-day/

3 https://primeminister.gr/2020/03/03/23447

4 https://primeminister.gr/2020/03/03/23447

5 https://ec.europa.eu/home-affairs/european-agenda-migration-press-material_en

6 https://primeminister.gr/2020/03/03/23447

7 https://ec.europa.eu/commission/presscorner/detail/en/statement_20_380

8 https://www.consilium.europa.eu/en/press/press-releases/2020/02/29/statement-by-the-president-of-the-european-council/; https://primeminister.gr/en/2020/03/03/23458

References

Akkerman, M. (2016) *Border Wars: The Arms Dealers Profiting from Europe's Refugee Tragedy*, Amsterdam: Transnational Institute.

Alexandris, A. (1983) *The Greek Minority of Istanbul and Greek-Turkish Relations 1918–1974*, Athens: Centre for Asia Minor Studies.

AlphaTV news (2020) 'M. Chrysochoidis: "2021 will be the year of security – the vaccine and the fence"', AlphaTV, [online] 29 December, Available from: https://www.alphatv.gr/news/politika/article/59851/m-hrusohoidis-to-2021-tha-einai-o-hronos-tis-asfaleias-to-emvolio-kai-o-frahtis/.

Angeli, D., Dimitriadi, A. and Triandafyllidou, A. (2014) 'Assessing the cost-effectiveness of irregular migration control policies in Greece', *Midas Policy Paper*, [online] October. Available from: https://www.eliamep.gr/wp-content/uploads/2014/11/MIDAS-Policy-Paper-EN.pdf [Accessed 9 July 2021].

ARSIS, Greek Council for Refugees, HumanRights360 (2020) 'The new normality: Continuous push-backs of Third country nationals on the Evros river'. Available from: www.gcr.gr/en/ekdoseis-media/reports/reports/item/1028-the-new-normality-continuous-push-backs-of-third-country-nationals-on-the-evros-river [Accessed 10 April 2022].

Balibar, E. (2009) 'Europe as borderland', *Environment and Planning D: Society and Space*, 27(2): 190–215.

Bass, M.J., Córdoba, D. and Teunissen, P. (2020) '(Re)searching with imperial eyes: collective self-inquiry as a tool for transformative migration studies', *Social Inclusion*, 8(4): 147–56.

Berry, M., Garcia-Blanco I. and Moore, K. (2016) 'Press Coverage of the Refugee and Migrant Crisis in the EU: A Content Analysis of Five European Countries', Report prepared for the United Nations High Commission for Refugees. Available from: www.unhcr.org/protection/operations/56bb369c9/press-coverage-refugee-migrant-crisis-eu-content-analysis-five-european.html [Accessed 10 April 2022].

Bush, R., Martiniello, G. and Mercer, C. (2011) 'Humanitarian imperialism', *Review of African Political Economy*, 38(129): 357–65

Carrera, S., Blockmans S., Grosand D. and Guild, E. (2015) 'The EU's response to the refugee crisis. Taking stock and setting policy priorities', *CEPS Essay*, No. 20: 16.

Casas-Cortes, M. and Cobarrubias, S. (2019) 'Genealogies of contention in concentric circles: remote migration control and its Eurocentric geographical imaginaries', in K. Mitchell, R. Jones and J. Fluri (eds) *Handbook on Critical Geographies of Migration*, Cheltenham: Edward Edgar Publishing, pp 193–205.

Collett, E. and Le Coz, C. (2018) *After the Storm: Learning from the EU Response to the Migration Crisis*, Brussels: MPI Europe.

De Genova, N. (2013) 'Spectacles of migrant "illegality": the scene of exclusion, the obscene of inclusion', *Ethnic and Racial Studies*, 36(7): 1180–98.

De Genova, N. (2017) 'Introduction', in N. De Genova (ed), *The Borders of "Europe": Autonomy of Migration, Tactics of Bordering*, Durham: Duke University Press, pp 1–37.

De Genova, N. (2018) 'The "migrant crisis" as racial crisis: do *Black Lives Matter* in Europe?', *Ethnic and Racial Studies*, 41(10): 1765–82.

Duncan, I. and Levidis, S. (2020) '"Weaponizing a river": at the border', *e-flux architecture*, [online] Available from: https://www.e-flux.com/architecture/at-the-border/325751/weaponizing-a-river/ [Accessed 26 December 2020].

Fairclough, N. (2001) *Language and Power*, London: Longman.

FIDH, Migreurop, REMDH (2014) *Frontex Greece-Turkey: The Borders of Denial*, Paris: FIDH.

Forensic Architecture (2020) 'Pushbacks across the Evros/Meriç river: situated testimony. Investigations', [online] Available from: https://forensic-architecture.org/investigation/evros-situated-testimony [Accessed 26 December 2020].

Frangiskou, A., Kandylis G., Mouriki A., Sarris N., Stathopoulou T., Thanopoulou M., Tsiganou J. and Varouxi C. (2020) *From Reception to Integration: Migrant Populations in Greece During and in the Aftermath of the Crisis*, Athens: National Centre for Social Research.

Gregory, D. (2004) *The Colonial Present: Afghanistan, Palestine, Iraq*, Oxford: Blackwell Publishing.

Hadjimichalis, C. (2018) *Crisis Spaces: Structures, Struggles and Solidarity in Southern Europe*, London: Routledge.

Hage, G. (2016) 'Etat de siege: a dying domesticating colonialism?', *American Ethnologist*, 43(1): 38–49.

Hall, S. and Massey, D. (2010) 'Interpreting the crisis', in R. Grayson and J. Rutherford (eds) *After The Crash: Re-inventing the Left in Britain*, London: Lawrence and Wishart, pp 37–46.

Hellenic Republic Ministry of Foreign Affairs, The (2020) Statements by Prime Minister Kyriakos Mitsotakis in Kastanies, Evros, following his visit with the heads of the EU institutions at the Greek-Turkish border. Available from: https://primeminister.gr/en/2020/03/03/23458 [Accessed 26 December 2020].

Hess, S. and Kasparek, B. (2017) 'Under control? Or border (as) conflict: reflections on the European border regime', *Social Inclusion*, 5(3): 58–68.

Hirschon, R. (2004) (ed), *Crossing the Aegean, an Appraisal of the 1923 Compulsory Population Exchange Between Greece and Turkey*, New York: Berghan Books.

Human Rights 360 (2020) *During and After Crisis: Evros Border Monitoring Report November 2019–April 2020*, Athens: Human Rights 360.

Human Rights Watch (2013) *Unwelcome Guests: Greek Police Abuses of Migrants in Greece*, New York: Human Rights Watch.

Ioannidis, S. (2020) 'Shields and Europe', Kathimerini, [online] 4 March, Available from (in Greek): https://www.kathimerini.gr/opinion/1067521/aspides-kai-eyropi/ [Accessed 20 November 2020].

Karadağ, S. (2019) 'Extraterritoriality of European borders to Turkey: an implementation perspective of counteractive strategies', *Comparative Migration Studies*, 7(12).

Karamanidou, L. (2015) 'The Securitisation of European Migration Policies: Perceptions of Threat and Management of Risk', in G. Lazaridis, et al. *The Securitisation of Migration in the EU*, London: Palgrave Publishing, pp 37–61.

Keyden, C. (2004) 'The consequences of the exchange of populations for Turkey', in R. Hirschon (ed), *Crossing the Aegean, an appraisal of the 1923 compulsory population exchange between Greece and Turkey*, New York: Berghan Books, pp 39–53.

Klein, B. (1994) *Strategic Studies and World Order: The Global Politics of Deterrence*, Cambridge: Cambridge University Press.

Lemberg-Pedersen, M. (2019) 'Manufacturing displacement: externalization and postcoloniality in European migration control', *Global Affairs*, 5(3): 247–71.

Loyd, J., Mitchell-Eaton, E. and Mountz, A. (2016) 'The militarization of islands and migration: tracing human mobility through US bases in the Caribbean and the Pacific', *Political Geography* 53: 65–75.

Mbembe, A. (2003) 'Necropolitics'. *Public Culture*, 15(1), 11–40.

Mbembe, A. (2019) *Necropolitics*, Durham, NC: Duke University Press.

McDonough P. and Tsourdi, E. (2012) 'Putting solidarity to the test: assessing Europe's response to the asylum crisis in Greece', Research Paper No. 231, Geneva: UNHCR.

Morrissey, J. (2013) 'The imperial present: geography, imperialism and its continued effects', in: N. Johnson, R. Schein and J. Winders (eds) *The Wiley-Blackwell Companion to Cultural Geography*, Chichester: Wiley-Blackwell.

Neilson, B. (2018) 'The currency of migration', *South Atlantic Quarterly*, 117(2): 375–96.

New Keyword Collective (2016) 'Europe/crisis: new keywords of "the crisis" in and of "Europe"', [online] Available from http://nearfuturesonline.org/wp-content/uploads/2016/01/New-Keywords-Collective_12.pdf [Accessed 20 November 2020].

Newsroom (2020a) 'From Afghanistan (comes) the 64% of those arrested at Evros', Kathimerini, [online] 5 March, Available (in Greek), from: https://www.kathimerini.gr/politics/1067745/apo-to-afganistan-to-64-ton-syllifthenton-ston-evro/ [Accessed 28 June 2022].

Newsroom (2020b) 'Undiminished the pressure at Evros: blockade to 4,600 entry attempts', Kathimerini, [online] 4 March, Available (in Greek), from: https://www.kathimerini.gr/politics/1067573/ameioti-i-piesi-ston-evro-mploko-se-4-600-apopeires-eisodoy/ [Accessed 28 December 2020].

Nielsen, N. (2012) 'Fortress Europe: a Greek wall close up', euobserver, Available from: https://euobserver.com/fortress-eu/118565 [Accessed 28 December 2020].

Oran, B. (2004) 'The story of those who stayed: lessons from articles 1 and 2 of the 192a Convention', in R. Hirschon (ed), *Crossing the Aegean: An Appraisal of the 1923 Compulsory Population Exchange Between Greece and Turkey*, New York: Berghan Books, pp 97–117.

Pallister-Wilkins, P. (2015) 'The humanitarian politics of European border policing: Frontex and border police in Evros', *International Political Sociology* 9: 53–69.

Reisigl, M. and Wodak, R. (2009) 'The discourse-historical approach (DHA)', in R. Wodak and M. Meyer, (eds) *Methods of Critical Discourse Analysis*, London: Sage.

Said, E. (1993) *Culture and Imperialism*, New York: Vintage.

Sardar, Z. (1999) *Orientalism*. Buckingham: Open University Press.

Saucier, P. and Woods, T. (2014) 'Ex aqua: the Mediterranean Basin, Africans on the move, and the politics of policing', *Theoria* 61(141).

Sheller, M. (2018) *Mobility Justice: The Politics of Movement in an Age of Extremes*. London: Verso.

Stoler, A. (2013) (ed) *Imperial Debris: On Ruins and Ruination*, Durham, NC: Duke University Press.

Stern, T. (2016) 'Responses to the "refugee crisis": what is the role of self-image among EU countries?', *European Policy Analysis*, 10: 1–16.

Tzimas S. (2020a) 'What is happening in Kastanies: a "letter" from Evros', Kathimerini, [online] 1 March, Available (in Greek) from: https://www.kathimerini.gr/society/1067125/ti-symvainei-stis-kastanies-ena-gramma-apo-ton-evro/ [Accessed 20 November 2020].

Tzimas, S. (2020b) 'A setting of tension at Evros after the respite', Kathimerini, [online] 5 March, Available (in Greek) from: https://www.kathimerini.gr/politics/1067596/skiniko-entasis-ston-evro-meta-tin-anapayla/ [Accessed 20 November 2020].

Üstübici, A. (2019) 'The impact of externalized migration governance on Turkey: technocratic migration governance and the production of differentiated legal status'. *CMS*, 7, 46.

Vaiou, D. and Stratigaki, M. (2008) 'From "settlement" to "integration": informal practices and social services for women migrants in Athens', *European Urban and Regional Studies*, 15(2): 119–31.

Walia, H. (2013) *Undoing Border Imperialism*, Chico, CA: AK Press.

Walters, W. (2011) 'Foucault and frontiers: notes on the birth of the humanitarian border', in U. Brockling, S. Krasmann and T. Lemke (eds) *Governmentality: Current Issues and Future Challenges*, New York: Routledge, pp 138–64.

Wodak, R. and Meyer, M. (eds.) (2009) *Methods of Critical Discourse Analysis* (2nd revised edn), London: Sage.

10

The Practice of 'Sanctuary' and Refugee Protection in India

Nasreen Chowdhory and Shamna Thacham Poyil

Introduction

Historically, sanctuary has been conceived as an uninfringeable space, which offered protection from violence or fear of potential violence. Protection involved a geographical transition of crossing borders from a territory of persecution or potential persecution to a territory of refuge. The idea of sanctuary and its practices have been associated with multiple religions including Buddhism, Christianity, Islam and Hinduism, or more specifically in the biblical 'cities of refuge' (Bagelman, 2016: 20). The 'practice of sanctuary' consolidates not just the act or exercise of providing sanctuary, but also the customs and principles on which such sanctuary was sought and provided. For example, Darling (2010) refutes the idea that sanctuary is a spatially rigid notion of providing protection, and argues that it should rather be seen as a qualified and dynamic act that was not tied to enclosed spaces, but extended to the protection authorized by churches and other places of worship.

This chapter conceptualizes 'sanctuary' not as the 'safe zone' or 'zones of peace' but rather as *indigenous practices* of various societies. We use India as a case study for exploring this. Countries such as India have opened their borders to refugees in a rather uncalculated manner, reflecting a culture of hospitality based on its legacy of repeatedly providing sanctuary. The chapter analyses the 'performativity' of the state in reproducing the figurative practices of extending hospitality to the various groups of people that have sought asylum within the Indian territory. It asserts that the provisions of sanctuary based on state performativity of hospitality eventually transmute to an identity-based protection. The chapter is divided into two sections: first, the historical practice of sanctuary is discussed, based on philosophical understanding and the state's performativity of hospitality. Second, the postcolonial understanding of 'citizenship as belonging' and practices of sanctuary in India is focused upon. The two are brought together in the conclusion.

The historical practice of sanctuary and the state's performativity of hospitality

The usage of the concept 'practice of sanctuary' attempts to consolidate not just the act or exercise of providing sanctuary, but also the customs and principles based on which such sanctuary was sought and provided. Mitchell (2007: 4) postulates that practices of sanctuary 'appear continuous and universal'. The author cites the early scholarly literature of Edward Westermarck (1909) to establish how 'Barotse in Southern Africa, the Acagchemen Indians in California, the Aruntas in central Australia, Ashanti in Ghana, Samoans in Pacific' were communities which engaged in practices of sanctuary. The works of Francisco Benet (1957) and William Lewis (1961) further support the existence of similar practices in Morocco (Mitchell, 2007: 4). England's Henry VIII is considered to have established seven permanent cities of refuge, with a criterion that sanctuary would be denied for those who have committed 'heinous' crimes such as murder, robbery or arson (Mitchell, 2007: 5) and that the nature of protection offered in sanctuaries would be 'limited and conditional, never absolute' (Mitchell, 2007: 6). The 'city of refuge' in Israel, where the semi-institutionalized practice of providing sanctuary in shrines, temples and other places of worship expanded the association between vulnerability and asylum.

In Greek, the notion of 'asylia' propounds the sacrosanct nature of a territory of sanctuary that was not to be breached (Sinn, 1993: 86), with the condition of 'hiketes' – wherein the claimant publicly declared reasons and conditions for seeking protection (Mitchell, 2007). Three types of sanctuaries existed in ancient Greece – urban sanctuaries within the polis, intra-urban sanctuaries in 'no man's land' but under administrative control of the polis, and extra-urban sanctuaries located in remote locations away from the city. According to Marinatos and Heagg (1993), protection in Greek sanctuaries was extended not just to vulnerable people such as political dissenters fearing persecution, but also offenders of crimes.

The Christian biblical reference of God's provision of sanctuary to Cane, and the Old Testament indication of Hebrew establishment of cities of refuge, showcase the Western tradition of offering sanctuary. Ancient Greek works such as the writings of Homer and the classical Roman scripts of Cicero indicate the conditions in which asylum is sought and sanctuary is provided, along with the rights of incumbent 'foreigners' (Isayev, 2017).

The Christian Church's practices of sanctuary in the European Middle Ages embodied the idea that there was no offence that God would not absolve, if a person asked for salvation. The practice of sanctuary provided by the Church during the Roman empire entailed the 'right to sanctuary' as much as the accompanying customary provision of protection, with certain regulations to claim refuge (Mitchell, 2007: 12). In medieval Europe, sanctuary cities provided protection that was on a par with freedom to the erstwhile serfs and slaves who had escaped from bondage (Schwarz, 2008). Bauder (2017) equates such a practice with the contemporary practice of offering asylum to the stateless non-citizen.

The erosion of older religious sites of sanctuary and sanctuary cities demarcated for protection with the enforcement of state sovereignty in the post Westphalian order, led to new forms of sanctuary such as political asylum being practiced from the 20th century onwards. The proliferation of the language of 'illegal' migrants and anti-asylum policy during the late 20th century, created due to the politics of exclusion institutionalized by certain states, caused churches in countries including Norway, Sweden and Germany to again provide sanctuary to the rejected asylum seekers (Bauder, 2017; Millner, 2013). This new discourse and practice of sanctuary protection had 'illegal immigrants' and refugees as its focus, rather than including political dissenters or criminals (Bauder, 2017). Areas referred to as 'zones of peace' and safe havens also emerged in other contexts. They tried to provide protection and ameliorate suffering in the aftermath of wars and civil conflicts, thereby maintaining tentative spaces of peace (Hancock and Iyer, 2007).

The hyphenation of the concept of hospitality with the practice of sanctuary is necessary, as sanctuary involves the transgression of borders. The crossing of sovereign borders creates the categories of 'guest' and 'host' who seek and, in turn, provide sanctuary; thus, bringing the notion of hospitality into the frame. The idea and tradition of hospitality can be traced to the Greek custom of hospitality called 'Xenia'; mentioned in classical literature such as the Iliad and the Odyssey (see also Chapter 9). But African epic Sundiata or Sanskrit couplets from Taittriya Upanishad, were also rooted on the notion that God would visit masquerading as a stranger. Hospitality, or 'hospitium',[1] was perceived to be the deific right of the guest, and an obligatory duty for the host to perform. In the Indian tradition, Hindu rituals of worship are based on the premonition that god is the divine guest who deserves the utmost hospitality from the host. Thus, across all cultures, offering hospitality to those who seek refuge was based on conscientious compulsion, kinship-based affinity or even strategic reciprocity (Chowdhory and Poyil, 2019a).

The theological histories of almost all religions involve accounts of migration – both voluntary and forced. In Islam, the notion of 'hijra' which is translated as flight/emigration and concepts like 'muhajir' (emigrant/exile) or 'ibn sabil' (wayfarer) – those who are obliged to receive protection – reflects the tryst of forced migration and protection in Islam. Psalms 16, 27, 51 and 52 show similar relevance in Judaeo-Christian scripts (Marfleet, 2007). The exodus of almost 10,000 Jews from Spain due to their refusal to be forcibly baptized, and similar expulsions of the Protestant populace in France in 1590 causing them to seek refuge in Prussia (Dezayuas, 1988), depict the instances of transgression of established boundaries without state orchestration by the receiving state. The Zoroastrian population who fled to Gujarat in India in the 12th century due to the collapse of the Sassanid Empire were given refuge and eventually integrated within Indian society. The Jewish population who fled Roman persecution 2,100 years ago also found sanctuary in India. Thus, ancient and medieval practices of providing sanctuary prove that managing the collective influx of refugees or migrants once functioned outside the ambit of the legal institution of the state. Mobility is one of the most permanent attributes of humans. Migrating to distant lands for reasons including conquest, trade and cultural propagation have been recorded throughout history. In some cases, the relative ease with which people could find refuge elsewhere, leading to their eventual integration into the host society, has led to the understanding of some migrant groups as assets rather than liabilities; assets with the potential to contribute to the capital wealth of the territory, as producers and taxpayers (Marrus, 1988: 2; see also Chapter 3). With the emergence of the nation-state, managing and establishing control over such large-scale migrations became central to statecraft for 'imagining and socially producing the state's territorial order' (Soguk, 1999: 244).

In European philosophy, Levinias conceptualizes hospitality as a metaphysical relationship based on unconditional love for a fellow human, notwithstanding his/her complete otherness from the self. This conceptualization hypothesizes a scenario wherein the host becomes 'hostage' to the love reciprocated by the guest, precluding any possibility of 'possessively possessing' the guest (Isayev, 2017: 80), ultimately casting the guest into the domain of perpetual exile (Doukhan and Levinas, 2014). In a world where human exile is the perpetual reality (Levinas, 1999) and where no one can be a material possession of another, the strangeness in loving the stranger thus transmutes into a complex relationship of hospitality. Levinisian ethics of hospitality are the unconditional welcoming and love for the complete stranger – the utmost 'other'. In the Derridean view, Levinas imagines the strangeness of welcoming and then loving a stranger, that could lead to a hypothetical future relationship between the host and the guest (Makris, 2015). In conceiving hospitality as unconditional, Derridean philosophy suggests this constitutes an act of generosity that in turn generates a responsibility to the guest. It is an imperceptible connection that brings 'self' and 'other' towards a range of proximity conditioned by the permanence of perpetual exile that humans are caught in. Levinisian hospitality can be summed up as an amalgamation of both 'ethics of hospitality' and 'politics of hospitality' in which 'the right of man' has its relevance only in relation to the 'right of the other man' (Levinas, 1999: 128).

Derrida's conceptualization of hospitality as an ambivalent concept indicates an eagerness to invite or receive the other (Derrida and Dufourmantelle, 2000). In doing so, both guest and host intercede the 'border' as a zone of demarcation between two distinct spheres. Hence, hospitality cannot be reduced to an altruistic gesture embedded in compassion to the fellow human – it contains in itself the notion of colossal cordiality where the guest is treated no worse than any king. But the same unquestioned acceptance and welcoming of the stranger is inherent to the act of hospitality – which is covertly political. Even for legal immigrants, categorizations of 'visa required', 'visa not required', 'visa-on-arrival' and so on, shows that those who enter the territory, whether refugee or not, receive different levels of hospitality. Derrida therefore differentiates between the 'law of unconditional hospitality' and conditional 'laws of hospitality'. Indeed, the conditional laws of hospitality and law of unconditional hospitality are mutually constitutive (Chowdhory and Poyil, 2019a). To uphold conditional laws of hospitality is not to be mistaken with the beginning of complete erosion of unconditional hospitality. In relation to unconditional hospitality, it is implied that a state has to open its borders to welcome one and all, without any expectations in return. This indicates two aspects: as much as it demonstrates the power and capability of the host state to shelter and provide, it equally signifies the vulnerability of those who seek refuge. But the fortification of the nation-state as the cornerstone of the international political order, undermines claims to hospitality.

The sovereign authority of the state increasingly prioritizes national security over the principles on which sanctuary was provided and hospitality was offered in the past. It is here that it is necessary to move away from the meta-philosophical conceptualization of hospitality and to understand hospitality as a performative act of 'political responsibility' (Schiff, 2018). Parekh (2013) argues that the 'harm' done to refugees and stateless people is both 'legal/political harm' that entails the denial of citizenship and an 'ontological harm' that involves the denial of 'fundamental human qualities' (on the exclusion of refugees from theory-building in Ethics of Migration, see Chapter 11). This responsibility can be distinguished from the moral responsibility that is conceptualized in the works of Levinas and Derrida as the ethics of 'unconditional hospitality'. Irrespective of its resource base and strategic limitations, India, through its practice of sanctuary, has been demonstrating its share of 'political responsibility' to refugees and asylum seekers. In the absence of a regime of protection, the practice of refuge is based in deep-rooted customs and practices. The idea of humanitarianism that is based on morality, justice and mutual aid is central to this in relation to letting refugees enter India. The following section examines the idea of belonging based on the territorial notion of citizenship in postcolonial India and how this has shaped the practice of sanctuary.

The practice of sanctuary and the politics of belonging in postcolonial India

The practice of providing sanctuary is embedded in the cultural norms of individual nations, 'though their adaptations involve an inherent variation due to the differences in the modalities of laws, rules and regulations that are applied on an everyday basis' (Chowdhory and Poyil, 2019a). Yet, any hospitality provided 'constantly negotiates the spatial factor whereby "being inside" is privileged over "coming from outside", where inside and outside are constantly positioned against each other' (Chowdhory et al, 2019). Those who have been inside consolidate themselves to 'us' by constantly differentiating themselves from the 'Other' outsiders. The 'territorially trapped gaze' (Lax and Lemberg-Pedersen, 2019: 8) that is prevalent in demarcating individuals as 'us' and 'them' on the basis of spatial boundaries could be ascribed to the dominance of the modern nation-state (for a similar point concerning the postcolonial Greek/Turkish borderlands, see also Chapter 9). Practices of sanctuary in postcolonial India occur in the context of 'citizenship as belonging' but sanctuary provision eventually transmutes to 'identity-based protection' within this broader context.

It is imperative to note the trajectory of protection that evolved in the Indian subcontinent from the colonial to the later postcolonial period. The movement of migrant labour across the border to work in the plantations or other imperial military expeditions was determined by the imperial need to appropriate colonial resources of the British Crown. Interestingly, the strategic alliances with princely states and petty kingdoms did not necessitate protection or practices of political sanctuary. The consolidation of erstwhile imperial borders to the territory of an independent nation was coherent with the transition of 'colonial subject' to the 'political subject' of a sovereign nation-state (Samaddar, 2015). Unlike the homogeneous state formation in western nation-states, the newly independent nation-states (in this context India and Pakistan) formed out of the violent partition of British India. This created splintered identities with multiple fault lines along ethnicity, language and culture. Consequently, partition resulted in an ambiguous belonging for those political subjects who internalized as sacrosanct the territorial borders of their new nation-states. The vestiges of the same colonial legacy prove instrumental in understanding how India's postcolonial citizenship law has been a temporal and spatial project imbibing the essentialities of a modern nation-state that was habituated to 'exclude and limit' rather than 'include and embrace'. Thus, the construct of citizenship facilitated the perpetuation of the territorial gaze of distinguishing between 'us' and 'them' depending on which side of the India/Pakistan border one was located.

People's affinity with identities such as ethnicity and religion is significant in the constitution of Indian citizenship. Such affinities need to be viewed through a postcolonial lens to understand how the very same citizenship that is vital for political inclusion becomes vital in segregation, differentiation and repudiation, even for refugees who seek protection. In an overt illustration of how the colonial past still shapes and apprises the postcolonial present of these South Asian countries, the protection regime for refugees in India still conflates refugees with foreigners through the Foreigner's Act of 1946.[2] When analysed empirically, refugee status in these nations is often not based on legal refugee frameworks, but on kinship affinity or strategic relations with the country of origin of these refugees (Chowdhory et al, 2019). As Samaddar (2003: 22) points out, refugee policy for any country is an account of how it 'takes care and limits care' to a segment of people who are not its citizens. So having a concerted refugee policy or not having one at all is a reflection of how any nation-state wields and extends its power to include and exclude (Chowdhory et al, 2019, on the care/control nexus, see also Chapters 6 and 7).

Based on the relationship between 'us' and the 'Other' refugee groups, varying degrees of hospitality are performed by the Indian state. In the case of the Partition refugees and the creation of the 'Rehabilitation Finance Administration Act of 1948',[3] this transformed the 'regime of rights' into a 'regime of charity' for the refugees. Similarly, Tibetan refugees have been supported using various rehabilitation and resettlement plans along with the provision of registration certificates (RC) and have even been given permission to establish a 'Tibetan Government in exile' under the regulatory supervision of the Indian government. Such an approach can be considered a manifestation of a balancing act where the state's performativity of hospitality carefully weighs between a Derridean notion of the 'politics of hospitality' and the 'ethics of hospitality'. In comparison, the hospitality that the Tamil refugees from Sri Lanka received in India could be attributed to their cultural proximity with the Tamils in India, which overcame the fault line between 'us' and 'them' where the host could see a semblance of themselves in the guest. Arguably, protection or sanctuary has largely been based on a recognition of vulnerability, and can be understood as a continuation of the Indian state's obligation to the legacy of state performativity of hospitality.

The Citizenship Amendment Act of 2019 (CAA), which permits citizenship for Hindu, Buddhist and other non-Muslim minorities escaping religious oppression in the neighbouring states of Bangladesh and Pakistan, reflects a calculated appropriation of hospitality based on cultural affinity. The

Act is problematic in two ways – first, it overtly defines 'who can be a citizen in India' and second, it covertly envisages a highly restrictive framework of refugee protection by determining 'who is worthy of protection from *religious* persecution'. The CAA determines that protection is conditioned on the religious identity of the claimant, rather than the vulnerability that necessitated them seeking refuge in the first place.

An analysis of the political membership of the individual institutionalized through Indian citizenship is necessary to understand how provision of sanctuary is entwined with the identity of the claimant. There is an implicit relationship expressed in Indian citizenship law between citizenship, nationality and identity, such that despite being independent variables in the analysis of political membership, they occasionally act in mutual congruence to designate the contours of exclusion from the same political membership. If being a 'national' facilitates the default attainment of rights for a citizen, non-citizens will receive a very minimal and basic set of rights. In the Indian constitution the provisions of Part III such as Article 14 (the right to equality); Article 21 (the right to personal life and liberty); and Article 25 (the freedom to practice and propagate one's own religion), are guaranteed to non-citizens as much as citizens. Legally, the commonality between citizens and non-citizens ends there. For the South Asian countries such as India, 'national identities are tied to legal position by virtue of citizenship laws' and thereby facilitate the carving of boundaries of inclusion and exclusion based on the same citizenship laws (Chowdhory, 2019: 43). This is evident in the way the temporal and spatial constructs of citizenship instituted by the state become markers for enabling and disabling individuals from claiming the membership of the state.

The legality of citizenship discourses in India lets it 'oscillate ambivalently between encompassment and closure, creating a differential layering of citizenship' (Roy, 2008: 220). With the implementation of the CAA this ambivalence in citizenship spills over to the protection for refugees, which makes the non-citizen the 'constitutive outsider' now precluded from substantive protection (Roy, 2008: 221). If law cements the membership of individuals to a state through citizenship, and their relationship with immediate civil society is also then enforced through the rule of law, then law is instrumental in perpetuating the segregation of non-citizens from full members of the state, reducing their existence to the mere label 'refugee'. The postcolonial state of India has therefore inherited not just the administrative state apparatus of its colonial masters, but also the classification of its colonial subjects to distinct categories (Chowdhory, 2019). Such categorical segregation was based on a territorially rooted belonging as that can be visible in the branding of Chakmas in India, Biharis in Bangladesh or Estate Tamils in Sri Lanka. Citizenship, then, denotes not just the rights emanating from it, but also roots a person's belonging in the nation-state.

It effectively becomes the umbilical cord between the individual and the body politic.

The conflation of cultural, racial or ethnic markers with national identity has led some scholars to examine the 'politics of belonging' (Favell, 1999; Yuval-Davis, 2006; Antonsich, 2010; Chowdhory, 2018). Nira Yuval-Davis (2007: 7), for example, views citizenship as an 'abstract category', an 'embodied category involving concrete people who are differentially situated in terms of gender, class, ethnicity, sexuality, ability, state in the life cycle etc'. The categorization focuses on the relationship between the individual and the state; as a means to achieve the ends of rights bestowed and guaranteed by full membership in any nation-state. The 'embodied category' corresponds to the notion of 'multi-layered citizen' (Yuval-Davis, 1997) who has affiliation of varying degrees to multiple political communities. The impact of such a multifarious connection is more problematic for refugees and stateless individuals than others. Such a perspective refutes the liberal notion of citizenship that emphasizes the prominence of the nation-state in citizenship, and is more in alignment with the cosmopolitan framework of citizenship. Hannah Arendt's conceptualization of citizenship as the 'right to have rights' reflects the importance of this rudimentary requisite for anyone to survive (Arendt, 1973: 296).

Yuval-Davis (2007: 11) perceives belonging as denoting the 'emotional dimension' which entails 'love' for one's own country, 'hatred' for the 'Other' who has the potential to pollute it and 'fear and anxiety' regarding the perpetual threat that the 'Other' constitutes to 'our' cultural purity. Roy (2010) opines that amendments to the Indian Citizenship Act of 1955 showcase the centrality of migrants to the discourse of citizenship. The cataclysm of partition and the subsequent state-building of postcolonial India required the Citizenship Act of 1955 to be perceived as a limited, but largely inclusive definition of citizenship that validated associational belonging (Rodrigues, 2005). The provisional and temporary protection these groups received on entry as refugees can be attributed to the performativity of hospitality that involved both the political responsibility and humanitarian concerns of the state. But the eventual amendments in 1986, 2003 and 2005 brought about a negative bias to the category 'migrant', conflating it with 'illegality' and thereby casting the migrant as the 'Other' (Roy, 2010).

The CAA of 2019 is a further departure from the pluralist notion of citizenship brought about by the democratic constitution of India. It brings in segregation and exclusion based on religious difference and simultaneously sets in motion a paradigmatic shift from the principle of *jus soli* to *jus sanguinis* based on religious identity (Jayal, 2017). By excluding certain categories of migrants from claiming citizenship, but permitting other persecuted minorities the same privilege, the CAA challenges the democratic ethos of equality. There exists a continual incongruity between a democratic ethos of equality and the notion of inclusion. Normatively, the notion of inclusion is embedded in the democratic attributes of equality and representative government. But this often sanctions a recurrent practice of *exclusion* when realized through the platform of citizenship. Román (2010: 11) argues that the history of citizenship is to 'extol[s] the virtues of equality for all members within a given society' despite the fact that citizenship has 'legitimated a millennia-long practice of forbidding many members of those societies from enjoying that equality'. They constitute the subservient individuals of the polity who undergo the 'alien-citizen paradox' (Román, 2010: 11) that constantly reminds them of their otherness. Creation of such hierarchies of subordinated co-existence through systematic inclusion and exclusion is 'citizenship's dark little secret' (Román, 2010: 6).

As noted previously, the notion of 'vulnerability' itself has undergone a paradigmatic shift, morphing into 'identity centric vulnerability' claims. The idea of 'vulnerability' in refugee discourse involves fear, denial, deprivation, powerlessness, ambiguity and invisibility; all emanating from the structural exclusion and persecution that precipitated their perilous forced migration (Zolberg et al, 1989; Kibreab, 2004). UNHCR (2010: 4) measures vulnerability based on variables including 'exposure to trauma, human rights violations and other hardships and conditions. Additionally, various humanitarian agencies backed by various international conventions have put forth 'hierarchical categories of vulnerability' (Moritz, 2012: 123) brought about by the combination of variables such as 'age, sex, ethnicity, health' (Morawa, 2003: 140). The Indian CAA asserts that Hindus, Sikhs, Jains, Buddhists, Christians and Parsis from neighbouring Afghanistan, Pakistan and Bangladesh would be considered as individuals of 'minority communities' and hence 'shall not be treated as illegal migrants for purposes of this act' enabling them to apply for citizenship within 6 years of residence, as opposed to the usual 12 years residence criteria. The qualification of vulnerability in the CAA would in turn exclude undesirable refugees from claiming protection and sanctuary by juxtaposing the inclusion of those who voluntarily claim to have entered the country by 'illegal' means (that is, without proper paperwork and documentation).

The precarity of asylum seekers encompasses the anticipation and uncertainty that the state will be compassionate and provide care to some, while excluding others based on a well-curated narrative of territorialized belonging (Chowdhory and Poyil, 2019b). David Farrier (2011: 157) argues that while providing asylum through its authority to include and exclude, the sovereign state also showcases its inherent power to constitute a 'legitimate narrative'. This legitimate narrative presupposes the one who seeks refuge as someone who does not typify the stark contrast between 'us' and 'them', but rather is a 'knowable and nameable figure' (Malkki, 1995: 498) who doesn't pose a threat. It is the narrative of being the 'absolute other' that causes the state to offer conditional hospitality to many refugee groups that cross its borders. To the host, the 'absolute others' are guests who have the potential to upset the very existence of the household (Deutscher, 2001: 94). Any permanence to the protection offered to them will cause the margins between guest and host to become obsolete both spatially and temporally. The space where they co-exist, and the duration for which they co-exist, and even the medium such as language through which they negotiate such co-existence, all of these contrive a common platform that diminishes the fault lines. The 'absolute other' is to always be on the other side of the margin that should never be breached.

Conclusion

The state performs hospitality by opening its borders to the vulnerable and thereby providing them sanctuary, but later institutes hierarchical practices of protection to various groups (Chowdhory et al, 2019). Such discretion of the sovereign state, which demonstrates the practice of 'inclusion through exclusion', (Agamben, 1998: 18) should not be considered as an upgrade from their earlier plight and deprivation, but rather as a perpetuation of 'bare life' in a different form. Changes that occurred with the formation of nation-states also brought a corresponding change in the nature of sanctuary practices. As rightly observed by Philip Marfleet (2011), the idea of protection nominally remained similar, but the nature and pattern of protection changed drastically. Unlike the sanctuary cities of the past which exerted their own pastoral or theological authority, the notion of sanctuary is now completely under the sovereign control of the state. The legal subjectivity of the refugee reinforces de-politicization to ensure the continuation of 'bare life'. Agamben (1998: 144), in making a distinction between 'bare life' and 'full life', claims that bare life is a manifestation of the covert sovereign power of the state. The precarious existence of the refugee exposes them time and again to the prevalent sovereign state power that construes restrictive and categorical protection to refugees, essentially converting the 'humanitarian' underpinnings of sanctuary to a politically driven 'religious identity' based protection.

The Indian CAA of 2019 can be seen as an effort to enforce such a politics of belonging, wherein territories are demarcated according to the religious collective identity of individuals. If not emphasizing the rightful people who belong to the nation, the Act emphasizes 'who does not belong' and construes a hierarchy of unequal rights to refugees and forced migrants seeking refuge from persecution. We have argued that the CAA was an organic extension of existing exclusions of some of different faith and religion, thereby making the Muslim migrants the 'absolute other'. The Indian practice of sanctuary where the state performs hospitality based on humanitarianism is now withering away only to be replaced by calculated political acts of 'selective protection' to those who conform to the state narrative of 'homogeneous nationhood'.

Notes

1 http://penelope.uchicago.edu/Thayer/E/Roman/Texts/secondary/SMIGRA*/Hospitium.html

2 https://indiacode.nic.in/bitstream/123456789/6803/1/foreigners_act_1946.pdf

3 http://legislative.gov.in/actsofparliamentfromtheyear/rehabilitation-finance-administration-act-1948

References

Agamben, G. (1998) *Homo Sacer: Sovereign Power and Bare Life*, Stanford: Stanford University Press.

Antonsich, M. (2010) 'Searching for belonging – an analytical framework', *Geography Compass*, 4(6): 644–59.

Arendt, H. (1973 [1951]) *The Origins of Totalitarianism* (Revised edn), New York: Harcourt Brace Jovanovich.

Bagelman, J.J. (2016) 'Still waiting: security, *temporality*, population', in *Sanctuary City: A Suspended State*, London: Palgrave Macmillan.

Bauder, H. (2017) 'Sanctuary cities: policies and practices in international perspective', *International Migration*, 55(2): 174–87.

Benet, F. (1957) 'Explosive markets: the Berber highlands', in K. Polyani, K. Arensberg and H.W. Pearson, *Trade and Markets in the Early Empires: Economies in History and Theory*, New York: Collier-Macmillan, pp 188–217.

Chowdhory, N. (2018) 'State formation, marginality and belonging: contextualising rights of refugees in India, Bangladesh and Sri Lanka', in *Refugees, Citizenship and Belonging in South Asia: Contested Terrains*, Singapore: Springer Nature Singapore, pp 43–69.

Chowdhory, N. (2019) 'Citizenship and membership: placing refugees', in N. Uddin and N. Chowdhory (eds) *Deterritorialised Identity and Transborder Movement in South Asia*, Singapore: Springer, pp 37–54.

Chowdhory, N. and Poyil, S.T. (2019a) 'Conceptualising hospitality in refugee management in India', *Asia Dialogue* [online] 20 November, Available from: https://theasiadialogue.com/2019/11/20/conceptualising-hospitality-in-refugee-management-in-india/ [Accessed 28 June 2022].

Chowdhory, N. and Poyil, S.T. (2019b) 'The global compact of refugees: a viewpoint of global South', *Refugee Watch*, 54: 1–14.

Chowdhory, N., Poyil, S.T. and Kajla, M. (2019) 'The idea of *protection*: norms and practice of refugee management in India', *Refugee Watch*, 53: 36–54.

Darling, J. (2010) 'A city of sanctuary: the relational re-imagining of Sheffield's asylum politics', *Transactions of the Institute of British Geographers*, 35(1): 125–40.

Derrida, J. and Dufourmantelle, A. (2000) *Of Hospitality* (trans. R. Bowlby), Stanford: Stanford University Press.

Deutscher, P. (2001) 'Hospitality, perfectibility, responsibility [questions to Jacques Derrida]', in P. Patton and T. Smith (eds), *Jacques Derrida: Deconstruction Engaged, The Sydney Seminars*, Sydney: Power Publications, pp 93–97.

DeZayuas, A.M. (1988) 'A historical survey of twentieth century expulsions', in A. Bramwell (ed.) *Refugees in the Age of Total War*, London: Unwin Hyman.

Doukhan, A. and Levinas, E. (2014) *A Philosophy of Exile*, London: Bloomsbury.

Farrier, D. (2011) *Postcolonial Asylum: Seeking Sanctuary Before the Law*, Liverpool: Liverpool University Press.

Isayev, E. (2017) 'Between hospitality and asylum: A historical perspective on displaced agency', *International Review of the Red Cross*, 99(1): 75–98.

Jayal, N.G. (2017) 'The 2016 Citizenship Amendment Bill consolidates a trend towards a majoritarian and exclusionary concept of Indian citizenship', *The CARAVAN* [online], Available from: https://caravanmagazine.in/vantage/2016-citizenship-amendment-bill-majoritarian-exclusionary [Accessed 28 June 2022].

Kibreab, G. (2004) 'Pulling the wool over the eyes of the strangers: refugee deceit and trickery in institutionalized settings', *Journal of Refugee Studies*, 17(2): 1–26.

Lax, V.M. and Lemberg-Pedersen, M. (2019) 'Border-induced displacement: the ethical and legal implications of distance-creation through externalization', *Questions of International Law*, 56(1): 5–33.

Levinas, E. (1999) *Alterity and Transcendence*, New York: Columbia University Press.

Lewis, W.H. (1961) 'Feuding and social change in Morocco', *Journal of Conflict Resolution*, 5(1): 43–54.

Makris, S. (2105) 'Jacques Derrida and the case of cosmopolitanism: "cities of refuge" in the twenty-first century', in D. O'Byrne and S. De La Rosa (eds) *The Cosmopolitan Ideal. Challenges and Opportunities*, London: Rowman and Littlefield International, pp 177–94.

Malkki, L. (1995) 'Refugees and exile: From "refugee studies" to the national order of things', *Annual Review of Anthropology*, 24: 495–523.

Marfleet, P. (2007) 'Refugees and history: why we must address the past', *Refugee Survey Quarterly*, 26(3): 136–48.

Marfleet, P. (2011) 'Understanding "sanctuary": faith and traditions of asylum', *Journal of Refugee Studies*, 24(1): 440–48.

Marinatos, N. and Haegg, R. (eds) *Greek Sanctuaries: New Approaches*, London: Routledge.

Marrus, M.R. (1988) 'Introduction', in A.C. Bramwell (ed) *Refugees in the Age of Total War*, London: Unwin Hyman, pp 7–32.

Millner, N. (2013) 'Sanctuary sans frontieres: social movements and solidarity in post-war Northern France', in R.K. Lippert and S. Rehaag (eds) *Sanctuary Practices in International Perspectives: Migration, Citizenship and Social Movements*, Abingdon: Routledge, pp 57–70.

Mitchell, C.R. (2007) 'The theory and practice of sanctuary: from asylia to local zones of peace', in L.E. Hancock and C.R. Mitchell (eds) *Zones of Peace*, Bloomfield, CT: Kumarian Press, pp 1–28.

Morawa, A. (2003) '"Vulnerability" as a concept in international human rights law', *Journal of International Relations and Development*, 6(2): 139–55.

Moritz, A. (2012) 'Supporting refugee women's strategies for coping with challenges during maternity in resettlement: shifting the focus from vulnerability to agency', *Revista Iberoamericana de Salud y Ciudadanía*, 1(1): 119–56.

Parekh, S. (2013) 'Beyond the ethics of admission: stateless people, refugee camps and moral obligations', *Philosophy Social Criticism* [online], DOI: 10.1177/0191453713498254.

Rodrigues, V. (2005) 'Citizenship and the Indian constitution', in R. Bhargava and H. Reifeld (eds) *Civil Society, Public Sphere and Citizenship, Dialogues and Perceptions*, New Delhi: Sage, pp 209–35.

Román, E. (2010) *Citizenship and its Exclusions: A Classical, Constitutional, and Critical Race Critique*, New York: New York University Press.

Roy, A. (2008) 'Between encompassment and closure: the "migrant" and the citizen in India', *Contributions to Indian Sociology*, 42(2): 219–48.

Roy, A. (2010) *Mapping Citizenship in India*, New Delhi: Oxford University Press.

Samaddar, R. (ed) (2003) *Refugees and the State: Practices of Asylum and Care in India*, 1947–2000, New Delhi: Sage.

Samaddar, R. (2015) 'Returning to the histories of the late 19th and early 20th century immigration', *Economic and Political Weekly*, 50(2): 49–55.

Schiff, J.L. (2018) 'Welcoming refugees: mindful citizenship and the political responsibility of hospitality', *Signs* 43(3): 737–62.

Schwarz, J. (2008) *Stadtluft Macht Frei: Leben In Der Mittelalterlichen Stadt*, Darmstadt: Primus Verlag.

Sinn, U. (1993) 'Greek sanctuaries as places of refuge', in N. Marinatos and R. Haegg (eds) *Greek Sanctuaries: New Approaches*, London: Routledge, pp 88–109.

Soguk, N. (1999) *States and Strangers: Refugees and Displacements of Statecraft*, Minneapolis: University of Minnesota Press.

UNHCR (2010) *The Heightened Risk Identification Tool (User Guide)* (2nd edn), [online] Available from: https://www.unhcr.org/4aa76c279.pdf [Accessed 28 June 2022].

Westermarck, E. (1909) 'Asylum', in J. Hastings (ed) *Encyclopedia of Religion and Ethics*, Volume II, Edinburgh: Collier, pp 161–4.

Yuval-Davis, N. (1997) *Gender and Nation*, London: Sage Publications.

Yuval-Davis, N. (2006) 'Belonging and the politics of belonging', *Patterns of Prejudice*, 40(3): 197–214.

Yuval-Davis, N. (2007) 'Intersectionality, citizenship and contemporary politics of belonging', in J. Bennet (ed) *Scratching the Surface: Democracy, Traditions, Gender*, Lahore Cantonment: Heinrich Boll Foundation.

Zolberg, A.R., Suhrke, A. and Aguayo, S. (1989) *Escape from Violence: Conflict and the Refugee Crisis in the Developing World*, New York, Oxford: Oxford University Press.

11

Refugees and Political Theorists: The Problem of Complicity

Phillip Cole

Introduction

In much political and media discourse, and humanitarian discourse, refugees and other displaced people are framed as helpless and passive victims, in need of rescue.[1] Nando Sigona observes that these discourses construct 'the refugee as an agency-less object of humanitarian intervention' (Sigona, 2014: 370). Prem Kumar Rajaram similarly points to humanitarian representations in which the forcibly displaced 'are rendered speechless and without agency' (Rajaram, 2002: 251). In this chapter I examine whether the same framing is taking place at the level of theory. My spotlight is relatively narrow, as I work in the field of political theory which discusses the ethics of membership, migration and displacement, a field which can be described as the ethics of migration, and which largely emerges from the discipline of political philosophy (for different examples spanning nationalistic to cosmopolitan variants of work in the ethics of migration, see: Walzer, 1983; Miller, 1995; 2016; Cole, 2000; Wellman and Cole, 2011; Carens, 2013; Blake, 2020). Discussions of refugees, border control, asylum and displacement are central themes of this work and my concern is the way in which these discussions are ethically framed here.

The important point is that what emerges from this literature are not only conceptual frameworks aimed at representing forced displacement as a phenomenon, but also recommendations in the form of policy proposals: as these works are primary about the *ethics* of migration, they are concerned with *what ought to be done*. In other words, some of these writers aim to represent the forcibly displaced in a *political* sense, of representing their interests. The question is, of course, in what sense are they qualified to do that, and to what extent does their position disqualify them from doing so? To an extent the focus is even narrower, as this chapter can be understood as a work of self-criticism, a questioning of my own position as a political theorist located in the global North who is working on the ethics of forced displacement, and how this may compromise my ability to come up with proposals for how the international community should approach this issue. However, despite this focus, I believe this discussion is relevant to wider academic fields of political theory, political science and social theory where these issues are discussed, and that it will raise questions and challenges that other theorists from these fields will find of interest, as the question of ethics, of *what ought to be done*, is by no means confined to the literature I have identified here. It may be that these other academic fields are more advanced than the Ethics of Migration literature in thinking about these challenges (see, for example, Mayblin and Turner, 2021), but I do think that despite some progress in those areas there is still a great deal still to do in 'displacing' the global North/Western perspective from its central position in much work on forced displacement.

Alexander Betts and Paul Collier provide an example of the problematic framing I am concerned with, explicitly identifying the provision of refuge as 'fulfilling a duty of rescue' (Betts and Collier, 2018: 6); Michael Walzer refers to 'helpless and desperate people' (1983: 51); and Christopher Heath Wellman seeks to answer the refugee question through an analogy of a baby abandoned on a doorstep in the dead of winter (Wellman and Cole, 2011: 120). Here, as in political and media discourse, refugees are often framed as helpless and passive victims in need of rescue. An alternative framing is through the concept of 'resiliency', through which refugees *are* constituted as agents but of a limited and non-political kind – I do not discuss this version of 'resiliency humanitarianism' here but it is becoming increasingly dominant in the field (Ilcan and Rygel, 2015).[2] My argument here is that there is a tendency for this body of literature to frame refugees in ways that deprive them of political agency. What is in play in all these kinds of framings is a relationship of power – refugees are framed in specific ways by the media, by Western/Northern politicians and by international humanitarian agencies and NGOs, and that framing is largely uncontested because refugees are denied the power to constitute themselves. The same relations of power are in play, I argue, in mainstream Western political theory, and have the same effect, but shifting those relations of power is not straightforward.

Importantly, it is not that the displaced are silent and powerless, but that they are in many contexts *silenced* and *disempowered* by the processes through which their life-prospects are determined. They have voices and they have agency, but those voices are not always listened to, and that agency can be constrained (for this point in the case of displaced Afro-descendant communities in Colombia, see Chapter 12). What they lack is *political* agency, which I take to be the capacity to participate in political debates and processes that bring about change in the political landscape as an equal with other participants. This may be the case, for example, where people find themselves encamped for a long period of time and without prospects for local political participation in the host country. Though, of course refugee experiences globally are diverse and some refugees do achieve political inclusion.

To move to the realm of theory, which is the focus of this chapter, in much of the literature I've described, refugees are taken to lack *theoretical* agency, by which I mean the capacity to participate in the processes that bring about change in the theoretical landscape. Of course, many scholars have had a refugee background: Hannah Arendt, Isaiah Berlin, Ernest Gellner, Judith Shklar and Isaac Deutscher are famous examples in political theory, but there are many others across academic disciplines. Behrouz Boochani is a contemporary example, and personally I have worked with students with refugee backgrounds at all levels of study who are entering academic careers, including Ali Zalme (2021), whose doctorate on Kurdish refugees living in the United Kingdom was published recently. However, in much of the ethics of migration literature, forcibly displaced people continue to be constituted as objects not subjects. They are the objects of policy, having their life-prospects determined for them by governments and international agencies – by an international regime of humanitarian governance. They are similarly objects of theory, and indeed of wider academic study.

The key issue here is representation – who gets to represent refugees? (see also Chapter 13). It seems obvious to me as a matter of justice that refugees should represent themselves, and so should participate as full political agents in the processes of decision-making about their lives, and yet the extent to which they have been excluded from the policy-making processes that deal with refugee questions is breath-taking. There have been attempts to address this, mostly recently in relation to the Global Refugee Compact (Drozdowski and Yarnell, 2019). The idea of the 'Refugee Voice' has received a great deal of attention, both from humanitarian organizations and theorists (Owen, 2018; Fine, 2019). My own view is that the debate needs to move beyond a concern for the Refugee Voice towards Refugee Agency in its political sense, such that 'we' no longer listen to refugee voices in reaching policy conclusions, but that the 'we' that reaches those conclusions is acknowledged to include refugees themselves.[3]

How this is to be done in practice is a hugely important question, but my project in this chapter is much more limited. The focus is on how similar exclusions are apparent in political theory when it addresses refugee questions, and how political theorists can meet these challenges. Again, there is a question of representation here. The title of this chapter refers to political theorists rather than political theory, and this is deliberately done in order to raise the question of position, and my own position in writing it, which I share with most scholars of immigration ethics based in European universities. I am a White middle class male European academic who has not had any of the experiences of being displaced and needing to seek protection elsewhere.[4] In what sense, then, can I represent refugees when theorizing questions of justice regarding displacement and refugeehood? 'Representation' here is ambiguous between *describing* refugees as an object of study and *speaking for* them as a normative theorist. Both are relevant here, because in the process of seeking to speak for refugees I at the same time constitute them as objects of discourse, whether I am conscious of that or not. Here I am taking seriously the feminist and postcolonial critique of much 'western' academic work (for example see Spivak, 1988; Mohanty, 2003; Young, 2001), and the argument that important dimensions of theory are determined by relationships of power. This does require me to examine my own position as the content of theory may be influenced to some extent by who gets to do it, and I have to be conscious of my role in the constitution of refugees as a specific kind of object.

One of the challenges here is that of complicity, that the conceptual framework I am working with may be in some sense complicit in the oppressive systems I am working to overthrow, and that, however benign my intentions, I may be contributing to that oppression. In Part 1 of the chapter, I examine the questions of framing, representation and agency, and I discuss the problem of complicity and the relevance of the postcolonial critique for political theorists working on refugee questions. In Part 2, I examine this challenge, and the prospects for a political theory in which refugees are not only represented, but are also present.

Part 1: Framing the refugee

As we have seen, when it comes to humanitarian discourse, the concern is that refugees are framed as helpless and passive victims, without voice or agency, and even where refugee voices are used in humanitarian discourse, there are concerns about how those voices themselves are framed (Woods, 2019; Khosravi, 2010). My interest here, however, is in the ways in which this framing of refugees and asylum seekers is also present in the ethics of migration literature, and theory's role in constituting them in this way. However, much more widespread among these theorists is not so much the *presence* of these themes, but the *absence* of the theme of political agency. In other words, the theorists working on the question of borders and protection, I would suggest, often set about their normative task of arriving at ethical solutions to refugee questions without ever entertaining the possibility that refugees could be political agents with a role to play in arriving at those solutions. David Owen notes: 'In some of my earlier work on refugees, I failed to appreciate adequately the significance of the issues of refugee choices and refugee voices to the provision of refugee protection in a way that acknowledges the dignity of refugees' (Owen, 2018: 26, n 14). I think this is an acknowledgement that I, and other political theorists who have written about refugee issues, need to sign up to (see Fine, 2019 for the kind of approach I am advocating here).

However, in this chapter I move the challenge of the presence of refugee agency beyond political processes and into theoretical ones. The problem here is a lack of realization that refugees themselves could be agents of theory. We need to be careful not to essentialize a unique refugee experience, especially given the wide understanding of who is a refugee that I am using in this chapter. This would not only be a false step, but would also create the danger of 'compartmentalizing' refugee scholars as experts on only a narrow range of theorizing about forced displacement, or indeed a narrow set of questions in political theory in general. However, their experiences of being displaced, during displacement, and after finding 'refuge', may enable them to arrive at important theoretical insights, insights which may shift the meanings and roles of fundamental concepts, and introduce new ones. For example, more complex understandings of 'home' and a more sophisticated grasp of the experience of exile are elements that have emerged from my readings of such texts. Shahram Khosravi writes eloquently of his experience of exile (Khosravi, 2010: 73–4), while Behrooz Boochani's *No Friend but the Mountains: Writing from Manus Prison* advances Manus Prison Theory as a means of understanding the relationship between Australia and its island camps (Boochani, 2018). There is, of course, a central element of autobiography in these writings and texts that are not strictly 'academic' but constitute storytelling by people with refugee backgrounds that have also been significant for me here, such as Dina Nayeri's *The Ungrateful Refugee* (2019), Gulwali Passarlay's *The Lightless Sky* (2015) and Viet Thanh Nguyen's *The Displaced* (2018).

In the field of policy and practice there is a movement towards the recognition of the importance of meaningful refugee participation. James Milner writes that since 2016 there has been 'a commitment to enhancing the role of refugees in the making and implementation of policies that affect them' (Milner, 2021: 1). Paragraph 34 of the Global Compact on Refugees states: 'responses are most effective when they actively and meaningfully engage those they are intended to protect and assist'. While Milner recognizes the challenges that still remain here, he says: 'This is a potentially significant area of innovation for the governance of the global refugee regime, especially given the regime's history of claiming that the core institution of the refugee regime has the moral and expert authority to represent the needs and interests of refugees' (Milner, 2021). At the very least, many Western political theorists working on forced migration do not seem to acknowledge that their lack of displacement experiences might limit *their* moral and expert authority to represent the needs and interests of refugees in proposing policy solutions for displaced people. This raises the challenge that political theory is a discourse of power, constitutes its subjects and objects in ways that may be limiting if not oppressive, and excludes those subjects and objects from the discourse that constitutes them.

The challenge here is to understand the processes through which political theory constitutes the refugee by operating as a discourse of power. Through these processes, political theory on immigration not only fails to comprehend that refugees could have political agency and so play a central role in arriving at value- and justice-based derived guidelines to their situation, it also fails to comprehend that refugees could be agents of theory, contributing central insights based on their experiences of being refugees. By 'discourse' here I mean a Foucauldian system of power that constitutes subjects and objects in a specific field: by 'subjects' I mean those constituted as agents with the capacity to shape the discourse itself; by 'objects' I mean those constituted as passive, without agency, who have no role in shaping the discourse of which they are the object.[5] The suggestion is that in the kind of political theory dealing with refugee questions, citizens of nation-states are constituted as subjects and so as political agents, while refugees are constituted as passive objects of control. Foucault's approach is helpful here as it provides an account of 'how human beings constitute themselves as subjects and how they treat one another as objects' (Hoy, 1986: 4).

A problem with alleging that political theory constitutes this kind of discourse is that this body of theory is extraordinarily diverse with many conflicting accounts and disagreements. However, this in itself is not an overriding challenge to seeing it as a Foucauldian discourse, as Robert Young points out. For Foucault 'discourses operate in an unstable environment of change and transformation. The objects of a discourse are quite capable of being contradictory' (Young, 2001: 403, see also Chapter 9). The important point is that: 'Discourse … constitutes the unifying force of an anonymous field whose configuration defines the possible position of speaking subjects' (Young, 2001: 404), and also 'constitutes the very objects that occupy its field' (Young, 2001: 405). Even here, Young points out, Foucault's account of discourse pushes against a simplistic division between the subject and object in the way I have characterized it. He comments: 'Within a single discourse … all sorts of strategic options, many of them distinct from and even incompatible with each other, will be developed at the peripheries' (Young, 2001: 405, on strategic use of anti-colonial discourse, see also Chapter 8).

Political theory should, then, be understood as a discourse that constitutes a field of study, and that constitutes the subjects and objects of that study, predominantly constituting the refugee as an object with the problematic aspects this brings with it. This raises challenges for those political theorists, including myself, who do not have the experiences of being a refugee. As I pointed out in the introduction, as a normative theorist addressing the question of refugees, I am representing refugees in two senses: first, I am constituting them as objects of study; and, second, I am seeking to *speak for* refugees through suggesting normative prescriptions to be applied to their situation. Both of these acts of representation are problematic, as both of them indicate a relationship of power. If I acknowledge this relationship of power, how then can I continue to speak on refugee issues?

However, before we can address the question of whether the political theorist can speak, we first have to ask: Who is the political theorist? In this context, the question has to do with the division between the political theorist as the person who contributes towards the constitution of political theory and the refugee as the object of that theory, and I am questioning that division because it assumes that political theorists and refugees are two distinct bodies of people. But as stated, the simple point is that a good many political theorists – and many other academics – have had a refugee background of one kind or another; and a good number of people with refugee status are in the process of becoming political theorists and other kinds of academic. I have noted a tendency at academic conferences and workshops, and indeed in classrooms, to assume that the 'refugee' is always outside of the room; or if there is someone with a refugee background in the room, they are present as a 'refugee' and not as an 'academic', and are therefore not in a position to make a 'proper' contribution to proceedings.

This brings us to the other question: Can the political theorist speak? More accurately, the question is: Can the political theorist speak legitimately about the oppressed, in the absence of any experiences of oppression? My previous point goes some way to answering this, as it seems to assume that the political theorist is never a member of the oppressed group. But still, I would hazard a guess that most political theorists working on refugee questions have not been refugees, and that at least some of them, such as myself, are 'White', male and middle-class. Of course, what intersectionality tells us is that we are all being oppressed by gender, global capitalism and neo-colonialism, but still that oppression takes very different forms and gives rise to very different experiences depending on your background and where you are located; and the experience of being a refugee looks to be a distinct form of oppression, with distinct oppressions giving rise to distinct refugee experiences.

And so, I, as a 'White', male, middle-class academic, do have to address the question about the extent to which I can theorize about the injustices done to those whose experience of oppression I have not shared. As Linda Alcoff points out in relation to social theory:

> As social theorists, we are authorized by virtue of our academic positions to develop theories that express and encompass the ideas, needs, and goals of others. However, we must begin to ask ourselves whether this is ever a legitimate authority, and if so, what are the criteria for legitimacy? In particular, is it ever valid to speak for others who are unlike me or who are less privileged than me? (Alcoff, 2008: 119)

One quick answer to the question is that I must be *able* to do this, because I *must* do it – I have an ethical obligation to pay close attention to certain injustices and put them at the centre of political theory and action.

However, in spite of this the question still remains: how can someone with no experience of specific forms of oppression (recognizing, of course, that there is no universal refugee experience of oppression), and who occupies a privileged and powerful position because of the system that causes and perpetuates that oppression, legitimately speak about it without working with, and quoting, refugees themselves? To the previous reply that they must, the disturbing response is that the *way* they speak about it may, despite their good intentions, perpetuate the oppression they seek to criticize, because the structures of 'knowledge' they deploy in their critique are built upon the ideology of oppression. The conceptual framework they are working with may in some sense be complicit in the oppressive system they are working to overthrow.

This challenge has been articulated strongly within postcolonial theory. As Cheryl McEwan points out, postcolonial theory constitutes a radical challenge to the 'power to name, represent and theorize' (McEwan, 2019: 34). For postcolonial theory, says McEwan: 'Knowledge is never impartial, removed, or objective, but is always *situated*, produced by actors who are positioned in specific locations and shaped by numerous cultural and other influences. This determines what counts as knowledge, who creates it, where it is generated and how and for whom it is disseminated' (McEwan, 2019: 46–47).

One aspect of this is the privileging of theory: 'subalterns tell stories and researchers theorize for them' (Spivak, 1988: 275; McEwan, 2019: 261). This involves a twin denial – firstly that the subaltern can do theory; and secondly that the production of theory is itself a political practice (Kapoor, 2004). McEwan points to the agency/passivity binary here:

> Even when the subaltern does speak, her voice is relayed, filtered, reinterpreted, appropriated and even hijacked by intervening institutional structures. Some attempts have been made to circumvent this by using direct testimonials, but there is no avoiding who edits and translates the stories, how they are presented, for what

> purposes and so on. ... The subaltern voice is always being mediated. (McEwan, 2019: 309, on processes construing mobile subjects from the global South, see also Chapter 7)

For Spivak, the western-located academic *must* speak, but must understand their responsibilities and the limitations of their position. While I acknowledge the problematics of referring to 'we' here, I will phrase what follows in that register. First, we can engage in critique from within. For Spivak, we can change and transform discourses from the inside, 'transforming conditions of impossibility into possibility' (Spivak, 1988: 201; McEwan, 2019: 350); we must be aware of the ways in which the theoretical framework within which we are embedded is complicit in the systems of oppression we seek to critique, and seek to transform that framework into a genuinely egalitarian and emancipatory discourse. Second, we must be prepared to acknowledge *our* complicity, not only the complicity of the dominant framework – the theorist is located within a discourse of power, which includes our locations in institutions, and we must be hyper-self-reflexive about our complicities in maintaining particular relations of power within and through that discourse and within and outside of those institutions.

Third, we have to experience the unlearning of privilege as loss, through recognizing the limits of our knowledge – there are parts of the world and of people's lives and experience that we cannot know and so cannot represent in any straightforward way, and some of those parts of the world may be located in our own neighbourhoods; in seeking to speak about oppression, we must nevertheless remain aware of that about which we cannot speak. Fourth, we must learn how to learn from below. This means that we cannot simply 'listen' to the voices of refugees and other displaced groups; rather, we need to learn *how* to listen without constraining the meaning of what we are listening to within the confines an 'old' framework, but instead being open to the richness of the meaning and import of the words – this does not require us to have a 'new' framework already to hand, but it is to open up space for different voices and to learn new ways of speaking. Fifth, we need to learn how to work without guarantees. 'Working without guarantees means being aware of the blind spots of one's powers and representational systems, and either accepting failure or learning to see it as success' (McEwan, 2019: 352). Those we need to listen to and learn from may not wish to speak to us; those we want to enter into partnership with may not wish to enter into partnership with us.[6]

And so, the conclusion is that the political theorist *must* speak, has a moral responsibility to speak (and act), but must be aware of the effects their position (whatever that is) has on how they can speak in order to contribute to an answer to refugee questions. As McEwan says, this moral responsibility has to be 'reformulated in ways that do not replicate neo-colonial power relations' (McEwan, 2019: 316). Rather than the exclusive owners of refugee questions in political theory, we must understand ourselves as making a specific kind of contribution to answering those questions in partnership with others. Rather than only speaking for, we must learn how to speak with. But a genuine and constructive partnership may involve giving up some of the authority political theorists believe they have in arriving at answers to refugee questions. In the final section of this chapter, I examine some of those limitations on what political theory can do here, and what kinds of partnerships need to be developed.

Part 2: What is to be done (by political theorists)?

How, then, can political theorists approach refugee questions in their work? One of the key themes that has emerged has been that of speaking *with* rather than *for* others. We need to work in partnership with others. The first kinds of partnerships we need to make are with other academic disciplines working in the field of Refugee or Forced Migration Studies. There is a tendency for political theorists, mostly emerging from the discipline of philosophy, to work in isolation from other disciplines on these questions, and there is a danger in doing so that we fail to grasp the complexities of some of these issues. This criticism applies to my own work. Sarah Song makes a similar point in relation to political theory's engagement with the ethics of migration more widely: 'Normative debates about migration rest in part on empirical claims, and if political theorists want their work to offer practical guidance in real-world debates, they must engage with the best empirical scholarship on the subject' (Song, 2018: 399).

For me, the need for engagement with a wider range of empirical research goes beyond the need to offer practical guidance to policy makers. Even in its most 'ideal' form, political theory must be based on a firm understanding of who refugees are and the root causes of refugee movements: what forms those movements take, what drives them, what impact they have, their historical roots and connections with colonialism and enslavement, and the nature of the global political and economic system within which they now take place. Mihai calls for an honest and diligent engagement with evidence from the social sciences and history rather than selecting pieces of evidence that support one's preformulated proposals. 'In failing to engage with the most recent findings in bodies of work relevant to their normative proposals, philosophers' claims lose plausibility and socio-political relevance. Gestural references to strands of research in say, economics or sociology, are insufficient: only patient, rigorous yet critical attention to the existing knowledge produced by other fields fits the picture of responsible theory I advocate here' (Mihai, 2020: 590). What we need is what I call 'dirty political theory', a political theory which is prepared to jump into the mix with other disciplines, to engage with data in all its forms, and to learn from sociology, economics, anthropology and other disciplines which are closer to the ground, as it were, rather than maintain a somewhat lofty position above such matters.

However, it is not simply that different fields of political theory and different disciplinary fields should connect and talk and learn from each other when it comes to issues of displacement.[7] The academic space where displacement is studied must also be open to diverse voices which may transcend disciplinary boundaries, especially what could be termed postcolonial, global South and 'indigenous' voices, and indeed the voices of the displaced themselves. Aurora Vergara-Figueroa, writing about displacement in Colombia, observes that 'the concepts of forced migration and forced displacement are limited in their ability to explain the complexities of the world-historical realities they are expected to capture. Their analytical scope is too narrow'. She comments on the 'lack of historicity underneath the concept of forced migration' (Vergara-Figueroa, 2018: 2) and writes: 'I would go further and suggest that it is a notion that has proven dubious, narrow-minded, destructive and dangerous' (Vergara-Figueroa, 2018). She highlights 'the theoretical infirmity in the concepts underlying the research and policies produced in the field of forced migration' (Vergara-Figueroa, 2018: 4), and voices the suspicion that 'the main rationales in which this concept is founded can contribute to the continued exploitation and pillage of the populations it meant to protect' (Vergara-Figueroa, 2018: 4; see also Mayblin and Turner, 2021, and Chapter 12).

A greater challenge is the need to make partnerships with those directly affected by the events we are engaging with, refugees themselves. Fine points out that the 'we' in political philosophy tends to be a shorthand for 'we who are not refugees; we who are not from the Global South' (Fine, 2020: 17). Elena Fiddian-Qasmiyeh comments on the importance of 'centralizing the knowledge and the conceptualizations of people who have migrated, been displaced, and/or who are responding to migration in different ways' (Fiddian-Qasmiyeh, 2020: 12). Such people are 'active agents whose capacity to act is restricted by diverse systems of inequality and violence', and this makes it 'essential to go beyond collecting, or documenting, such experiences, voices, and acts' (Fiddian-Qasmiyeh, 2020: 12). She says: 'it becomes necessary to challenge rather than reproduce the assumption that migrants and refugees merely experience, are affected by, and/or respond to migratory processes, and that it is only through scholarly attention that these experiences can be analysed, for "us" to make sense of "their" lives and worlds' (Fiddian-Qasmiyeh, 2020: 12). We need to 'recognize that analysis and theorization are not the preserve of academics and practitioners' (Fiddian-Qasmiyeh, 2020: 12).

There needs to be a multifaceted conversation here. As I have argued, this goes beyond the need to listen to 'refugee voices' – it involves the realization that refugees have a fundamental right to political *agency* (see also Chapters 12 and 13). Political theorists have to build a framework which embodies the idea of political agency for refugees in arriving at normative answers to refugee questions. Even then, that framework must be one that recognizes the equality not only of the position of the refugee alongside other political positions that constitute it, but also of refugee agency in the process of deciding what the ethical framework should look like. In other words, it is not good enough for political theorists to construct an ethical framework for answering refugee questions that recognizes the role of the political agency of refugees in arriving at an answer – we must also recognize the role of the agency of refugees at the level of theory: refugees themselves are agents of theory, and their experiences of being refugees may enable them to arrive at essential theoretical insights into what that ethical framework should look like. I made the point earlier that many academics, including political theorists, have a refugee background, and many people with refugee backgrounds are engaged in academic study in their host communities, including political theory (Fine, 2019: 31).[8] An example of the kind of work I have in mind here is that of Shahram Khosravi (2010), and the fact that Khosravi describes himself as an anthropologist should not, given the previous discussion about the need to transcend disciplinary boundaries, be a reason for political theorists not to engage with his work.

It may sound from what I have said so far that I want political theory to be grounded firmly in empirical research and the real experiences of refugees, so that it can, in some sense, be more 'realistic' in what it puts forward as normative solutions to refugee questions. However, there is a sense in which I am arguing for a 'pure political theory', by which I mean one free of the need to come up with policy proposals that those in power will take seriously. I agree with Wendy Brown when she says that 'we must … beware of capitulating to a certain pressure on theory itself today – to apply, to be true, or to solve immediate real-world problems' (Brown, 2002: 573). Rather, I am suggesting that what political theory provides – and this is perhaps its singular contribution to an interdisciplinary project – is a framework for radical imagination in which anything is possible. My argument is that these acts of 'pure' radical imagination have to be grounded in a realistic understanding of what it is to be a refugee or forced migrant, not constrained by a 'realistic' understanding of what political leaders and policy makers take to be 'feasible' in relation to what they present as a refugee 'crisis'. The reality we need to be engaged with is the reality of the experiences of refugees, their motivations, their desires, their hopes and fears. Sarah Fine has pointed to 'how listening to and engaging with voices of refugees and other migrants might contribute to a more nuanced understanding of refugee and other migrant experiences and thus help inform a "realistic" (in the straightforward sense of "in touch with reality") and sympathetic approach to refugee movements' (Fine, 2019: 29). This is a radical realism, not a pragmatic one. This means our discussion cannot be limited by states, citizens and nations as we find them in the world, nor by the 'political will' attributed to what are taken to be the key agents of change – liberal nation-states and their citizens.

Conclusion

All of this requires a series of radical and disruptive displacements. The first is that of the citizen of the liberal democratic state from the centre of the picture, a position they dominate at present so that the refugee is constructed as a 'problem' that must be solved on behalf of that central figure. We must be willing to problematize the power of the liberal citizen to determine the answer to refugee questions rather than refugees themselves, and place their safety and security on an equal plane with that of refugees and other forced migrants, rather than holding that they are non-negotiable. We must also, of course, displace the liberal democratic state from the centre, such that the interests of such states in 'managing migration' no longer determine the abilities of refugees to reach safety.

The second displacement, and the main point of this chapter, is that of the political theorist from the global North as the exclusive owner of the process of arriving at normative answers to refugee questions. As I said in the introduction, this can be understood as a process of personal self-criticism as I work on the ethics of forced displacement. If other global North academics working on forced displacement, whatever their disciplinary background, believe that they have fully addressed these challenges, or that they do not apply, then this chapter does not speak to them, and so I address these final thoughts to myself alone. I need to problematize my power to determine and answer these questions – ask by what right I believe I can make normative recommendations for policies that determine the life-prospects of refugees, however 'progressive' I believe those recommendations to be. And I must problematize my own complicity in the silencing and disempowerment of the refugee voice and refugee agency, through hyper-self-reflexivity about my role in constituting the refugee as an object of study. I can no longer go about my normative task without working in partnership with other disciplines; nor without advocating that refugees must be political agents with a role to play in arriving at those answers; and that refugees themselves must be and often are agents of theory, that their experiences of being refugees enable them to arrive at essential theoretical insights that would otherwise be missed. I must learn how to speak with, rather than to only speak for, and I must also learn when to remain silent.

Notes

[1] This chapter was written with the support of a Senior Research Fellowship provided by the British Academy, the Thank Offering to Britain Fellowship, 2019–2020. It was presented at the conference 'Postcoloniality and Forced Migration: Displacement, Protection and Control', held at Aalborg University, Denmark, 11–13 December 2019, and I am grateful for the comments I received at that conference. Thanks also to Kerri Woods, Martin Lemberg-Pedersen, Lucy Mayblin, Nina Sahraoui and Sharla Fett for commenting on draft versions of this chapter.

[2] Throughout this chapter I use the term 'refugee' broadly, not confined to the definition in the 1951 Refugee Convention. I agree with Serena Parekh when she says 'we ought to interpret the term as broadly as possible' (Parekh, 2017: 11). She follows Joseph Carens in taking the term to cover people outside of their home state and unable to return 'owing to serious and indiscriminate threats to life, physical integrity or freedom resulting from generalized violence or events seriously disturbing public order' (Carens, 2013: 201; Parekh, 2017: 13. See Cole (2020) for a discussion of the limits of international protection for the forcibly displaced.

[3] They are, of course, also framed in terms of threats to security and as illegal and in some sense criminal. I do not look at this kind of framing here. See Jones et al (2017) and Kirkwood et al (2016).

[4] It may well be that Owen, and others who refer to refugee voices, mean it in this sense of political agency, of course.

[5] This is not the clearly false claim that White, male, middle class, European academics cannot be refugees. The crucial point seems to be that I do not have the relevant experiences, and on the face of it, my identity position does not determine that I can never have those experiences. However, my identity position does seem to have wider relevance when it comes to the question of who gets to do political theory.

[6] Paul Patten usefully distinguishes between two senses of 'subject': first, 'a being endowed with certain capacities or possibilities for action'; and second, a being 'subjected to power relations' (Patten, 1998: 66). In this chapter I use it in the first sense, and use the term 'object' to stand for the second sense.

[7] Thanks to Kerri Wood for clarifying many of the points in this paragraph.

[8] Thanks to Lucy Mayblin for pointing this out to me.

References

Alcoff, L. (2008) 'The problem of speaking for others', in A.Y. Jackson and L.A. Mazzei (eds) *Voice in Qualitative Inquiry: Challenging Conventional, Interpretive, and Critical Conceptions in Qualitative Research*, London and New York: Routledge.

Betts, A. and Collier, P. (2018) Refuge: Transforming a Broken Refugee System, London: Penguin Books.

Blake, M. (2020) *Justice, Migration, and Mercy*, New York: Oxford University Press.

Boochani, B. (2018) *No Friend But the Mountains: Writings from Manus Prison*, Sydney: Picador.

Brown, W. (2002) 'At the edge', *Political Theory*, 30(4): 556–76.

Carens, J. (2013) *The Ethics of Migration*, New York: Oxford University Press.

Cole, P. (2000) *Philosophies of Exclusion: Liberal Political Theory and Immigration*, Edinburgh: Edinburgh University Press.

Cole, P. (2020) 'Global displacement in the 21st century: towards an ethical framework', *Journal of Global Ethics*, 16(2): 204–19.

Drozdowski, H. and Yarnell, M. (2019) 'Promoting refugee participation in the Global Refugee Forum: walking the walk', *Refugees International Issue Brief*, Washington, DC: Refugees International.

Fiddian-Qasmiyeh, E. (2020) 'Recentering the South in studies of migration', *Migration and Society: Advances in Research*, 3: 1–18.

Fine, S. (2019) 'Refugees, safety, and a decent human life', *Proceedings of the Aristotelian Society*, CXIX(I): 25–52.

Fine, S. (2020) 'Refugees and the limits of political philosophy', *Ethics and Global Politics*, 13(1): 6–20.

Hoy, D.C. (1986) 'Introduction', in D.C. Hoy (ed) *Foucault: A Critical Reader*, Oxford: Blackwell, pp 1–26.

Ilcan, S. and Rygiel, K. (2015) '"Resiliency humanitarianism": responsibilizing refugees through humanitarian emergency governance in the camp', *International Political Sociology*, 9: 333–51.

Jones, H., Gunaratnam, Y., Bhattacharya, G., Davies, W., Dhaliwal, S., Forkert, K., Jackson, E. and Saltus, R. (2017) *Go Home? The Politics of Immigration*, Manchester: Manchester University Press.

Kapoor, I. (2004) 'Hyper-self-reflexive development? Spivak on representing the Third World "Other"', *Third World Quarterly*, 25(4): 627–47.

Khosravi, S. (2010) *'Illegal' Traveller: An Auto-Ethnography of Borders*, Basingstoke: Palgrave Macmillan.

Kirkwood, S., Goodman, S., McVittie, C. and McKinlay, A. (2016) *The Language of Asylum: Refugees and Discourse*, London: Palgrave MacMillan.

Mayblin, L. and Turner, J. (2021) *Migration Studies and Colonialism*, Cambridge: Polity.

McEwan, C. (2019) *Postcolonialism, Decoloniality and Development* (2nd edn), London and New York: Routledge.

Mihai, M. (2020) 'Engaging vulnerabilities: an outline for a responsive and responsible theory', *Journal of Social Philosophy*, 51: 583–607.

Miller, D. (1995) *On Nationality*, Oxford: Clarendon Press.

Miller, D. (2016) *Strangers in our Midst: The Political Philosophy of Immigration*, Berkeley: Harvard University Press.

Milner, J. (2021) 'The politics and practice of refugee participation in the governance of the global refugee regime', Canadian Political Science Association Annual Conference 'Diversity and the Discipline of Political Science', June.

Mohanty, C.T. (2003) *Feminism Without Borders: Decolonizing Theory, Practicing Soldarity*, Durham, NC and London: Duke University Press.

Nayeri, D. (2019) *The Ungrateful Refugee*, Edinburgh: Canongate Books.

Nguyen, V.T. (ed) (2018) *The Displaced: Refugee Writers on Refugee Lives*, New York: Abrams Press.

Owen, D. (2018) 'Refugees and responsibilities of justice', *Global Justice: Theory, Practice, Rhetoric*, 11(1): 23–44.

Parekh, S. (2017) *Refugees and the Ethics of Forced Displacement*, London and New York: Routledge.

Passarley, G. (2015) *The Lightless Sky*, New York: Harper Collins.

Patten, P. (1998) 'Foucault's subjects of power,' in J. Moss (ed) *The Later Foucault*, London, Thousand Oaks, New Delhi: Sage, pp 64–77.

Rajaram, P. (2002) 'Humanitarianism and representations of the refugee', *Journal of Refugee Studies*, 15(3): 247–64.

Sigona, N. (2014) 'The politics of refugee voices: representations, narratives, and memories', in E. Fiddean-Qasmigeh, G. Loescher, K. Long and N. Sigona (eds) *The Oxford Handbook of Refugee and Forced Migration Studies*, Oxford: Oxford University Press, pp 369–82.

Song, S. (2018) 'Political theories of migration', Annual Review of Political Science, 385–402.

Spivak, G.C. (1988) 'Can the subaltern speak?', in C. Nelson and L. Grossberg (eds) *Marxism and Interpretation of Culture*, Chicago: University of Illinois Press, pp 271–313.

Vergara-Figueroa, A. (2018) *Afrodescendant Resistance to Deracination in Colombia: Massacre at Bellavista-Bojayá-Chocó*, Cham: Palgrave Macmillan.

Wellman, C.H. and Cole, P. (2011) *Debating the Ethics of Immigration: Is there a Right to Exclude?* New York: Oxford University Press.

Walzer, M. (1983) *Spheres of Justice*, New York: Basic Books.

Woods, K. (2019) 'Refugees' stories: empathy, agency, solidarity', *Journal of Social Philosophy*, 51(4): 507–25.

Young, R. (2001) *Postcolonialism: An Historical Introduction*, Oxford and Malden: Blackwell.

Zalmi, A. (2021) *Home and Sense of Belonging Among Iraqi Kurds in the UK*, Washington, DC: Lexington Books.

12

Singing Historical Reparations: Alabaoras Challenging the Spectacle of Forgiveness in Communities Affected by Deracination in Colombia

Aurora Vergara-Figueroa and Jerónimo Botero Marino

Introduction

In this chapter, we address three issues of contemporary as well as postcolonial significance for the field of forced migration. First, how do Afro-descendent communities having experienced violence face requests for forgiveness from their aggressors? Second, how does the field of knowledge that is forced migration consider the role of race when forgiveness and reparations are requirements for a peace process? Third, does this illustrate a need to move beyond the concept of forced migration to consider categories such as deracination?

Previous research has argued that the concept of forced migration needs to be un-thought, both epistemically and politically, from a Black feminist perspective, in order to integrate into our scholarship a historical analysis of how territories, where land dispossession constantly occurred, are produced (Hill Collins, 2000; Arboleda, 2016; Vergara-Figueroa and Arboleda Hurtado, 2016; Vergara-Figueroa, 2018). This is crucial for comprehending the empirical significance of deracination as a category of analysis, social mobilization and reparation. The concept of deracination can be valuable for articulating how local conceptions of territory are constructed historically, the impacts when people are being dispossessed from it, and the connections to similar experiences across the world through the concept of diaspora.

This chapter operationalizes such an analysis through the case of the survivors of the massacre of Bellavista-Bojayá, and their claim that they ask the government for the reparation of their souls. We argue that this demonstrates how deracination can point to an irreversibility and irreparability in experiences of being uprooted from territory, a sociological aspect that the concept of forced migration does not capture (Vergara-Figueroa, 2018). Based on ethnographic and documentary research, including field notes conducted in Bojayá between 2016 and 2019, we analyse how the Colombian government, Revolutionary Armed Forces of Colombia (henceforth FARC) members and paramilitary groups struggle to be forgiven by the community of Bellavista-Bojayá-Chocó in the aftermath of the massacre of 2 May 2002, where more than 80 people were killed (CNRR-GMH, 2010).

In this chapter, we consider the case of postcolonial politics on deracination in the Colombian Bojayá region. We then problematize how standard typologies of forced migration focus on external forces inducing displacement, but leave out local and regional complexities and socio-economic processes preceding the conflicts and political violence. For a sociology of deracination, we need to consider the social poesis that sustains the dispossessed (Hartman, 2019: 227). This case offers grounds for a more nuanced analysis of the realities of deracinated populations condemned to be ignored either because they are considered 'hard to quantify' (Castles, 2003: 15) or because the complex causes that inform them are not easily captured in the prevailing labels and are therefore left out of the mainstream debate. By exposing the historical and colonial roots behind epistemological erasures of such complexities, the chapter unveils constellations of knowledge and power in the prevailing understandings of and research into forced migration (Vergara-Figueroa et al., 2017). It offers an analysis of how racial grammar is manifested as a consequence of movements of people across and within borders and regions imbued with local historicity, and, more specifically, in the request of forgiveness in the Colombian peace process of 2012–16 signed on 26 September 2016.

Our analysis departs from the figure of the 'Black Christ of Bojayá', which is given by members of FARC to this community in the purse of forgiveness. Such political forgiveness can be a manifestation of the power of a victim, but it can also place a burden and function as a form of reconstituted racial domination (Mosquera and Barcelos, 2007; Mosquera and Lao-Montes and Rodriguez, 2010; Bonilla, 2012). We base this analysis on Lefranc's (2005: 275) argument that:

> Forgiveness appears to be an action that establishes a new relationship, a relationship that frees the offender from the burden of debt (from his/their guilt) and the offended from the stigma of the prejudice suffered and his status as a victim. Although it does

> not equalize the relationship, it renews it with a foundation no longer that of violence, or the offense suffered. Forgiveness does not restore a previous relationship. It allows a restart from scratch. This restart can always be interpreted as a restoration.

Through socio-historic and ethnographic interventions, we examine how the case of Bojayá in Colombia illustrates that the reproduction of the coloniality of dominant understandings of how belonging – and who is seen to belong – can be represented as *only provisional*. Accordingly, we argue that this case illustrates how even though the concept of forced migration can be helpful for formulating policies of temporal protection, it holds limited analytical power to understand intersections of structural, institutional and everyday developments (Vergara, 2018).

The chapter is divided into four sections. First, we describe the signing of the peace agreement on 26 September 2016, with a group of traditional singers from Bojayá. Second, we explain the significance of this case through the symbol of the 'mutilated' Christ of Bojayá. Third, we describe the attempts made by different armed actors to ask forgiveness from this community. As a symbol of this moment, we refer to 'the Black Christ of Bojayá' given by members of FARC to this community asking for their forgiveness. The fourth and final section discusses what Bojayá's case can add to the literature on forgiveness within racialized and postcolonial contexts of violence and to the core ideas of the field of forced migration.

The peace agreement

> We want justice and peace that comes from the heart.
>
> Excerpt of song by Alabaoras of Pogue, 2017

On 26 September 2016, the Colombian government signed a peace agreement with FARC in Cartagena after almost 60 years of armed struggle and 4 years of negotiation in Havana, Cuba. This event was attended by different members of the Colombian government, the FARC, the international community (such as presidents, delegates and the UN), as well as representatives of the victims. At the event, Juan Manuel Santos, the President of the Colombian government, spoke, as did the commander of the FARC, and the 'alabaoras'[1] (group of singers) of Bojayá,[2] 'singing to hope', in order to represent the victims of the conflict. What did they say? They stated that they are happy that the FARC surrendered their arms, that the President had been brave in his efforts to achieve peace. They said:

> We must never forget the victims of the armed groups; there should be justice, reparation, and non-repetition; for over 500 years, we

> have been living in terror in our territories [meaning the continuity of the conflict with slavers and enslavement], the signature of the peace agreement is not the complete transformation of the territory into a peaceful space; still, there are other violent groups in the zone, and the government cannot abandon us now.[3]

For the alabaoras of Bellavista-Bojayá, the heart is the primary source of truth and forgiveness, which is therefore not strictly, or legally derived. On the contrary, it is this subjective source that the process seems to need to guarantee reconciliation. Was it not, perhaps, what was expected on that day from the victims? Were they expected to play their part and offer forgiveness? Or was this, rather, the only part of the process that belonged only to the victims, who seemed to be in their full power, since neither the state nor any force, could sanction forgiveness by them?

Forgiveness is not disputed, like memory, nor sanctioned by laws, like justice. Nor is it decided by some bureaucratic agency as reparation is. Only the victim grants forgiveness; it is indisputable but also necessary for a transformative peace process. It is the victims' contribution to the progress of things, but in that sense, there is also a certain mandate on the victim to forgive. Forgiveness is thus a power of the victim, but a power circumscribed. In these circumstances, one might think that racialized communities will, finally, be able to alter longstanding power dynamics. It is, at least, what negotiators expected from the victims and perhaps what they expected from the alabaoras of Pogue-Bojayá. However, the case of Bojayá demonstrates that this form of power can also be a burden and an instance in which racial grammar can reappear.

Thirteen days before this event, on 19 September 2016, the people of Bojayá faced the difficulty of receiving and accepting an offer of forgiveness from FARC as a symbol of forgiveness for grievances. At a community meeting called to discuss the matter, a state official said, 'Bojayá is no longer Bojayá; it is the whole nation giving a message of reconciliation'. Even though the 2 October 2016 popular referendum denied the ratification of the Colombian peace agreements, it was Bojayá that would show the highest favourable vote to the agreements: 96 per cent said 'yes' and 4 per cent said 'no'. One of the most important political magazines in Colombia, *Semana*, titled one of its issues with the exclamation of Father Antún, who was at the local church of Bojayá the day of the massacre: 'We believed in the pardon of the FARC, and we granted it in the polls'. Why would the pardon of Bojayá symbolize reconciliation in this national process, as evidenced by the statement of the official? Is a vote favourable to the national process also a concession of forgiveness to FARC? In short, why is forgiveness so important for the peace process in Colombia? And why are women in Pogue-Bojayá singing to demand historical reparations?

The Mutilated Christ: the massacre

> And this was a tough blow
> That frightened everybody
> They formed that fight
> And the peasant suffered
>
> Cañola, 2017. Excerpt of song by Alabaoras of Pogue

The setting of the spectacle of forgiveness in Bojayá?

The empirical evidence of this chapter was collected between 2016 and 2019 based on the production of the documentary and CD *Voices of Resistance*.[4] This is an audiovisual project of the Center for Afrodiasporic Studies (CEAF) of the Icesi University of Cali, financed by the Ford Foundation and carried out in alliance with the Center for Ethics and Democracy (CED) of Icesi. CEAF seeks to make visible and strengthen organizational processes of Afro-descendant women, and the audiovisual project seeks to disseminate, circulate and promote alabao as a musical expression of Afro-Colombian communities in the Pacific. In this sense, the university wants to address the need of the Pogue group of singers to create audiovisual records which reflect their efforts to preserve the songs and traditions of their community. The first volume compiles 12 songs and a documentary by the Pogue-Bojayá group of praisers. It was co-produced by Phenomena and Pacífico Records. Herrera Valencia et al (2019) describe how the project was undertaken and the details of the ethnographical processes. Marin and Alzate (2021) analyse the ethical and political implications of the performance of the alabaoras of Pogue. Ohmer (2019) states that this documentary is an example of epistemic justice.

According to the last population census recorded by DANE (Colombian National Administrative Department of Statistics), the municipality of Bojayá has 9,941 inhabitants. 58.4 per cent are Afro-Colombians and 41.4 per cent are indigenous people. 95.86 per cent of the population has their basic needs unsatisfied, a figure that has been maintained since 1993. 61.4 per cent of the population have changed their residential address due to life threats, 20.4 per cent due to the difficulty of obtaining employment and 10.8 per cent for family reasons. Only 38.2 per cent of the population between 3 and 5 years old attend a formal educational establishment, 59.4 per cent of the population between 6 and 10 years old, and 56.4 per cent of the population between 11 and 17. In the capital of the municipality, where 50.4 per cent of the population is concentrated, there is no hospital (DANE, 2021).[5] There is one school, and no university. There is one Catholic Church and close to five Churches in which protestant Christians meet.

These religious spaces are a central part of life in Bojayá. After almost 60 years of guerrilla presence in the territory, in 1997, a paramilitary incursion began in the municipality of Bojayá. The presence of guerrilla and paramilitary groups increased the pressure, torture and terror on the civilian population always suspected of allying with the enemy. Paramilitaries established the practice of 'cleansings', where they killed selected people within the community and threw them into the Atrato River with warning signs, so locals would not collect them and give them a proper burial. Paramilitaries established curfews and several regulations to control human and food circulation. To strengthen their control, they disappeared people, threatened their relatives, robbed their houses and placed land mines in the territories, among other acts of terror. These events resulted in massive deracination –uprootings from the land (Vergara-Figueroa, 2018). This context of massive deracination is another component of the spectacle of forgiveness.

On 1 May 2002, the FARC began an offensive against the paramilitary in Bellavista. The population, in panic, sought refuge in the house of the Augustinian sisters and the church. They chose the few brick buildings, which could better protect them from bullets. They also chose a sacred place that offered spiritual protection. On 2 May, however, the FARC threw three bomb cylinders aiming at the paramilitaries who took refuge near the civilian population. One of the cylinders exploded on the altar of the church. Over 80 people died, 55 per cent of them children, not counting six that were in their mother's bellies. Those who could leave, abandoned the town. Some took refuge in houses; others ran to the forest, and the rest, guided by Father Antún, crossed the Atrato River to Vigía del Fuerte with bullets flying past them (which is what most of the population ended up doing).

The mutilated and dismembered bodies of the dead and those wounded and unable to move remained in the church. The survivors had to stay in the now roofless church for over 4 days, enduring burning sunlight during the day and torrential rain at night. Minelia, the so-called *loca del pueblo* ('local fool') remained in the church, talking to the dead, carrying water with salt to the wounded and moving them to the sacristy that still had a roof. Piece by piece, Minelia also began to re-group the mutilated bodies, gathering the parts that she believed belonged together. The confrontation between the armed groups lasted 4 more days. During this time, there were partial attempts to remove and help the wounded in the church and bury the dead. During the hostilities, men volunteered to bury the bodies in a mass grave. The victims went to the grave without mortuary rites and were unidentified. As a symbol of this massacre, a mutilated figure of the Christ of Bojayá was collected from the ruins of the church and erected in a square wooden urn by the nuns, who are now its custodians along with three afrocolombian leaders from the community of Bellavista.

Singing for reparations in this setting: the alabaoras

'Alabaos' are traditional songs in the Colombian Pacific region which are part of mortuary rites (Quiceno, Ochoa Sierra and Villamizar, 2017). They are syncretic expressions of multiple traditions. However, in the difficult conditions of threat, death, abandonment and violence experienced in this area, alabaos would also become one of few oral manifestations of political autonomy by the communities. These are traditional expressions of the community's aesthetic, and seem to present no threat to the armed groups. However, we hypothesize that alabaos represent a counter-hegemonic narrative of violence, and so that these songs are a cultural text allowing us to read both political violence and Black subjectivity. For these reasons we will offer an analytical chronology of the development of alabaos (see Table 12.1). We present a summary of this hypothesis through a chronology that starts in 1997 when paramilitary groups entered Bojayá and finishes in 2016. We divide this temporality into four moments, according to the characteristics we identify in a series of 12 alabaos. In the following tables, we describe the major challenges the community was up against, how this manifested in the lyrics of alabaos, and their resources of resistance and challenge to how forgiveness has been displayed as a spectacle in Bellavista-Bojayá.

Consequently, they sing their territory, inhabit it with their songs, and re-appropriate it symbolically. In this way, the community began to use traditional religious songs and the alabaos as a strategy of memory

Table 12.1: Alabaos' challenges, resistance and resources, 1997–2002

Challenges	How do they defend themselves from these events of deracination?	Resources of resistance
Transformation: The territory of Bellavista-Bojayá as a battlefield.	Women start inserting names of dead or missing people into their traditional songs to register events in the collective memory.	To re-inhabit the territory singing.
Disintegration: The subjection of the population to the friend/enemy dichotomy of armed groups.		To defend the sense of the 'us' (as community members) other than the 'aggressors'. Self-representation against this usurpation of representation.
Disappearance: Continuous anguish that something serious could happen.		Early alerts

Table 12.2: Alabaos' challenges, ritualization and resources, 2002–7

Challenges	Who, to whom, how and when is this unpublished fact ritualized?	Resources of resistance
* The dead cannot go to rest in peace, and the living cannot stay. * The collective and diffuse character of the dead. * The unfinished nature of the deaths.	*Social organization:* The group of alabaoras is created. *Production:* They begin to compose new lyrics with their traditional lyrics.	* Those who stay (at Bellavista) accompanied the dead. * Transition from the dead to the massacre. * Transition from the traditional funeral to the commemoration.
* The us: the collective character of the aggrieved subject. * New interlocutor: the welfare state. * New discourse: help, displaced, returned.		* The government owes us. * Bellavista is a part of Bojayá along with more than 30 other communities of Afrodescendants and indigenous. * They demand rights, not help. * The community keeps its memory, not official records and expert evidence.
* Disappearance. Banishment of the community in the territory.		Return and reinstall.

and to denounce, in these songs, the violent events that took place in the territory. At the same time, they issued early warnings to require government intervention.

The massacre of 2002 was materially and spiritually traumatic, and an unprecedented threat to the continuity of the community of Bellavista. The survivors of the massacre fled the community. The dead in the church remained in limbo since it was not possible to identify them, sing their praises and give them mortuary rites until after 2018. This was contrary to the logic of life in this community, which was dismembered. Its living members were gone, dispersed and with an unpaid debt to its dead members who had not been able to depart peacefully. Five months after the town's abandonment due to the massacre, most of the old settlers returned to rebuild their lives in the territory. Given the dramatic and unprecedented violence, the community thus responded by reinterpreting its social and expressive resources, and some significant changes in the tradition of the alabaos began (see Table 12.2).

First, the social organization developed, people began to organize a group of alabaoras. Second, they began to sing alabaos on the day of the commemoration of the massacre and have as a subject the whole community of Bojayá (including those who died). Third, the production of new alabaos by some alabaoras began. Fourth, new vital themes emerged, including that the massacre became a symbol of the alabaos. Moreover, the alabaos would also come to function as a form of interlocution to the state. As such it was framed and imbued with a new vocabulary promoted by the state, including 'aid', 'internally displaced', and 'returned'. The alabaoras, however, challenged this new narrative.

After the massacre of 2002, the funeral rite turned into a commemorative rite; from this tragedy, the need arose for the alabaoras, until now an unorganized group of women (and some men) who sang in funeral rites, to organize themselves. Many had lost their loved ones on the day of the massacre. Alabaoras began to formalize and sing the tragedy, interpreting and performing the meaning of the massacre in their songs. They demonstrated that the whole municipality of Bojayá was a victim, and not only the inhabitants dead, wounded and bereaved by the attack in Bellavista.

In the new structure of alabaos, there is continuity in the musical form; the religious theme is maintained with a spirit of denunciation, but the alabaos become autonomous. They continued to have ceremonial mortuary roles and acts, but now it is the commemoration of the massacre that is sung. The alabaoras argue that the souls of those who died on 2 May 2002 have not been able to leave because they were not adequately identified and did not receive the appropriate ceremony. This is the reason why they demand reparation of the soul. The alabaoras consolidated a leading role in the process of collective mourning and in the elaboration of the significance of the community presence in political processes (see Table 12.3).

During this period, a new discourse of the process emerged, one of *forgiveness*. More precisely, the triad of *recognition-forgiveness-reconciliation*. It is interesting to note that the communities of Bojayá did not claim as a priority the recognition of the fact and forgiveness of the perpetrators. Their claims were different, namely to attend to the victims and identify the dead. However, the climate of public opinion and the discursive and political structure of the agreement introduced the need for forgiveness. Furthermore, the inhabitants of Bojayá, victims of the massacre, and the alabaoras as their representatives, quickly became subjects whose forgiveness would occupy an essential place in interpreting the possibilities of success of the national Colombian peace process.

In this case, we argue that power is manifested in the granting of forgiveness and that this balances out the previous relationships of power in the area. It is a power that allows communities to take the initiative on the agenda, including, as we shall see, being able to set the points of discussion, in some

Table 12.3: Alabaoras' challenges, response to representability and resources, 2007–12

Challenges	How to respond to this growing political demand to represent the interests and demands of the community before this range of intervention actors	Resources of resistance
⋆ Security in the territory (still populated with illegal actors and armed groups). ⋆ The 'registry' of victims. ⋆ The breach of the promises of the state (exhumation and identification of corpses). ⋆ Struggles with compensation proceedings. ⋆ The community is increasingly interfered with by practices and discourses of the state, NGOs and academia. ⋆ The alabaoras and alabaos begin to reference the memory and claims of the people of Bojayá.	The group of alabaoras begins to compose lyrics for occasions other than the commemoration of the massacre. This includes for occasions of political interlocution inside and outside the territory.	⋆ The alabaos have thus passed from the family-communal space (burial) to the public-community (commemoration) and now, finally, to the public-political: strategic representation. ⋆ They sing the memory and mourning: a community supporting the grievance and becomes resilient to tell it and process the consequences. ⋆ Claims and debts are sung: the community is now more empowered, defined not only by the massacre but also by the taint of 500 years of oppression and the ethnic, social and cultural rights it claims (now the Afrodescendants and the Indians). ⋆ The survivors become subjects of the claims in memory of the dead.

aspects. Because the peace process and its actors need forgiveness and cannot force it out or punish its lack by law, forgiveness becomes a good bargaining resource for aggrieved communities.

At the same time, as illustrated by the case of Bojayá, a burden is also manifested, since being agents of forgiveness with a level of political representation as the ones impacted, also means accruing greater political responsibility at the national and international level. The personal and collective drama of the community of Bojayá and how they want or can handle their anger, resentment, mourning, or forgiveness, now seems to append the surprising fact that their forgiveness is a powerful signal about the possibility of the peace process – before it is granted or denied. It is transformed and no longer only a sincere personal process of forgiving in private, but also of telling all Colombians whether forgiveness can and should be given, and thus if national coexistence and peace are possible. Thus, forgiveness becomes demandable by political responsibility. In Bojayá, this required a public manifestation that turned into a spectacle, which we argue ultimately served to silence the victims. To be a representative of forgiveness thus became a defining feature of this new community identity for the bereaved of Bojayá.

As we have seen, the first step is the innovation of using alabaos to defend the community, to denounce, build memory and manifest its autonomy. Every commemoration, in effect, is funereal but cyclical, repeated every year because it accompanies the dead who have not been able to leave and therefore has to accompany them permanently. From the memorial service to the commemoration, it produces a displacement of a familiar-communitarian fact (the individualized mortuary rite) to a more political-public ritual (the commemoration) because the dead are not fully identified and because the whole community of living is indebted. An overlap of political subjects is also construed in order to ask for vindication of their rights (victims of violence).

The Christ offered: the forgiveness

> Just because we are Black
> They treat us that way
> Ay, they declare war on us
> To 'get us out of their land.'
>
> Excerpt of song by group of alabaoras of Pogue

The gift of the FARC: the Black Christ of Bojayá

During the peace process, the FARC in Havana commissioned a Cuban artist to design a Black Christ as a symbol of repentance and a request for forgiveness (Cagüeñas, 2022). While conducting the ethnography, we participated in the meetings in which community leaders were debating whether or not to receive the gift. We were able to interview the Cuban artist in charge of the symbol. He said to us that he made a 'Caribbean Christ' using an 'Afro-descendant' model that he explained was not a faithful representation, since he used his features as a reference when having doubts about what a 'Black person looked like'[6]. Given its size, to transport the statue to the territory, it was necessary to disarm it (to remove its arms) and to put it in a box. It arrived, then, not ordered by any member of the community, not consulted, disarmed and dismembered, in a box by the river.

This episode, the arrival of a dismembered Christ, replicated the image of the inhabitants that were systematically killed in the previous decades, and escaped across the river. Its arrival, without previous consultation, is representative of the impositions on the community and the occupation of these territories. And disputes arose in the community, as this so-called gift generated confusion and grievance. Later, FARC leaders and the sculptor went to Bellavista to present their gift. But when they arrived, there was no one to receive them, and they were – at least momentarily – expelled from Bellavista. The victims' committee then met and discussed whether or not to accept the Christ as an offer of forgiveness, even though the community never asked for or consented to this offering.

The gift was experienced as an imposition by the community, akin to the ones they had suffered for decades in their territories. Many questions emerged. One of the victims of the massacre asked if the new Christ would now challenge the place of the mutilated Christ of Bojayá. She also inquired if FARC leaders wanted to replace the symbol of the mutilated Christ, to change the meaning of the tragedy. As we conducted participatory observation during the meeting, we also inevitably identified the rise of several questions about forgiveness. We wondered if it was a disinterested offering or whether it was meant to generate an obligation to forgive. Along the lines of the reflections of Mauss (1966), perhaps it would work as a gift: a gift that catches one in gratitude and generates an obligation to forgive. A gift then also going back from the indebted to the debtor. Or was it, finally, an imposition that instructed the community on how to forgive and what grievances they should be able to forgive? Did it replace the material and symbolic reparation that the community had asked from FARC and the government for so long? And if they chose to forgive, wouldn't they lose their newly gained power, which no one could expropriate or replace? A power with which they could, perhaps, get what they need from the national peace process? Or would it be reparative and part of the mourning to forgive in that way?

On the other hand, during the meeting, a series of alternative questions also presented themselves: Did those who wanted to accept it – a minority – truly accept it freely, or were they living in areas of guerrilla control, where they feared the release of information of what was said by whom at the meeting? In other words: Were they receiving the gift as a precaution to protect themselves against possible retaliation? The representatives of the state, who were also in the meeting, suppressed the terrible political, national and international impact that it would have to not accept the offering. Accordingly, the state representatives insisted on arguing that Bojayá should act as an example of reconciliation for the nation. This, of course, created a dilemma for the community. Did they have a political obligation, with the country, to the peace process, to accept this offer of forgiveness, this symbol of repentance, regardless of what their hearts said – which is allegedly where forgiveness lies? In addition: would it be an intelligent strategy and not, instead, a loss of agency in what was going to follow? Accepting this gift without consultation or negotiation was, unquestionably, a new form of violence against the community.

During these discussions, a state official suggested that the community accept the gesture of repentance but not the object. Consequently, the committee agreed to receive the Black Christ who, provisionally and while discussions of his future continue, remained in the Loma de Bojayá, a nearby community but not in Bellavista. How can this compromise be understood? What does it mean to receive the gesture but not the object? We argue that the best way to understand it, is to understand the meaning and strategy that the community of Bojayá has managed to impose on the political urgency of forgiveness that has been asked of them.

Conclusion

The case of Bojayá illustrates who have been the victims of violent events, forcibly removed from their territories, are not forced migrants; they are deracinated. We need to make room in our field to consider their voices and experiences, and to carefully re-consider categorical frameworks used to analyse the historical conditions tied to structural and institutional inequalities; otherwise, we will continue silencing their voices and experiences from our analysis of society. Our preceding analysis also shows how Afro-descendant communities in Colombia that have experienced violence can be forced to relive the trauma of violence once more, when faced with requests for forgiveness from their aggressors, if it is portrayed in the form of a political spectacle that leaves little room for them to heal.

The women of Bojayá educate us to see the footprints of sociology in their songs. They teach us that race plays an essential factor when historically oppressed and disadvantaged communities are asked to forgive during a national and mediatized peace process. Through the songs, the women of Bojayá sing historical reparations and show us a form of political agency and revindication. They claim a just society, but their alabaos also tell of over 500 years of oppression, and exposure to such horrific events, because they are Black (Mosquera Palomeque, 2017). Accordingly, they sing historical reparations, and by doing so, demonstrate the linkages between a current, postcolonial moment and encounters of the colonial era.

Singing historical reparations is their way of producing knowledge so that the world can bear witness to what happened and happens to them. With their songs, they join the political debate and create spaces for liberation, and with Hartman (2019: 227) we argue that these alabaos are the social poesis that sustains the dispossessed. They create a moral account so that violence perpetrated against them does not get erased, and as such, alabaos are material manifestations of 'the social poesis that sustains the dispossessed. They can make sense of their experiences, turn what they are living into the written (or sung) word. By contrast, when decontextualized, the sociology of forced migration risks failing to understand, and even also erasing, such complexity, because it fails to capture the power and beauty and history in the lives of the deracinated populations where violence is not an exception but a definition of their existence (Hartman, 2019).

Alabaos are one of the few spaces left for them to express their dreams and pain without risking being silenced, disappeared, or killed. Through traditional songs such as alabaos, the women at Bojayá, and with them, their communities, sing their territory, symbolically re-inhabiting and re-appropriating it with their songs, after the heinous event of the massacre. The alabaos become a strategy to defend their sense of community and to re-group it. The requests for forgiveness from the community has come to balance the power relationships between it, the Colombian government and the armed groups. This newly gained power allows communities to take the initiative on the agenda of the national peace process since the actors involved need forgiveness to move on and cannot force it out or decree it by law. Forgiveness thus becomes a bargaining resource for bereaved and aggrieved communities. In the case of Bojayá, we argue that forgiveness is a process more than an act and learn that singing forgiveness can become a political act that restores a broken dignity. However, the case of Bojayá also reveals the tensions and silences preventing the advancement of a more complex understanding of this problem and its implication for today's realities of violence and deracination in Colombia, which stand in continuity with colonial and racial logics.

The repertoires of forgiveness used in Bojayá, and state actors' attempts to impose a new and decontextualized narrative of forced migration or forced displacement as a one off and exceptional event on the process, demonstrates how epistemological silence and erasure work. This case, therefore, offers an analytical contribution that allows us to revisit the sociology of forced migration, post-conflict and political reconciliation in the context of a peace agreement. In doing so, it opens up new avenues for viewing contemporary processes of deracination as placed on a continuum of historical, racial, gender and spatial formations (Tovar Rojas, 2007; CNMH, 2014; Arboleda, 2016).

The case of Bojayá offers us an opportunity to revise how a sociology of forced migration can consider the stories and voices of Black women by showing how the women of Bellavista think historical reparations and forgiveness have been turned into a spectacle more than a dignified process. Demonstrating that they are critical thinkers producing knowledge, the women of Bojayá open the doors for an understanding of forced migration that is more engaged and attuned to their sorrows, pain, dreams and cries for justice. Through their songs, which form a reservoir of knowledge, and through how they articulate what is happening in the territory, we can read how they are waiting for a discipline and a political landscape which are still not ready to respect the power of their knowledge, the validity of their experiences as lives that matter. Their story thus illustrates a need to think beyond the concept of forced migration and to consider categories such as deracination. Unthinking the notion of forced migration seems to us to offer the opportunity to reinforce communities' claims to have been deracinated from their ancestral lands again and again and again. It allows us to link their history of land tenure, territory making and dispossession of land, to world-historical conjunctures of local/regional/global cycles of colonial and capitalist exploitation.

Notes

1 This name is used for women and men who sing at community funerals. At the Pacific coast, this is a traditional practice.

2 For the ceremony, see: https://www.youtube.com/watch?v=cKKch6N639g&feature=youtu.beO

3 Documentary Voices of Resistance. Vol. 1. Cantadoras de Pogue. Icesi University, Cali, producer. 2016–2017. https://www.icesi.edu.co/vocesderesistencia/e/vol-1-cantadoras-de-pogue.php

4 Voices of Resistance https://www.icesi.edu.co/vocesderesistencia/sobre-el-ceaf.php

5 Colombian National Administrative Department of Statistics (DANE): https://www.dane.gov.co/

6 Vergara Figueroa, Fieldnotes.

References

Alabaoras of Pogue (2017) Alabao Por La Paz. Available from: https://centrodememoriahistorica.gov.co/alabao-por-la-paz/ [Accessed 26 April 2022].

Arboleda, S. (2016) *Le han florecido nuevas estrellas al cielo. Suficiencias Íntimas y Clandestinización del PensamientoAfrocolombiano*, Cali: Asociación Casa Cultural El Chontaduro y Poemía: Su casa editorial.

Bonilla-Silva, E. (2012) 'The invisible weight of whiteness: the racial grammar of everyday life in contemporary America', *Ethnic and Racial Studies*, 35(2): 173–94.

Cagüeñas Rozo, D. (2022) 'Cristo en el Atrato: un episodio en la historia de la facultad mimética', in D. Ruiz-Serna and C. del Cairo (eds) *Humanos más que Humanos y No Humanos: Intersecciones críticas en torno a la antropología y las ontologías*, Bogotá: Editorial Pontificia Universidad Javeriana.

Cañola, L. (2017) '"Décimo Quinto Aniversario": Voces de Resistencia Capítulo 1. Cantadoras de Pogue', *Voces de Resistencia*, [online] Available from: https://www.icesi.edu.co/vocesderesistencia/sobre-el-ceaf.php [Accessed 2 August 2021].

Castles, S. (2003) 'Towards a sociology of forced migration and social transformation', *Sociology*, 37(1): 13–34.

CNMH (2014) 'Un río de voces que clama. Bojayá. Consultado el 16 de mayo del 2016', [online] Available from: http://www.centrodememoriahistorica.gov.co/centro-audiovisual/audios/un-rio-de-voces-que-claman-bojaya [Accessed 2 August 2021].

CNRR-GMH (2010) 'Bojayá. La guerra sin límites. Bogotá: Tauros y Semana', [online] Available from: www.centrodememoriahistorica.gov.co/descargas/informes2010/informe_bojaya.pdf [Accessed 2 August 2021].

DANE (Colombian National Administrative Department of Statistics) (2021) https://www.dane.gov.co/index.php/en/ [Accessed 2 August 2021].

Hartman, S. (2019) *Wayward Lives, Beautiful Experiments: Intimate Histories of Riotous Black Girls, Troublesome Women, and Queer Radicals*, New York: W.W. Norton, p 348.

Herrera Valencia, M., Mosquera Lemus, L., Cagüeñas Rozo, D. and Vergara-Figueroa, A. (2019) 'El objeto-relato como dispositivo de memoria: el caso del Grupo de Alabao de Pogue, Bojayá, Chocó', in L.F. Durán, D.V.T. Rojas Roa, L.G. Martínez, E.C. Puentes and D.J.L. Cediel (eds) *Lugares, recorridos y sentidos de la memoria histórica Acercamientos metodológicos*, Chía: Universidad de la Sabana.

Hill Collins, P. (2000) *Black Feminist Thought: Knowledge, Consciousness, and the Politics of Empowerment*, New York and London: Routledge.

Lefranc, S. (2005) *Políticas del perdón*, Bogotá: Grupo Editorial Norma.

Mauss, M. (1966) *The Gift: Forms and Functions of Exchange in Archaic Societies*, London, Cohen & West.

Marín, P. and Alzate, G. (2021) 'Ethical and political implications of "performance" in a rural cultural practice: Afro-Colombian women singers from the town of Pogue', *Tiyatro Eleştirmenliği ve Dramaturji Bölümü Dergisi*, 32: 1–22.

Mosquera Palomenque, E. (2017) '"Siempre seas bendito": Voces de Resistencia Capítulo 1. Cantadoras de Pogue', *Voces de Resistencia*, [online] Available from: https://www.icesi.edu.co/vocesderesistencia/sobre-el-ceaf.php [Accessed 2 August 2021].

Mosquera Rosero-Labbé, C. and Barcelos, L. (eds) (2007) *Afro-reparaciones: memorias de la esclavitud y justicia reparativa para negros, afrocolombianos y raizales*, Bogotá: Universidad Nacional de Colombia. Centro de Estudios Sociales (CES).

Mosquera Rosero-Labbé, C., Laó-Montes, A. and Rodríguez Garavito, C. (eds) (2010) *Debates sobre ciudadanía y políticas raciales en las Américas Negras*. Bogotá: Universidad Nacional de Colombia, Universidad del Valle.

Ohmer, S. (2019) 'Afro-Latin American documentary resistance from the Pacific coast: how Voces de Resistencia (2017) changes the landscapes of aesthetics, academia/community collaboration, and Black feminist activism during the Colombian "peace process"', *Afro-Latin/American Research Association (PALARA)*, 23(Fall): 49–59.

Quiceno, N., Ochoa Sierra, M. and Villamizar, A. (2017) 'La política del canto y el poder de las alabaoras de Pogue (Bojayá, Chocó)', *Estudios Políticos* (Universidad de Antioquia), July-Dec, 51: 175–95.

Tovar Rojas, P. (2007) 'El cementerio africano en Nueva York: enseñanzas de un ejercicio de reconciliación', in C. Mosquera Rosero-Labbé and L. Barcelos (eds) *Afro-reparaciones: memorias de la esclavitud y justicia reparativa para negros, afrocolombianos y raizales*, Bogotá: Universidad Nacional de Colombia. Centro de Estudios Sociales (CES).

Vergara-Figueroa, A. (2018) *Afrodescendant Resistance to Deracination in Colombia. Massacre at Bellavista-Bojayá-Chocó*, Cham: Palgrave Macmillan.

Vergara-Figueroa, A. and Arboleda Hurtado, K. (2016) 'Afrodiasporic feminist conspiracy: motivations and paths forward from the first international seminar', *Meridians: Transnational Feminisms*, 14(2): 118–129.

Vergara-Figueroa, A. and Cosme Puntiel, C. (2018) *Demando mi libertad: Mujeres negras y sus estrategias de Resistencia en la Nueva Granada, Venezuela y Cuba, 1700–1800*, Cali: Universidad Icesi.

Vergara-Figueroa, A., Ramírez Vidal, L., Valencia Angulo, L.E., Agudelo Henao, L.M., Mosquera Lemus, L.M., Rojas Mora, S. (2017) *Descolonizando Mundos: Aportes de intelectuales negras y negros al pensamiento social colombiano*, Ciudad Autónoma de Buenos Aires: CLACSO.

13

The Subaltern Can Speak: The Mobility Strategies of Forced Migrants in Kenya's Kalobeyei Integrated Settlement

Felicity Atieno Okoth

Introduction

Migration research has largely privileged the analysis of migrants primarily as subjects needing to integrate into migrant-receiving societies, but has failed to adequately address migration against the backdrop of power, and specifically postcoloniality (Casas-Cortes et al, 2015b; c). A postcolonial approach to understanding migration evokes questions on the exploitative elements of border regimes and goes further to link migration to the inequalities which migrants from the global South – here conceptualized as subalterns – encounter in transit and Europe (De Genova, 2016). At a policy level, the racial fact of border regimes in Europe has rarely been acknowledged as it forces a face-to-face encounter with the violent postcoloniality of contemporary Europe where a large number of migrants from formerly colonized countries have been rendered 'illegal' (Lemberg-Pedersen, 2019). These migrants are, however, challenging the borders set up by The European Union (EU) by adopting different subversion strategies, beyond the Union's intensified externalized border controls (Papadopoulos and Tsianos, 2013).

In the context of increasing border controls at the edge of the European Union (EU), this chapter casts its lens on Kalobeyei Integrated Settlement, a project funded largely by the European Union (EU) to facilitate the local integration of refugees and asylum seekers being hosted in Kenya (Betts et al, 2019). Kenya has for a long time been considered a country of transit by forced migrants, given its encampment policy. Consequently, migrants' aspirations are often oriented towards moving to a third country in the global North, as opposed to settling in Kenya (ECDPM, 2019). Using a postcolonial lens, this chapter aims to explore the mobility strategies of refugees within Kalobeyei settlement against the backdrop of the delocalization and externalization of Europe's borders. This is in line with growing interest in migration research that favours a postcolonial approach to border regimes (Mayblin and Turner, 2021). EU's border externalization, for instance, has been conceptualized in relation to the 'colonial matrix of power', where the refortification of borders has been equalized with the disposability of lives that are particularly Black and/or brown (Lemberg-Pedersen, 2018; Darder and Griffiths, 2018).

Postcolonial approaches to understanding migration include perspectives that focus on the periods between colonialism and independence as chronological markers. Focus here is largely on the migration flows that occurred post-independence and the transnational ties that continue to bind colonized and colonizing countries to date (Bleich, 2005; Darian-Smith, 1996; Loyal, 2009). Others, including subaltern scholars, view postcolonialism as a continuation of colonialism through discourses and rhetoric that tip power in favour of the West. Here, claims of how and who can talk and write about formerly colonized people are questioned (Said, 1978; Spivak, 1998). This chapter however adopts Frilund's (2018) and Blunt and McEvan's (2002) conceptualization: '[T]he "post" of "postcolonialism" takes up two meanings, first, a temporal aftermath – a period of time after colonialism – and a critical aftermath – cultures, discourses, policies and practices that lie beyond but remain closely influenced by, colonialism' (Blunt and McEvan, 2002: 4). This conceptualization is taken up in this chapter as it avoids the structural categorization of the terms 'colonial' and 'postcolonial' which otherwise hinge themselves on temporality.

The chapter is divided into four broad sections. It begins by exploring the link between migration and postcoloniality, and the dynamic impact of colonial encounters on both colonizing and colonized societies. The current politics of externalization within Europe and the racial fact inherent in these practices are specifically explored (Balibar, 1998, 2001; De Genova, 2010, 2016; Lemberg-Pedersen, 2019). Next, I present Kalobeyei Settlement as a border and as an EU delocalization project (Barbero, 2012; den Hertog, 2016; Cuttitta, 2018; Lemberg-Pedersen, 2018). The third section presents the field and finally highlights the mobility strategies adopted by forced migrants in Kalobeyei Settlement while analysing these using the concept of subaltern voice construction (Spivak, 1998; Papadopoulos et al, 2008; Darder and Griffiths, 2018). I conclude by summing up the most critical aspects of my arguments.

Forced migration and postcoloniality: temporal and critical aftermaths

Despite the official end of colonialism in Africa 50 years ago, the former colonial powers of Europe are yet to fully acknowledge the colonial legacies on the continent, particularly in relation to the current challenges of globalization, migration and minority politics. The EU's immigration and asylum agenda and current border externalization policies are blind to the scramble and partition of Africa following the Berlin Congress of 1884–85 and how this has affected migration today. Loyal (2009) and Bourdieu and Wacquant (2000), for example, highlight how colonialism disenfranchized Algerians of their land and pushed them to urban areas. This consequently influenced their migration to France. According to Loyal (2009: 416), the current condition of the Algerian, that is, their 'psychosocial equilibrium, self-identification and cognitive dissonance' is undergirded by colonialism and continues to inform their migration aspirations to France.

Balibar (2001), highlights three phenomena that can be observed in this context. First, the resurgence of systematic migration rooted in the colonial era. Second, the use of colonial methods of administration aimed at governing human mobility whereby EU member states are setting up headquarters in various municipalities and capitals of formerly colonized countries (see also Chapter 4). Third, and as a result of these, a shift back to the citizen-subject colonial government schemes where some ethnicities are hierarchized and in effect dominated based on their strata in the hierarchy. Fortification efforts are not meant to act as a barrier to all but rather there exists hierarchization and differentiation where entry is determined based on the groups migrants are seen to belong to (Frilund, 2018). Migrants from former colonies often find themselves in the lower strata.

Despite Balibar describing this hierarchization 20 years ago, there has been inadequate engagement with the migration-postcoloniality nexus and [im]migration from a historical standpoint. Academic and public discourses have instead favoured social and economic lenses to explaining migration. The movement of persons from the global South (both forced and voluntary) as such, has been conceptualized as largely driven by economic hardships and represented to be taking place on an extraordinarily unmanageable scale, conveniently forgetting refugee regimes within Western contexts and displacement within colonial territories produced by European powers (Mayblin, 2017; Danewid, 2017). Because of a lack of historical perspective in migration rhetoric, many EU citizens construe immigration as a temporary, accidental, recent phenomenon that is a threat to their existence. Yet, migration is constituted by, and an extension of, Europe's colonial and postcolonial reality (Thomas, 2013). The place of the 'Other', in this case 'Africa', in the EU's political and social imaginary is key, especially when exploring the role such constructs and perceptions continue to play in migration policymaking, and in shaping perceptions of Africa (as a continent) and Africans (as a people) (Thomas, 2013; Hansen and Jonsson, 2014).

Academic and political discourses that highlight the connectedness of Europe and Africa have frequently represented the two as an unmediated pairing of opposites: White over Black or North over South. These categorizations, it has been argued, perpetuate dominant epistemologies of displacement and reinforce colonial modes of governance and power (Thomas, 2013). The refortification of borders in the context of these discourses manifest in the re-drawing of the global colour line (De Genova, 2018) rendering Black and brown lives disposable, in order that European life might flourish (Darder and Griffiths, 2018). The element of power inherent in this process is conceptualized by Mbembe (2003: 17) as necropolitics, where:

> Power defines itself in relation to a biological field—which it takes control of and vests itself in. This control presupposes the distribution of human species into groups, the subdivision of the population into subgroups, and the establishment of a biological caesura between the ones and the others. This is what Foucault labels with the (at first sight familiar) term racism.

Race, according to Mbembe, undergirds Western practices and political thoughts, especially when it comes to ruling over others or imagining others – often people from the global South – as less human. De Genova (2018), in the same vein, posits that anyone concerned with questions of race and racism currently must recognize that contemporary migration contexts in Europe are an extension of the continent's racial colonial past. Racism in this sense is manifested in border and security measures of locking out the other and internalized through discourses on race/ethnic relations (Thomas, 2013, see also Chapters 7 and 10). The racial fact of migration has however not deterred the colonized from the lure of former colonial centres. Fanon (1967), in trying to explain this double-edged phenomenon, posits that:

> When the settler and the native's glances meet, the settler ascertains bitterly 'They want to take our place'. And it is indeed true for there is no native who does not dream of setting himself up in the settler's place. It is always in place of the other that the colonial desire is articulated. (p. xxvii)

Fanon's account foregrounds the need to explore how African migrants' colonial desires inform their subversion strategies. The strategies adopted by African migrants are conceptualized here as the subaltern speaking. Borrowing from Spivak (1998), the Subaltern is defined broadly as a minority with a colonial past. Cognisance is, however, given to the fact that minorities are often hierarchized with those in the lowest strata, for example, women, the disabled and the elderly exposed to further epistemic violence from within. Spivak (1988) and Chakrabarty (2000) both argue that the essentialization of subalterns as a unified one ignores the inherent differences within the colonized body politic, which in itself is an act of violence. In this chapter I use the term subaltern not as a fixed category, but as a heuristic tool aimed at analysing the actions of the forced migrants in the case study. The subaltern is conceived here as having the ability to speak back based on their border subversion actions (on the need to represent the political agency of refugees, see Chapters 11 and 12).

Spivak's (1988) question on whether the subaltern can truly speak was taken up by the Subaltern Study Group (Chatterjee, 1989, 1993; Chakrabarty, 2000) and other thinkers who explore subaltern subversion as speaking against the backdrop of postcoloniality. Agency has been linked here to subaltern resistance undergirded by power dynamics. Linking subaltern resistance to migration, Papadopoulos et al (2008), have similarly theorized subaltern mobility as being at the centre of the configurations of power and practices of resistance. Casas-Cortes et al (2015a) go further to highlight the constituent power of migrant journeys using Autonomies of Migration (AoM). The concept of AoM challenges the dominant interpretations of migration by favouring an analysis that focuses on the process of subjectification in its different forms. Here, the diversification of migrant practices becomes political organization and mobilization sites.

AoM sees the act of migration as a political act, and links migratory acts in the context of border controls to expressions of migrant agency. That is not to suggest that AoM advocates view migrant agency as equivalent to power. Casas-Cortes et al (2011), for example, argue that the AoM approach does not downplay the role of power. Rather, it aims to point at resistance and struggle as constitutive elements of border power simultaneously. This draws on Foucault's (1982) theory of power from a broad perspective. The symbols of social order (in this case, the border) simultaneously becomes inhibitory and stimulating as they do not convey the message 'do not dare budge' but rather cry out for subversion. Mobility across these established borders is thus considered a political act of power that transgresses the economic logics of migration. From an AoM standpoint, Papadopoulos and Tsianos (2013) argue that border controls are subject to the logics, motivations and trajectories of the subalterns which derail and delegitimize sovereign control.

AoM has been critiqued for romanticizing mobility and ignoring the realities of detention and deportation inherent in EU states' desires to control migration. This control desire has seen the Union push global South 'neighbouring' and 'neighbours of neighbouring' countries into containing migrants within their territories through financial incentives (Barbero, 2012; Cuttitta, 2018). This has consequently resulted in a myriad of actors and agencies being tasked with migration management in countries of origin and transit (Andersson, 2014a; Casas-Cortes et al, 2015a). These interventions have particularly been in anticipation of migration and thus act to shift borders to the points where migration processes begin – way before the external borders are reached. Cuttitta (2018: 785) conceptualizes this phenomenon as 'delocalization' – a process whereby border enforcement gradually moves away from the cartographical line of state borders. This is accompanied by other necessary activities such as asylum processing increasingly occurring within countries of transit or origin resulting in what is termed extra-territorialization and externalization (see Cuttitta, 2018). He further argues that delocalization coupled with humanitarianism is instrumental to restrictive migration management and often acts to exonerate European states from their legal responsibilities (on trajectories of externalization in French and Italian colonialism, see, respectively, Chapters 5 and 8. On Anglo-American colonial-imperial externalization practice, see Chapter 2).

The AoM approach clearly is helpful in explaining subalterns' subversion strategies in the context of externalized border controls, bearing in mind the need not to overly romanticize such strategies. However, the approach falls short in linking such phenomena with postcoloniality. This chapter thus acts to bridge these two approaches. In the next section I introduce the case study setting through which these dynamics will be explored.

Kalobeyei Integrated Settlement as a site of border subversion

In May 2019, I started my PhD fieldwork in Kalobeyei Settlement having previously been part of a team that had, a year earlier, conducted a midterm review of EU projects within the settlement. I specifically sought to explore intercultural relations between refugee traders and host populations against the backdrop of the settlement's integration agenda. An ethnographic case study was the method of inquiry adopted by the study and I spent 1 month in the field conducting semi structured interviews, having informal conversations and observing the day-to-day interactions between refugee traders and the host community, in Village 1 market – the biggest market in the settlement. I stayed in Kakuma town, the nearest centre to the settlement, and made daily morning and evening 30-minute commutes to the field. I spent the last week living with a Congolese family, as both spouses were traders who I had formed close relationship with during my previous visit to the location. In return, I assisted with the daily domestic chores and bought subsistence goods that were needed by the family.

An ethnographic case study was appropriate because it allowed for an in-depth understanding of the phenomena under study within set time boundaries – while still acknowledging that the study is located within a richer, wider context (Parker-Jenkins, 2018: 25). Further, it benefited from the prior development of theoretical prepositions while still allowing for the employment of ethnographic techniques. I was thus able to interview 26 refugee traders, six of them women from different nationalities, with those of Congolese descent being the majority. I conducted three focus group discussions (one male, one female and a mixed focus group) with different refugee traders where their lived experiences were discussed in the context of their intercultural encounters with the host community. It was during these discussions that it came out that a majority of these traders were keener on migrating to third countries as opposed to remaining in the settlement. They were specifically adopting different mobility strategies – despite Kenya's encampment policy, and against the EU's vision of Kalobeyei Settlement.

Kalobeyei Settlement and specifically the Kalobeyei Integrated Social and Economic Development Program (KISDEP) is funded largely by the EU's Emergency Trust Fund for Africa (EUTF). The EUTF allocated €4.6 billion to Africa in order to foster better migration management within the continent and limit irregular migration to Europe (Coggio, 2021). €24.9 million have been specifically allocated to Kenya as of 2020 (European Commission, 2021), with the funds largely geared towards efforts to locally integrate refugees and to strengthen local institutional and technical capacities to facilitate local integration. External border management, as seen in the case of Kalobeyei, has remained a top funding priority for European policymakers. This phenomenon has been highlighted by den Hertog (2016) who, having mapped the funding instruments associated with the EU's external migration control, found out that the budgets are massive and that they have been increasing over time.

The United Nations High Commissioner for Refugees (UNHCR), together with the Government of Kenya, are the EU's major KISDEP partners. UNHCR works together with other 'implementing partners' – mostly International Non-Governmental Organizations (INGOs) in order to ensure the vision for Kalobeyei Settlement (local integration and refugee self-reliance) are met. The local integration of forced migrants in Kalobeyei is being pushed by the EU outside Kenyan legal and policy frameworks, as Kenya still officially has an encampment policy (Refugee Act, 2006) that limits employment opportunities and the free movement of refugees outside camps. In this way, the EU is incentivizing the Kenyan government to implement policies which are in contradiction with national refugee policy. Such external migration controls according to Lemberg-Pedersen (2019), are part of the EU's initiatives to complement their regional policies with the control of migration outside their territorial borders, and in so doing interfere with the sovereignty of countries in the global South.

The strategic, economic and geopolitical interests maintained in countries of migrants' origin and transit can, then, be understood as part of a colonial project on the part of the EU (Barbero, 2012; Lemberg-Pedersen, 2018). The humanitarian rhetoric of fostering 'social cohesion' and 'self-reliance' in Kalobeyei Settlement acts to contain refugees within a country of transit, reinforcing Cuttitta's notion that 'humanitarianization and delocalization are in a relationship of mutual support and influence' (2018: 785). In this way, refugees are subjected to humanitarian care with the aim of preventing onward migration, thus controlling the borders of countries far away remotely.

Kalobeyei Settlement in effect can be categorized as a border based on Agier's (2011: 50) position that the border is 'everywhere that an undesirable is identified', with the travellers' bodies becoming enforcement sites in themselves. Novak (2017), in the same vein, discusses the embodiment of the EU–Africa border within different localities by different individuals. This casts light on the fluidity of the border and how it is differently constructed by various social agents in everyday life. As such, borders are not static but rather part of dynamic, continuous b/ordering processes. This conceptualization helps to move away from the essentialization of borders and territories as fixed entities (Collyer and King, 2015). In this way, Lemberg-Pedersen (2018) conceptualizes borders as a 'processual shift' where 'bordering' denotes ongoing socially regulative functions linked to trajectories of racism and power. This is discussed in the context of the colonial subject – the subaltern, speaking back at EU's border externalization in the next section.

The subaltern can speak

While stricter border controls and neocolonial projects that go beyond the EU's immediate borders are intensifying, migrants from the global South (subalterns) are adopting strategies to bypass these extended controls. The logic behind these strategies is not merely social, political or economic but can be traced to postcolonial desires. This position is buttressed by Fanon (1967) who posits that the psychopathology of the African, his alienation and his desires in relation to the colonizer (EU) does not emanate from a socio-economic sense but from a psycho-existential complex that transcends conscious reason. This is illustrated by a conversation that I had with a 32-year-old Congolese clothing trader who had been in Kalobeyei for 4 years. He posited that:

> Now we read on social media and from organisations working here that they do not want refugees in Europe anymore. It makes you feel bad that the same people who caused problems in your

> country do not want you ... that you bother them ... no one wants to go where they are not welcomed but I will not focus on this for now. All my life I have thought of going to Belgium to have a better life so simple racism will not stop me. ... I will try to get there even if it takes 20 years.

The respondent was doing comparatively well economically in relation to other traders in the settlement and had used his profits to establish a larger business for his wife in the settlement. Despite being well established in the settlement, the respondent still desired to go to Belgium using any means possible and was currently saving money for a mission geared towards Belgium. He refused to disclose this mission but promised to send me pictures of his soft life when he got there. I asked him why Belgium, and he mentioned that it is because they speak French, and that he has a right to live there given that 'Belgium plundered my homeland and killed my ancestors'. It is from this tension, both psychological and political, that strategies of border subversion by migrants emerge. The 'point of Europe' conjured by the respondent highlights the ambivalence of Europe both as an imagined concept, and as a project to be accomplished. The subaltern refuses the predetermined space put up for him/her by the EU. Borders in this sense, rather than stopping the subaltern, then invite him/her into Europe's presence where power relations are played (Bhabha, 1994). This is contextualized by a respondent who posited that:

> I do not see myself being here for more than 2 years. UNHCR says resettlement has been streamlined ... that we have to consider local integration, but no sane person would agree to this kind of life out of their free will. Just look around you. What are we integrating to? A desert? I do not plan to stay here for long. ... I plan to file for protection from domestic violence from my husband. Women on the protection list are often given resettlement priority. If not, I will go back to my country and find other ways. ... I also know people I can pay to get there but this will be my last option.

The respondent was a Congolese female trader who has been in the settlement with her husband and two young children. The couple run the shop and have both agreed on filing a domestic violence case if Kalobeyei remains a local integration settlement. The husband is okay with going back to his hometown if the wife and kids are resettled under the protection banner. It is noteworthy to mention that less women are currently being taken into protection shelters by UNCHR as there are now stricter follow up sessions to ascertain the veracity of domestic violence claims (ECDPM, 2019). It can then be said that border regimes in themselves are not transformative, rather they are brought to life by migrants' subversion strategies aimed at overcoming them (Casas-Cortes et al, 2015b). Migration policies then are subject to migrants' mobilities rather than the actions of states or border control actors.

This power dynamic is further illustrated by a refugee community leader that I had an informal conversation with in the market. He explained that:

> It is not strange to have a Congolese asylum seeker registered in Tanzania, moving to Uganda then Kenya just hoping that their relocation case will go through eventually. They usually crisscross these country borders annually and some have managed to beat the system and get to Europe. But now UNHCR says the donors are not happy with this. ... They are looking at how to integrate the registration system to capture single registration like the one in Europe ... but people will still find a way to reach Europe.

This statement points to the fact that migrants take up different routes, identities and status while on the move based on the border regimes they encounter at different points of their journey (Casas-Cortes et al 2015a; b). This dynamic identifies with Andersson's (2014b) arguments that the EU does not prevent the migrant from entering its borders rather it also helps bring their target, the postcolonial migrant, into being. Thus, instead of taking up a totalizing or restrictive approach to power, postcolonial approaches need to foreground how power is complexly constituted and distributed along migration corridors, specifically migrants' desires and efforts to go beyond spaces and territories defined for them by the postcolonial masters (Heidenreich and Vukadinovc, 2008: 141).

The migration aspirations and desires of the interviewees in Kalobeyei reflect mobility trajectories that they aspire to pursue, but cannot; unlike migrants from the desirable parts of the globe. This brings to fore the logic of capital, but not in a way intended to brush away migrants' complex subaltern subjectivities (see also Chapter 12). That migrants migrate for economic reasons strengthens the postcolonial logic rather than counters it (Novak, 2017). The subaltern recognizes that their position of disadvantage is caused by the colonial master, and in turn desires to take up the position of the master (Bhahba, 1994). The subalterns have consequently reinvented themselves and found new ways of reaching Europe. Andersson (2014b) highlights similar subterfuges in the Mediterranean that point to the fact that border regimes do not in themselves have the ability to transform but rather they are rendered dynamic by the various forms of migration acts (Casas-Cortes et al, 2015a). As such, the erroneous supposition that migration policies are solely decided by states and various institutions of border control needs to be re-examined. Borders react and respond to subaltern mobility strategies as opposed to demarcations of sovereign administrative units. In the postcolonial sense, subaltern hybridity – neither being here nor there – destabilizes Europe's ambitions of confining the body of the migrant within its borders, outside Europe's internal borders.

Conclusion

This chapter has used a postcolonial approach to understand the border subversion strategies adopted by African migrants in their quest to reach Europe. Using Kalobeyei Integrated Settlement as a case study, the chapter conceptualizes the settlement as a border given its role in containing the bodies of African migrants (subalterns) in Kenya and effectively outside EU's borders. These steps have, however, not deterred African migrants from desiring and attempting to reach Europe as seen in the strategies the research participants are adopting, in an aim to bypass humanitarian systems of control within the settlement. Kalobeyei, as a border, thus does not prevent the postcolonial African migrant from entering EU's borders; rather, it helps bring the postcolonial migrant into being – it invites him into Europe's presence. This chapter foregrounds the need to consider colonial histories when analysing migration from the global South, in this case Africa. This is because the African migrants' migration logic transcends social and economic necessities with migration revealed by the respondents to be less an instrumental undertaking than a 'valued and yearned for' thing in its own right.

This chapter has revealed that the desire and imagination of somewhere is undergirded by temporal and critical postcolonial rhetoric that sustains the migrants' desire in that they may fail to migrate but still partake actively in these geographical imaginations. The chapter further highlights how the EU has to constantly re-examine its borders based on the subversion strategies that subalterns adopt –that is, being registered in multiple countries, adopting different identities and creating new narratives at different points of their journeys. Consequently, better technologies and mechanisms are being adopted at borders to effectively contain the subaltern within the global South with the help of humanitarian actors. Nevertheless, the EU's borders are constantly being transgressed, resisted and reappropriated by African migrants. The possibility of the subaltern speaking does not, however, negate the need to pay attention to the structures that have been facilitated by colonial legacies currently manifested through unequal access to rights and opportunities. A postcolonial approach to migration, in this sense, has enabled this chapter to highlight how delocalization coupled with humanitarianism, is currently instrumental in extending migration governance that is colonial in nature. This is done under the guise of better migration management in the global South and thus should be further theoretically explored from a postcolonial standpoint.

References

Agier, M. (2011) *Managing the Undesirables: Refugee Camps and Humanitarian Government*, Cambridge: Polity.

Andersson, R. (2014a) *Illegality, Inc.: Clandestine Migration and the Business of Bordering Europe*, Oakland: University of California Press.

Andersson, R. (2014b) 'Hunter and prey: patrolling clandestine migration in the Euro-African borderlands', *Anthropological Quarterly*, 87(1): 119–49.

Balibar, E. (1998) 'The borders of Europe', in P. Cheah and B. Robbins (eds) *Cosmopolitics: Thinking and Feeling Beyond the Nation*, Minneapolis: University of Minnesota Press, pp 216–32.

Balibar, E. (2001) 'Outlines of a topography of cruelty: citizenship and civility in the era of global violence', *Constellations*, 8(1): 15–29.

Barbero, I. (2012) 'Orientalising citizenship: the legitimation of immigration regimes in the European Union', *Citizenship Studies*, 16(5–6): 751–68.

Betts, A., Delius, A., Rogers, C., Sterck, O. and Stierna, M. (2019) *Doing Business in Kakuma: Refugees, Entrepreneurship, and the Food Market*, Oxford: RSC.

Bhabha, H. (1994) *The Location of Culture*, London: Routledge.

Bleich, E. (2005) 'The legacies of history? Colonization and immigrant integration in Britain and France', *Theory and Society*, 34(2): 171–95.

Blunt, A. and McEwan, C. (eds) (2002) *Postcolonial Geographies*, London: Continuum.

Bourdieu, P. and Wacquant, L. (2000) 'The organic ethnologist of Algerian migration', *Ethnography*, 1(2): 173–82.

Casas-Cortes M., Cobarrubias, S. and Pickles, J. (2011) 'An interview with Sandro Mezzadra', *Environment and Planning D: Society and Space*, 29: 584–98.

Casas-Cortes, M., Cobarrubias, S. and Pickles, J. (2015a) 'Riding routes and itinerant borders: autonomy of migration and border externalization', *Antipode*, 47(4): 894–914.

Casas-Cortes, M., Cobarrubias, S. and Pickles, J. (2015b) 'Changing borders, rethinking sovereignty: towards a right to migrate', *REMHU Revista Interdisciplinar da Mobilidade Humana*, 23(44): 47–60.

Casas-Cortes, M., Cobarrubias, S., De Genova, N., Garelli, G., Grappi, G. and Heller, C. (2015c) 'New keywords: migration and borders', *Cultural Studies*, 29(1): 55–87.

Chakrabarty, D. (2000) *Provincializing Europe: Postcolonial Thought and Historical Difference*, Princeton: Princeton University Press.

Chatterjee, P. (1989) 'Caste and subaltern consciousness' in R. Guha (ed) *Subaltern Studies VI: Writings on South Asian History and Society*, New Delhi: Oxford University Press, pp 169–209.

Chatterjee, P. (1993) *The Nation and its Fragments: Colonial and Postcolonial Histories*, Princeton: Princeton University Press.

Coggio, T. (2021) 'Europe's tackling of "root causes" of African migration has a mixed record', *Migration Policy Institute* [online] 6 May, Available from: https://www.migrationpolicy.org/article/europe-migration-africa-eutf [Accessed 16 June 2021].

Collyer, M. and King, R. (2015) 'Producing transnational space: international migration and the extra-territorial reach of state power', *Progress in Human Geography*, 39(2): 185–204.

Cuttitta, P. (2018) 'Delocalization, humanitarianism, and human rights: the Mediterranean border between exclusion and inclusion', *Antipode*, 50(3): 783–803.

Danewid, I. (2017) 'White innocence in the Black Mediterranean: hospitality and the erasure of history', *Third World Quarterly*, 38(7): 1674–89.

Darder, A. and Griffiths, T.G. (2018) 'Revisiting "can the subaltern speak?" introduction', *Qualitative Research Journal*, 18(2): 82–8.

Darian-Smith, E. (1996) 'Postcolonialism: a brief introduction', Social & Legal Studies, 5(3): 291–9.

De Genova, N. (2010) 'Migration and race in Europe: the trans-Atlantic metastases of a post-colonial cancer', *European Journal of Social Theory*, 13(3): 405–19.

De Genova, N. (2016) 'The European question: migration, race, and postcoloniality in Europe', *Social Text*, 34(3(128)): 75–102.

De Genova, N. (2018) 'The "migrant crisis" as racial crisis: do Black Lives Matter in Europe?', *Ethnic and Racial Studies*, 41(10): 1765–82.

den Hertog, L. (2016) 'EU budgetary responses to the "refugee crisis" reconfiguring the funding landscape', *CEPS Paper in Liberty and Security in Europe*, 93: 1–20.

ECDPM (2019) *Regional Baseline Report, RDPP Learning and Evaluation Trajectory*, [online] Available from: https://ecdpm.org/wpcontent/uploads/small_RDPP_Baseline_LET_consolidated_reportpdf [Accessed 19 October 2020].

European Commission (2021) *EU Emergency Trust Fund for Africa: 2020 Annual Report*, Brussels: Publications Office of the European Union.

Fanon, F. (1967) *Black Skin White Masks*, New York: Grove Press.

Foucault, M. (1982) 'The subject and power', *Critical Inquiry*, 8(4): 777–95.

Frilund, R. (2018) 'Exploring (transit) migration through a postcolonial lens: Tibetans migrating to India and beyond', *Journal of Ethnic and Migration Studies*, [online] DOI: 10.1080/1369183X.2018.1501270

Hansen, P. and Jonsson, S. (2014) *Eurafrica: The Untold History of European Integration and Colonialism*, New York: Bloomsbury Academic.

Heidenreich, N. and Vukadinovc, V.S. (2008) 'In your face: activism, agit-prop, and the autonomy of migration – the case of Kanak-Attack in Halle', in R. Halle and R. Steingröver (eds) *After the Avant Garde: Contemporary German and Austrian Experimental Film*, Rochester: Camden House, pp 131–56.

Lemberg-Pedersen, M. (2018) 'Security, industry and migration', in A. Weinar, S. Bonjour and L. Zhyznomirska (eds) *European Border Control. The Routledge Handbook of the Politics of Migration in Europe*, London: Routledge.

Lemberg-Pedersen, M. (2019) 'Manufacturing displacement: externalization and postcoloniality in European migration control', *Global Affairs*, 5(3): 247–71.

Loyal, S. (2009) 'The French in Algeria, Algerians in France: Bourdieu, colonialism, and migration', *The Sociological Review*, 57(3): 406–27.

Mayblin, L. (2017) *Asylum After Empire. Colonial Legacies in the Politics of Asylum Seeking*, London: Rowman and Littlefield International.

Mayblin, L. and Turner, J. (2021) *Migration Studies and Colonialism*, Cambridge: Polity.

Mbembe, A. (2003) 'Necropolitics', *Public Culture*, 15(1): 11–40.

Novak, P. (2017) 'Back to borders', *Critical Sociology*, 43(6): 847–64.

Papadopoulos, D. and Tsianos, V. S. (2013) 'After citizenship: autonomy of migration, organisational ontology and mobile commons', *Citizenship Studies*, 17(2): 178–96.

Papadopoulos, D. Stephenson, N. and Tsianos, V. (2008) *Escape Routes: Control and Subversion in the 21st Century*, London: Pluto Press.

Parker-Jenkins, M. (2018) 'Problematising ethnography and case study: reflections on using ethnographic techniques and researcher positioning', *Ethnography and Education*, 13: 18–33.

Said, E,W. (1978) Orientalism, New York: Pantheon Books.

Spivak, G. (1988) 'Can the subaltern speak?' in C. Nelson and L. Grossberg (eds) *Marxism and Interpretation of Culture*, Urbana: University of Illinois, pp 271–313.

Spivak, G. (1998) 'Race before racism: the disappearance of the American', *Boundary 2*, 25(2): 35–53.

Thomas, D. (2013) Africa and France: Postcolonial Cultures, Migration, and Racism, [online] Available from: http://ebookcentral.proquest.com [Accessed 12 October 2019].

14

Conclusion: Postcoloniality and Forced Migration

Martin Lemberg-Pedersen, Sharla M. Fett, Lucy Mayblin, Nina Sahraoui and Eva Magdalena Stambøl

Introduction

Across 12 chapters and the Introduction, this volume has showcased a broad range of approaches to researching the entanglements of forced migration with colonialism in the past and through to the present. Reflecting the volume's deep commitment to interdisciplinarity, the authors have done this differently: through historical research, through tracing current continuities of historical practices (for example migration control, surveillance, racial hierarchies) and/or through employing post and decolonial theoretical perspectives to illuminate current patterns of forced mobility and its control. The variety of approaches mirrors the authors' breadth of disciplinary backgrounds from across the humanities and social sciences, including history and historiography, sociology, anthropology and ethnography, political science and philosophy, international relations and criminology. This makes it clear that the trend towards historicizing current migration policies and patterns of forced mobility in light of a colonial past is – and needs to be – taking place across a wide range of intellectual traditions and scholarly literatures. This book is a contribution to that endeavor. We have identified seven cross cutting themes within the volume: the enduring power of ideas of race and racial hierarchy in responses to forced migration; postcolonial states managing mobile populations in their own interests; states seeking to spatially organize populations along modern/colonial lines; the role of private companies and non-state actors; the role of technologies for surveillance, categorization and control; and the fraught politics of sanctuary and hospitality. In the following sections we elaborate on these themes.

The enduring power of ideas of race and racial hierarchy in responses to forced migration

One of the crucial features of European colonialism was the mobilization of racial differentiation and hierarchy as a means of dividing and governing populations around the world. A postcolonial lens draws out the ways in which the instrumentalization of 'race' as a method of differentiation reshaped social and political relations globally, with long lasting implications. Across many of the chapters in this volume, then, we see race being used as a means of differentiating, controlling and prolonging the exploitation of certain populations. Historical and contemporary examples range from Adderley and Fett's chapter where people freed from slavery are resettled in Liberia simply because of the colour of their skin, over Vergara-Figueroa and Marino's analysis of revived exclusions of Afro-descendant communities in Colombia, to Okoth's discussions of how racialized and colonial mobility controls persist across former and current colonies in Africa, in order to contain Black Africans within particular territories. There are striking continuities from the colonial period here, with practices such as fences, walls, push-backs, immobilization tactics, encampment or resettlement, in Colombia, Ceuta and Melilla, Mayotte, Tanzania and Kenya.

While the contemporary period is sometimes narrated as post-racial (see Lentin, 2020 for a discussion), we see in these case studies, the ways in which colonial ideas of racial difference not only continue in social life, but also serve to organize the governance of human mobility. Indeed, the aims of fixing Burundians in Tanzania and the Congolese in Kenya through local integration (against national refugee policy), essentially because they are Black and African (Chapter 4), illustrates the continued logic that particular people belong in particular places because of the colour of their skin. It also illustrates the attached assumptions of immutable difference working through the racialization of their very being (Fanon, 2008 [1961]) and hence their presumed inability to exercise citizenship in Europe and its settler colonies. Teunissen and Koutrolikou's account of Turkey as the gatekeeper to Europe, and how transgressions of the Greek/Turkish border are represented by governments as a racial threat of invasion shows how the framing of certain groups of people on the move depicts them as fundamentally dangerous. And when found to be 'out of place', whether in Africa or Europe, they should be removed.

The actors behind the many efforts to contain in these ways also follow colonial patterns. The EU comes up time and again as an actor that, on behalf of European member states, seeks to quarantine or contain Black migrants on the continent of Africa, even those seeking sanctuary. This is no surprise since the history of the inception of the EU is very much entangled with European colonialism in Africa, be it for demographic exports of European workers and settlers to colonial territories, or for commercial-industrial extractive interests (Hansen and Jonsson, 2014). The containment practice is also undertaken by postcolonial member states. Boeyink et al. (Chapter 4) show how French people are free to visit and work in Mayotte (an island in the Indian Ocean under French jurisdiction) but people holding a Mayotte residency permit need to apply for a visa to travel to metropolitan France or to another French overseas department. They explain how the hierarchical structure of mobility controls in the area is designed to limit both the immigration of Black people to Mayotte, but also of Black Mahorans to metropolitan France. Meanwhile 'metropolitans' are free to visit and work in Mayotte as if it were a fully integrated French territory.

But of course, those who are the targets of these policies are neither blind to the racial colonial logics informing them, nor passive victims of migration governance efforts. As Okoth's chapter on such techniques of fixing in place in Kenya shows, refugees who find themselves encamped in Africa see these efforts, and actively plan to resist them through nevertheless migrating to Europe. As one participant in her research explains: 'we will not let simple racism stop us'. Okoth frames this in relation to subalterns speaking back, and in Chapter 12, Vergara-Figueroa and Marino relate how women from the Black community of Bojayá use the 'alabaos' songs to reclaim and indeed strengthen a critical-political voice, which larger, national peace processes are constantly undermining through requests for forgiveness. This can again be compared to Chapter 11, where Cole takes issue with the prevailing assumption in the Ethics of Migration to assume that refugees lack agency or voice when it comes to developing political theoretical solutions to forced migration situations. This tendency, which Cole also argues spans across a number of disciplines and political discourse in general, seeks to cast the refugee as a passive existence to be saved by others. But both the participants in Okoth's research, the Colombian Bojayá community, and the many scholars with refugee background who have influenced political theory on issues of migration illustrate that such pacification cannot be maintained. What is revealed in processes of speaking back is an understanding of the care we must take when describing displacement processes, as well as attention to the ways in which vast architectures of control are based on a racist hostility to African migrants in, as well as beyond, Europe.

But this is a hostility which is delegitimized by those colonial histories which have brought (for example) Belgium and the Democratic Republic of Congo to the present moment, as Okoth's research participants so astutely observe. Mayblin, too, seeks to delegitimize hostility to racialized migrants, which so often seeks a non-racial legitimation. The framing of Third World migrants as diseased and therefore threatening is rooted in colonial ideas of civilization and hygiene, which cast the colonial world as a diseased space, and migrants from that world as therefore themselves a contagion risk (Anderson, 2006; Chapter 7). Each in their own manner, the chapters by Cole, Vergara-Figueroa and Marino, Okoth and Mayblin therefore pose fundamental calls for questioning the conceptual and normative assumptions of Western or Northern positionalities which continue to structure research and policy in forced migration.

The notable absence of race as an organizing principle in migration management in Fratantuono's chapter on the Ottoman Empire speaks to the distinct nature of empires during the age of colonialism. Different from the European empires, Ottoman colonialism sought to include newcomers within the imperial polity and in that sense saw the various populations under its rule as racially equal, though stratified on the basis of class. This gave rise to large-scale migration schemes for social engineering purposes within the Ottoman Empire, and local debates about the useful migrants across it. By comparison, the colonialism of the European empires assumed a colonial/modern dichotomy that has carried into present policies, as discussed later. It was fundamentally organized on the basis of human hierarchy, where some were understood to be less human than others (and even non-human), and therefore subject to enslavement, indenture, violence and exploitation. Racial hierarchy in the European empires then, as Mayblin discusses in Chapter 7, included both physical and cultural understandings of racial difference. People with different skin colours and hair textures were understood as not only physically distinct but also culturally graduated. We see the interplay of these different articulations of modern/colonial differentiation – physical and cultural – very much at work in contemporary forced migration governance in a way that the Ottoman logic of economic inclusion is not (though see Chapter 9 on the influence of colonial/modern ideas in the Greek/Turkish borderland, and Chapter 8 on such differentiations in the Italian/Turkish/Libyan borderlands).

(Post)colonial states managing mobile populations in their own interests

Colonial powers were able to directly control migration across vast territories, altering the demography of different places from Liberia to the Caribbean to Rumelia to Libya. Of course, this is also undertaken against the backdrop of the kinds of racial logics discussed previously in the volume. Adderley and Fett's chapter on the resettlement of slave trade refugees (Chapter 2), and Fratantuono's chapter on migration management in the Ottoman Empire (Chapter 3) together opened the volume with historical perspectives on this theme. These chapters shift the viewpoint of contemporary forced migration research, illuminating both the ways in which migration management in colonial empires was distinct from the contemporary period, but also revealing parallels and continuity. The Ottoman Empire embraced refugee reception as an economic opportunity, while the modern/colonial authorities in the US and British metropoles sought to resettle people who had been freed from the illegal slave trade in ways which supported their own interests, either in military endeavours or in population management. It is clear that this migration management has been a tool for actualizing the aims of powerful (post)colonial states over several centuries.

As many of the chapters in this volume show, this is often undertaken under the guise of helping and protecting, while the primary aim so often remains controlling and spatially fixing undesirable populations. Here, 'helping and protecting' might involve encampment, local integration, or welfare provision, or indeed requests for forgiveness for past violence and displacement. In all cases, such practices are also conveniently oriented to governing who can be in which spaces, and who can be contained, and prevented from moving on. Teunissen and Koutrolikou's (Chapter 9) account of the crisis framing of border crossing between Turkey and Greece demonstrates the ways in which Turkey both represents itself as the sole bearer of responsibility for helping the Syrian people, and then strategically uses European fears of refugee arrivals to bargain for favourable privileges such as funding and promises of EU accession.

Historically, controlling mobility was more explicitly connected to economic enrichment through extractive practices including taxing colonial populations for the benefit of metropolitan societies. Some of the chapters in this volume show how the extractive incentive was in fact a central driving force behind colonization, and tended to manifest through partnerships between European colonial states and their private extractive industries (see Chapters 5 and 8). Moreover, the objective to drive racialized populations out of a territory is in focus across the chapters which connect the EU and Africa, and also in the Indian case study explored by Chowdhory and Poyil (Chapter 10). Here, we learn that Indian citizenship law is being changed in order to exclude Muslims from citizenship claims and to control the mobility of Muslim populations within the wider Sub-Continent.

Seeking to spatially organize populations along modern/colonial lines

The impetus to govern population mobility is not necessarily colonial, and that impetus in the present does not necessarily need to hold any colonial resonance. But what a distinctly postcolonial, or indeed decolonial, perspective brings is the recognition of how colonial ways of understanding the world continue to shape the present. There have been a range of conceptualizations proposed which seek to express the modern/colonial worldview. That is, the view that the world can be divided up into people and places which sit somewhere along a temporal spectrum of development or civilization (see Mayblin and Turner, 2021 for an overview). Drawing on Fanon, Grosfoguel et al (2015) articulate this in terms of the zone of 'being' and 'non-being', Santos (2017) in terms of 'the abyssal line', Said (1995 [1978]) in a slightly more limited conceptualization explored the idea of the 'Orient' and the 'Occident', while Du Bois talks of a global 'color line' (Du Bois 1994 [1903]). Third World Approaches to International Law (TWAIL) scholars continue to use the concepts of 'Third World' and 'First World' (Kanwar 2015; Mutua, 2000) to express both the imagined content of these referents (they are not actual places, they are symbolic geographies), and the material implications of them. What is being expressed in all of these conceptualizations is the sense of a distinction between the 'modern' world (the West), and the non-modern worlds (the 'rest' in Stuart Hall's terms) which emerged through colonialism and has come to hold profound material consequences in the contemporary period (Hall, 1996; Trouillot, 2003).

For forced migration scholars, as we can see across the contributions to this volume, the key insight is then to see efforts of mobility control and governance in relation to this modern/colonial worldview – the abyssal line. Thus, we see in multiple chapters, the expenditure and effort that the EU is willing to invest in preventing people moving from the continent of Africa, with the intention of seeking asylum in Europe. This includes large amounts of development aid being re-directed to controlling and policing African populations and their (potential) mobility through the building of surveillance technologies, databases and other instruments of migration government in African countries (Stambøl and Jegen, Chapter 5; Tjønn and Lemberg-Pedersen, Chapter 8). In the context of COVID-19, Mayblin (Chapter 7) demonstrates how the imperative to prevent people from crossing this line has grave implications for refugees. Teunissen and Koutrolikou (Chapter 9) show us how the Turkish/Greek borderland acts as a buffer zone with Europe, and how Turkish politicians clearly see their role in maintaining the integrity of the abyssal line. Even in India (Chapter 10) we see efforts to exclude Muslim others who are represented as dissimilar and inferior in ways which are redolent of the colonial period. Vergara-Figueroa and Marino (Chapter 12) show how the politically valuable ability of the Bojayá community to grant a forgiveness for past massacres that neither the Colombian state, FARC nor the paramilitaries can forcibly extract themselves, both imbues the community with power, but also imbricates it in forced migration governance along a dehistoricized, modern/colonial worldview. Okoth's participants in Chapter 13 see the logic of coloniality/modernity in efforts to keep them in Kenya. Indeed, while scholars of forced migration have tended to be reluctant to connect the politics of mobility to colonialism, those who experience restrictive policies often do make those links.

The role of private companies and non-state actors, past and present

Many European empires that first began as trading missions by private companies with royal charters, such as the Dutch West India Company, were pivotal in early colonial activities. In general, such private actors from across the various European empires were involved in colonial geopolitics and trade routes, such as the British East India company's role in the Opium Wars against the Chinese Qing Dynasty. Similarly, the Royal African company's role in the triangular trade in enslaved human beings (Pettrigrew, 2013) fuelled the westward expansion of the Atlantic capitalism, where European royal families, government ministers and transnational plantation, shipping, insurance and trading elites grew incredibly wealthy from a trade they referred to as the 'attractive African meteor' (see Williams, 1944: 37). Although Adderley and Fett (Chapter 2) focus on the government's military enlistment, officials also collaborated with private British estate owners to recruit emancipated Africans from the illegal slave trade for plantation labour in a Caribbean context where the lines were often blurred between different actors. Across this volume, the role of private businesses and other non-state actors working in collaboration with governments and supranational bodies to control migration along modern/colonial lines is also evident from the past to the present.

Tjønn and Lemberg-Pedersen (Chapter 8) and Stambøl and Jegen (Chapter 5) offer particularly stark case studies on this theme. The entanglement of energy companies with Italian and other colonial powers, as well as the national government after independence in the Libyan context (Tjønn and Lemberg-Pedersen) show how displaced populations can find themselves tangled up in geopolitical webs which are not primarily oriented to humanitarianism. Indeed, in Libya forced migrants were *created* by Italian settler colonialism. This is a pattern seen in many other settler colonial contexts (and discussed by Mayblin, Chapter 7), and is an under-acknowledged part of refugee history alongside enslavement and imperial abolitionism as instances of forced migration (Lemberg-Pedersen, 2019). What is fascinating about the role of private actors (notably the energy company ENI) in the Libyan context is its willingness to 'switch sides' between a fascist and pro-colonial position to seemingly anti-colonial discourses as the geopolitical situation and market shares shift. Often, however, the colonial and neocolonial activities of European states are to the direct benefit of private interests. From the architecture of immigration detention, to border control, biometric identification technologies and welfare administration, there is huge profit to be made in the refugee and migration governance sphere (see Lemberg-Pedersen, 2013). Stambøl and Jegen (Chapter 5) illustrate this with reference to the French company

Civipol, whose activities in creating civil registries, discussed in a later section, have enriched them at the same time as serving the interests of wealthy states. Vergara Figueroa and Marino (Chapter 12) invite us to consider the case of how paramilitaries feature alongside the Colombian state actor, in the complex, and historically ongoing negotiation and marginalization of Afro-descendant communities.

The role of technologies for surveillance, categorization and control, past and present

Technologies of categorization, identification and surveillance were central in managing colonial populations. While it can sometimes seem as though the present is distinct in the extent and nature of such practices, in fact contemporary biometric technologies are part of a long line of social control measures. Anthropometric and identification techniques, such as carding (forcing people to have an identification card) and fingerprinting, were developed during British colonization in India (see Ewert, Chapter 6), and also utilized in vast census and registration projects in the French Empire, for example (see Stambøl and Jegen, Chapter 5). Of course, private actors, as noted earlier, are often central in these activities. For example, Stambøl and Jegen show how the French company Civipol today is developing biometric civil registries in West Africa. Such registries support EU externalization policies in the region in that they render populations knowable and governable for the purposes of migration management. In this case, migration management entails re-fixing mobile populations in place, should they attempt to enter the EU (see also Boeyink et al, Chapter 4). The building of biometric civil registries from scratch is not a small or cheap endeavour, but the development of systems of identification such as slave logs, branding, passports and travel documentation has a long lineage through colonial activity, primarily in controlling where Black and brown people can go (see Browne, 2015).

Ewert (Chapter 6) shows how technologies of biometric identification can blur the boundaries between care and control with her case study of Syrian refugees in Jordan. Here, refugees are required to use biometric technologies to access certain cash benefits and welfare provision, rendering them complicit subjects in their own surveillance. Ewert draws on Mirca Madianou's concept of 'technocolonialism' (2019) in exploring how technologies such as these connect to historical methods of population administration and control. Here, the apparently benign implementation of technology to deliver support means that aid dependency is taking place within a context of conditional consent to share one's personal data.

The fraught politics of sanctuary, hospitality and forgiveness

While, as Chowdhory and Poyil (Chapter 10) show, sanctuary has a long history in theology and philosophy around the world, the politics of sanctuary, hospitality and also forgiveness has often been fraught. Fratantuono (Chapter 3), for example, shows how despite the keen interest of the Ottoman Empire in settling refugees in its territories, this settlement was not always warmly met by local people whose land was settled upon. In a similar vein, Adderley and Fett (Chapter 2), show how the resettlement in Liberia of emancipated people from slave ships intercepted in the Atlantic, perhaps unsurprisingly, led to hostilities between these settlers and the indigenous population. Attempts to resettle illegally trafficked Africans by putting them to work in the British West Indian regiments also (again unsurprisingly) led to revolt in some cases. For Vergara-Figueroa and Marino (Chapter 12), the way in which the Bojayá community would return to its territory without being able to identify and bury those killed in the 2002 massacre, and then experience the FARC's gift of a provisionally dismembered Black Christ, show how also an allegedly restorative notion of forgiveness can succumb to multiple actors' agendas and pressures

At times, then, and often in the global North (but not always, see Chapter 10 on the Indian context), the arrival of refugees is used by the state as an excuse to penalize and punish them in a cynical effort to garner support from citizens (as documented by Mayblin in Chapter 7). At other times, and usually in the global South, attempts are made to resettle refugees in contexts where they are met with ambivalence. This is the case for Burundians in Tanzania (see Boeyink et al, Chapter 4) and Congolese in Kenya (see Okoth, Chapter 13), but examples around the world abound. In some cases, such as that documented by Boeyink et al, (and see also Chowdhory and Poyil, Chapter 10), xenophobia towards particular nationalities follows logics established to divide and rule during the colonial era. At other times, attempts are made by powerful metropolitan states to settle people in inhospitable environments. As Okoth's participant points out in the Kenyan context, 'What are we integrating to? A desert?' Spaces which are either imagined to be empty, or are literally empty due to their inhospitability, have long been seen by the postcolonial powers as places to put 'undesirable' racialized populations out of sight, elsewhere, probably in the Third World. The EU's agenda to externalize the policing and detention of migrants in Libya discussed by Tjønn and Lemberg-Pedersen (Chapter 8) also speaks to this theme.

The care/control nexus (Agier, 2011) is often apparent in this ambivalent politics of sanctuary and hospitality. Teunissen and Koutrolikou's (Chapter 9) account, for example, of the Turkish state's strategic invocation of humanitarian care for refugees, while at other times refugee hosting (and leakage into Europe) is represented as an emergency to be solved through violent collaborations with EU border enforcers. Ewert (Chapter 6) discusses the biometric monitoring of Syrians in Jordan, and the shift between encampment and urban settlement in managing refugees in that context. Biometric technologies are used ostensibly to provide humanitarian support. Harm, however, may stem from remote identification without consent, or social sorting and discrimination based on social markers such as ethnicity or gender. Biometric identification also allows for the tracking of individuals across borders and contexts while the underlying databases facilitate cross-checking and linking of information. We know from mass atrocities such as the Holocaust and Rwandan genocide, that the alliance of biometrics with data storage in population registries can facilitate significant risks to people (Black, 2001). Connecting this to colonial histories allows us to recognize the ways in which the identification and classification of people for apparently benign purposes, has repeatedly been used as a means of racially based identification, quarantining, exclusion, subjugation, exploitation and violence.

Postcoloniality and forced migration: a research agenda

Having sketched out seven themes which emerge across the diverse contributions in this volume, this final section addresses postcolonial approaches to forced migration as an emerging research agenda. This book is not a stand-alone text, but part of a broader increase in interest in postcolonial research in forced migration studies, and of which several of the contributors are part (see, for example Cole, 2000; 2022; Mayblin, 2017; 2019; Vergara-Figueroa, 2018; Fratantuono, 2019; Lemberg-Pedersen, 2019, 2022; Boeyink, 2019; Bass, Córdoba and Teunissen, 2020; Mayblin and Turner, 2021; Sahraoui and Tyszler, 2021; Stambøl, 2021). As noted in the introduction, researchers in various disciplines and locations have begun to turn their attention to both colonial histories and their legacies in contemporary forced migration politics.

This volume seeks to make a contribution to this 'postcolonial turn' through a collection of responses to the question of what postcolonial perspectives can bring to forced migration and refugee scholarship. In that sense the volume contains its own omissions, limitations, internal contradictions, and is also certainly non-exhaustive. Limiting our contribution to 12 chapters necessarily forces us to omit multiple postcolonial contexts. For example, case studies from the Asia Pacific, about Arctic peoples, or the Sápmi in the Nordic countries, would have contributed geographical breadth as well as further problematized the discrepancy between the actual and symbolic geography of marginalization and dispossession. For instance, the trajectories between settler colonialism and present border policies in Australia, including the extraterritorialized migration controls of the 'Pacific Solution', accord with the volume's focus on brutal displacement practices towards indigenous populations performed by colonial empires in other regions (see Rajaram, 2003; Boochani, 2018; on the entanglement of resource extractivism and displacement politics, compare also Morris, 2021 with Tjønn and Lemberg-Pedersen, Chapter 8).

The limited space also means that not all imperial projects have been covered, even when it comes to those of European countries. While the British, French, Spanish, US and Ottoman postcolonial legacies have received most attention here, less has been afforded to Portuguese, German, Dutch, or Russian postcolonies. Furthermore, there are no perspectives from indigenous studies within the volume, even though several of the chapters detail implications of (post)colonial encounters for indigeneous populations across different temporal and geographical cases (see Chapters 2, 3, 4, 7, 8 and 12). Crucially, the perspective of the volume is not meant to indicate that indigenous studies do not constitute valuable perspectives capable of moving forward the study of postcoloniality and forced migration. However, as noted by Mayblin and Turner (2021, 18), while indigenous movements have been crucial in building anti-colonial resistance movement, indigenous studies have also been criticized for aligning with exclusionary nationalist agendas (see also Lawrence and Dua, 2004). The intricacies of such debates illustrate why such a perspective deserves more in-depth coverage than possible in this edited volume, with its focus on deepening the historicity of several case studies and their explorations of how local and colonial histories continue to shape contemporary forced migration policies and politics.

We can therefore see a range of themes beyond the scope of this volume which will be challenges for the field in the coming years. Climate justice in the present and future, and the legacies of colonialism in that sphere will be a key area of development, including the enduring ecological impact of colonial plantation complexes and extractivist economies, as well as climate-driven forced migration. Decolonizing curricula, and institutional practices and structures in universities, constituting a true reckoning with the past, not just tweaking the edges or adding in alternative perspectives, will be another worldwide challenge. This includes awareness and resistance to the ways in which research institutions can enter into strategic or funding partnerships with powerful policy institutions, and exacerbate relations of knowledge extractivism whereby displaced populations are mined for data, but not aided or empowered. Furthermore, the moving of these agendas into the political and policy domain is already happening in some spheres and will also be a key concern (for example when awareness of legacies of colonial racism feature prominently in social demands for institutional change in police work), but this is not yet happening to a significant degree in the sphere of forced migration governance, which is still prone to reproducing the epistemological erasure of colonial encounters and their effects.

While postcolonialism and related fields have been critical of policy-fetishizing research on migration generally, and refugee migration specifically, there must come a point where this understanding and critique enter into the discussion of policy-makers and shift the mainstream policy terrain. Could sanctuary as reparations as Achiume (2019) argues in the case of economic migrants, perhaps offer a discursive framework for change, particularly as the turbulence of climate change alters patterns of displacement and need? Beyond shifting the dynamics of inclusion and exclusion in particular policy fields (for example curricula, fora for policy-making) there is also a need to work towards breaking down the very structures of global inequality – including that of political economy – that continue to perpetuate the dependency and subjugation of postcolonies and their peoples by rich countries in the global North and their companies. We therefore welcome more research both on those structures and their empirical manifestations around the world, and crucially on 'bottom up' agency that can subvert control mechanisms and lead to change.

Necessarily, the postcolonial turn will be collaborative and interdisciplinary. As we discussed in the introduction, developing research methods which allow us to understand the continuities between past and present, as well as discontinuities and ruptures, is an ongoing challenge. But importantly, the aim is not to look backwards and in doing so get lost in the past. Rather, the aim is to look back in order to better understand the present, and to then look forwards, to imagine different futures which neither silence the past nor suggest that we are locked into path dependent patterns of behaviour. The coming decades will bring existential challenges for humanity and require new ways of imagining social life which recognize interconnection. Understanding the past and the present as both characterized by interconnection and deep inequality, we might envisage ways to overcome injustices in the interests of all Earth's inhabitants. But we can only overcome the mistakes of the past by first recognizing them, and their legacies in the present.

References

Achiume, E.T. (2019) 'Migration as decolonisation', *Stanford Law Review*, 71(6): 1509–74.

Agier, M. (2011) *Managing the Undesirables: Refugee Camps and Humanitarian Government*, Cambridge: Polity Press.

Anderson, W. (2006) *Colonial Pathologies: American Tropical Medicine, Race, and Hygiene in the Philippines*, Durham, NC: Duke University Press.

Bass, M., Cordoba, D. and Teunissen, P. (2020) '(Re)searching with imperial eyes: collective self-inquiry as a tool for transformative migration studies', *Social Inclusion* 8(4): 147–56.

Black, E. (2001) *IBM and the Holocaust: The Strategic Alliance Between Nazi Gemany and America's Most Powerful Corporation*, Washington, DC: Dialog Press.

Boeyik, C. (2019) 'A "worthy" refugee: cash as a diagnostic of "xeno-racism" and "bio-legitimacy"', *Refuge: Canada's Journal on Refugees*, 35(1): 61–71.

Boochani, B. (2018) *No Friend But the Mountains: Writings from Manus Prison*, Sydney: Picador.

Browne, S. (2015) *Dark Matters: On the Surveillance of Blackness*, Durham, NC: Duke University Press.

Cole, P. (2000) *Philosophies of Exclusion: Liberal Political Theory and Immigration*, Edinburgh: Edinburgh University Press.

Du Bois, W.E.B. (1994 [1903]) *The Souls of Black Folk*, New York: Dover Publications.

Fanon, F. (2008 [1961]) *Black Skin, White Masks*, New York: Grove Press.

Fratantuono, E. (2019) 'Producing Ottomans: internal colonization and social engineering in Ottoman immigrant settlement', *Journal of Genocide Research* 21(1): 1–24.

Grosfoguel, R., Oso, L. and Christou, A. (2015) '"Racism", intersectionality and migration studies: framing some theoretical reflections', *Identities* 22(6): 635–52.

Hall, S. (1996) 'The West and the rest: discourse and power', in S. Hall, D. Held, D. Hubert and K. Thompson, (eds) *Modernity: Introduction to the Modern Societies*, Oxford: Blackwell, pp 184–228.

Hansen, P. and Jonsson, S. (2014) *Eurafrica: The Untold History of European Integration and Colonialism*, London: Bloomsbury

Kanwar, V. (2015) 'Not a place, but a project: Bandung, TWAIL, and the aesthetics of thirdness', in L. Eslava, M. Fakhri and V. Nesiah, (eds) *Bandung, Global History and International Law: Critical Pasts and Pending Futures*, Cambridge: Cambridge University Press.

Lawrence, B. and Dua, E. (2004) *"Real" Indians and Others: Mixed Blood Urban Native Peoples and Indigenous Nationhood*, Lincoln, NE: University of Nebraska Press.

Lemberg-Pedersen, M. (2013) 'Private security companies and the European borderscapes', in T. Gammeltoft-Hansen and N.N. Sørensen (eds) *The Migration Industry and the Commercialization of International Migration*, London: Routledge, pp 152–72.

Lemberg-Pedersen, M. (2019) 'Manufacturing displacement: externalization and postcoloniality in European migration control', *Global Affairs*, 5(3): 247–71.

Lemberg-Pedersen, M. (2022) 'The contours of deportation studies', in R. King and K. Kuschminder (eds) *Handbook on Return Migration*, Cheltenham: Edward Elgar, pp 122–36.

Lentin, A. (2020) *Why Race Still Matters*, Cambridge: Polity.

Madianou, M. (2019) 'Technocolonialism – digital innovation and data practices in the humanitarian response to refugee crises', *Social Media and Society*, July–September: 1–13.

Mayblin, L. (2017) *Asylum After Empire: Colonial Legacies in the Politics of Asylum Seeking*, London: Rowman and Littlefield International.

Mayblin, L. (2019) *Impoverishment and Asylum: Social Policy as Slow Violence*, London: Routledge.

Mayblin, L. and Turner, J. (2021) *Migration Studies and Colonialism*, Cambridge: Polity.

Morris, J. (2021) 'Colonial afterlives of infrastructure: from phosphate to refugee processing in the Republic of Nauru', *Mobilitiesi*, 16(5): 688–706.

Mutua, M. (2000) 'What Is TWAIL?', *Proceedings of the ASIL Annual Meeting*, 94: 31–38.

Pettigrew, W.A. (2013) *Freedom's Debt: The Royal African Company and the Politics of the Atlantic Slave Trade, 1672–1752*, Chapel Hill: University of North Carolina Press.

Rajaram, P.K. (2003) '"Making place": the "Pacific solution" and Australian emplacement in the Pacific and on refugee bodies', *Singapore Journal of Tropical Geography*, 24(3): 290–306.

Sahraoui, N. and Tyszler, E. (2021) 'Tracing colonial maternalism within the gendered morals of humanitarianism: experiences of migrant women at the Moroccan-Spanish border', *Frontiers in Human Dynamics*, 3: 642326. DOI: 10.3389/fhumd.2021.642326.

Said, E.W. (1995 [1978]) *Orientalism: Western Conceptions of the Orient*, London: Penguin.

Santos, B.S. (2017) 'The resilience of abyssal exclusions in our societies: toward a post-abyssal law – Montesquieu Lecture', *Tilburg Law Review*, 22: 237–58.

Stambøl, E.M. (2021) 'Neo-colonial penality? Travelling penal power and contingent sovereignty', *Punishment & Society*, 23(4): 536–56.

Trouillot, M.-R. (2003) *Global Transformations: Anthropology and the Modern World*, New York: Palgrave.

Vergara-Figueroa, A. (2018) *Afrodescendant Resistance to Deracination in Colombia. Massacre at Bellavista-Bojayá-Chocó*, Cham: Palgrave Macmillan.

Williams, E. (1944) *Capitalism and Slavery*, Chapel Hill: University of North Carolina Press.

Index

Printed and bound by CPI Group (UK) Ltd, Croydon, CR0 4YY
17/09/2026
14964141-0005